Artists
on Recording
Techniques

Artists on Recording Techniques

Jeff Touzeau

Course Technology PTR
A part of Cengage Learning

COURSE TECHNOLOGY
CENGAGE Learning

Australia • Brazil • Japan • Korea • Mexico • Singapore • Spain • United Kingdom • United States

COURSE TECHNOLOGY
CENGAGE Learning™

Artists on Recording Techniques
Jeff Touzeau

Publisher and General Manager, Course Technology PTR: Stacy L. Hiquet

Associate Director of Marketing: Sarah Panella

Manager of Editorial Services: Heather Talbot

Marketing Manager: Mark Hughes

Acquisitions Editor: Orren Merton

Project Editor/Copy Editor: Cathleen D. Small

PTR Editorial Services Coordinator: Erin Johnson

Interior Layout Tech: ICC Macmillan Inc.

Cover Designer: Mike Tanamachi

Indexer: Kelly Henthorne

Proofreader: Kate Shoup

For product information and technology assistance, contact us at **Cengage Learning Customer & Sales Support, 1-800-354-9706**

For permission to use material from this text or product, submit all requests online at **cengage.com/permissions**
Further permissions questions can be emailed to **permissionrequest@cengage.com**

All trademarks are the property of their respective owners.

Library of Congress Control Number: 2008902398

ISBN-13: 978-1-59863-513-3

ISBN-10: 1-59863-513-1

Course Technology
25 Thomson Place
Boston, MA 02210
USA

Cengage Learning is a leading provider of customized learning solutions with office locations around the globe, including Singapore, the United Kingdom, Australia, Mexico, Brazil, and Japan. Locate your local office at: **international.cengage.com/region**

Cengage Learning products are represented in Canada by Nelson Education, Ltd.

For your lifelong learning solutions, visit **courseptr.com**

Visit our corporate website at **cengage.com**

Printed in the United States of America
1 2 3 4 5 6 7 11 10 09

For my mom—"You didn't have to be so nice...."

Foreword

It All Comes Back to Music

Capping each issue of the professional audio business and technology journal, *Pro Sound News,* is a regular feature titled "Music, Etc." The concept is simple. The preceding pages are filled with geek-speak and written in the vernacular particular to our industry. The magazine covers the technologies that drive our business and the companies and individuals who are the end users of those technologies, as well as those who develop and market the tools of the various audio trades. After immersion in the left-brain world of business and technology, "Music, Etc." provides a cleansing respite.

When audio engineers, studio owners, and gear makers alike are asked, "What motivated you to get involved in the music business?" the nearly unanimous reply is a love of music as key. The aptitudes that equip an individual to become a button-pushing, knob-twisting, mouse-clicking audio engineer might as easily be applied to, say, air traffic control or computer-assisted drafting. Electronic engineering skills necessary to design and build a high-fidelity microphone preamplifier could be practically applied to medical measurement equipment or to cell phone circuitry. Ah, but the music beckons, and the skills and passions of such individuals are thus focused on capturing the creative vision of the musical artist instead of other more mundane (though likely more lucrative) pursuits.

"Music, Etc." was created to make the connection back to the music by tapping into the artists' creative process. David McGee, the father of the column and its writer for many years, crafted "Music, Etc." to bring the motivations and methods of the artist into focus. A recent musical production project is typically the hook, with coverage of the musical aspects of the recording process, such as composing, instrumentation, and the musicians on the tracks. Beyond the creative end product, the perspectives of the music maker on the recording process can help build the bridge that links creativity and technology. How does a given artist think and work? Are artists oblivious to the technology, or do they use the recording infrastructure to enhance creativity? How is the creative process affected by physical surroundings, relationships between artists and their engineers and producers, an artist's understanding of technology (or lack of such understanding), and the workflow of a given project? Answering these extended questions is the role of "Music, Etc."

In recent years, Jeff Touzeau has stepped in as the regular author of "Music, Etc.," capably carrying on in the spirit of the tradition David established. *Pro Sound News* covers a huge volume of topics in a given issue, and though "Music, Etc." gets a healthy helping of our page real estate, it is inevitable that valuable material (including additional photography) would get left out of what is at heart a short-form magazine. That's where this book, *Artists on Recording Techniques,* comes in. Jeff's extensive interviews are available here for the first time in their full, unabridged depth. Jeff's questions and the back-and-forth between interviewer and artist give an additional dimension to the dialogue that can be sacrificed in the short form of "Music, Etc." Jeff is given fairly free rein in the selection of artists to interview for his monthly missive. He's brought an eclectic blend of perspectives to our pages, ranging from the mainstream of contemporary music to the more esoteric and niche artists. Jeff has done an excellent job of dipping into a varied array of genres. The blend you'll find here, which includes some artist interviews that were not found in shorter form in "Music, Etc.," includes well-known pop and rock icons such as Pink Floyd, Duran Duran, America, and Barenaked Ladies, with a focus on where creative expression has led them in a modern media market and production environment. Contemporary artists such as Clap Your Hands Say Yeah and Sevendust share the stage with stalwart artists in a process of continual reinvention, such as Joe Jackson, Tony Bennett, and John Fogerty. Musician's musicians are given voice, including John Scofield and Kaki King.

When the electronic and software engineers developing audio production tools set out to develop a product, it behooves them to understand not only what a device or program might do, but how the human interface enhances (or, heaven forbid, detracts from) the creative process. When audio engineers approach a project, they are by necessity both a technological facilitator of the process as well as a counselor, confidant, and advisor to the artists. When producers assemble the team of musicians and engineers to help artists achieve their vision, they balance encouraging and promoting creativity with the choice of personnel, resources, physical environment, and the mundane but necessary budgetary considerations. What makes an artist comfortable? What provides inspiration without distraction? Are there genre-specific considerations that can affect production decisions? Are the traditional approaches to recording giving way to an artist-centric approach where the mechanical functions no longer dictate the process? Is technology reaching an oft-stated goal of enhancing and promoting creativity, rather than being merely a vehicle to capture performance? How do artists, when given the opportunity to drive the process, choose to work? In *Artists on Recording Techniques*, Jeff brings to light the artist's perspective on these issues and more.

Those of us involved at various levels in the recording process can learn a lot from the artist's-eye view. Be the reader of *Artists on Recording Techniques* an audio technician, engineer, studio owner, producer, equipment manufacturer, hardware or software designer, or even a music fan or an intern aspiring to a loftier role in the process, taking the time to listen to the artists is time well spent. Given that music is the motivation, and ultimately the artists are the source of that music, who better to share insights into capturing the creative process than the artists themselves? In the pages of *Artists on Recording Techniques*, Jeff Touzeau continues and expands on his established role of creating a dialogue with musical artists. Your role is not only to read and enjoy the dialogue, but to learn from it and then apply the lessons learned to your participation in the creation and capture of creative expression. Till the fertile soil of your mind in preparation for the planting of a new crop of ideas, then turn the page and dig in.

Frank Wells
Editor, *Pro Sound News*

Preface

In my eighth grade English class, my teacher, Mr. Chupka, asked each student a simple question: "If you could have a conversation with anyone, living or dead, who would it be?" Most of the students offered more or less predictable responses…Jesus Christ, Abraham Lincoln, Shakespeare. When Mr. Chupka called on me, I said, "Roger Waters." "Roger Waters?" he replied, with a quizzical look on his face.

I was a teenybopper when I first heard *The Dark Side of the Moon,* yet the album (yes, it was vinyl) had such a deep impact on me that it forever changed my outlook on life—possibly even my DNA. No other piece of art—visual, literary, or musical—has ever moved me to that degree, possibly for the very reason that I was so impressionable at that age. I can even attest to the fact that I lost…er, as Nirvana so eloquently put it, *Nevermind.*

Fast-forward to a rainy October in 2005. I'm a few years older and have further exercised my senses; I've studied classic literature in Oxford, examined Impressionist art in Paris, and smelled the stew of scents in New York City. In fact, right now I'm trudging up 48th Street through the rain with a plastic bag in hand, headed toward Roger Waters' apartment near St. Patrick's Cathedral for an interview. What's in the bag? My fourth or fifth (I can't remember which) copy of *The Dark Side of the Moon*—which, if I have the nerve, I will ask Mr. Waters to sign directly following the interview.

As I wait in Waters' living room, it is surreal. The view from his apartment is nothing short of spectacular—I can see the entire East Side of New York City laid out before me. Finally, Roger comes out and greets me with genuine warmth, looking focused, fit, and smartly dressed. I am offered a glass of wine, we sit down, and I conduct the most memorable interview of my life.

I never could have imagined the pleasure I would derive from interviewing not just Mr. Waters, but all of the other subjects in this book. It has been a great privilege to talk about their passions and learn about what makes each of their recording experiences unique. I feel really lucky—and they are *paying* me for this?

Jeff Touzeau
May 2008

Acknowledgments

When you start a book, it's hard to realize the web of support that is required to take it to the finish line. Now that the book is complete, this web is becoming clearer. First and foremost, I would like to thank Kim, Caroline, and Ashton for their loving support—there is no way this book could exist if it was not for each of you.

Second, I'd like to thank Frank Wells, Janice Brown, Fred Goodman, Deb Greenberg, and everyone at *Pro Sound News*—writing "Music, Etc." each month has been a great privilege, and I've leaned on each of you for support at one time or another. Thanks also to John Storyk and Duncan Potter, both of whom are my friends and important mentors in my career. Also, I'd like to thank Ian Catt—my favorite producer, my very first interviewee, and someone I can now call my friend. Thanks also to Richard Barone, Steve Berlin, Roger Waters, Nick Mason, and Mark Fenwick—a class act.

This book would not have been possible without the help of many publicists, including Ken Weinstein, Tom Muzquiz, Arlin Pulijal, Kissy Black, Bobbie Gale, Amanda Cagan, Christopher Moon, Julie Murray Porter, Julie Calland, Susan Clary, Patti Conte, Angelica Cob, Adam Smith, Diana D'Angelo, Renee Harrison, Kate Jackson, Catherine Herrick, Jill Strominger, Pam Workman, Amber Haeckel, Katherine Deatrick, Christine Morales, Alicia Karlin, Paula Erickson, Sylvia Weiner, Steve Manning, and many others—I thank you for your time, effort, and patience in helping me pull together these interviews and related artwork.

I would like to thank all the photographers who let me use their work, including Jimmy Ienner, Jr., Reuben Cox, Brian T. Silak, Cory Lashever, Taylor Crothers, and so many others. I am also grateful to all the artists who I interviewed for this book and who were so gracious with their time and interest. Thanks also to the record company and management personnel who helped me in various ways during the different phases of this project.

Finally, thanks to my family: Mark, Lynda, Mom, Dad, Marcy, Bing, Cathy, Rob, Debbie, Eric, and Nana for your continued encouragement. Also, thanks to Orren Merton and Cathleen Small, who provided invaluable guidance and editing in the shaping of this book. Thanks to Stephanie Susnjara and David Miles Huber for providing me with overall moral support as a writer. Thanks to Matt Harper, Michael Filer, and Larry Crane—editors in the audio field for whom I have the greatest respect.

There are doubtless many others who I haven't named, and I would like to take this opportunity to thank them now. While you aren't personally named here, you can be assured that I am most grateful.

About the Author

Jeff Touzeau is a writer and musician living in New York. His book entitled *Making Tracks: Unique Recording Studio Environments* (Schiffer, 2006) was released to critical acclaim, and he is also the author of *Careers in Audio* (Cengage Learning, 2008). As a journalist, Touzeau's work has appeared in *EQ, Pro Sound News, Tape Op, Performing Songwriter, Professional Sound,* and many other magazines. When he isn't writing, he enjoys composing and recording music at his studio, Hummingbird Sound.

Contents

Introduction

Pro Sound News is an audio-industry trade magazine, widely read by producers, engineers, live sound professionals, manufacturers of audio equipment, and many other people involved in the audio field. I have been an avid subscriber to *Pro Sound News* for many, many years. I would wait for my copy each month with great anticipation, and when it finally came, I would immediately thumb through to the last page, where there was a column called "Music, Etc."

"Music, Etc." always gave me insight into recordings that no other magazine could provide—and always from the artist's perspective. The feature column, which covered nearly every conceivable musical genre, was always done in interview format and written in a very familiar tone. I would often daydream about what I would do if I ever had a shot at writing that column.

One Fall day in 2005, my daydream became reality. Janice Brown, who was the recording editor at *Pro Sound News,* asked me if I would like to write a "Music, Etc." piece on Sevendust, the alternative metal band based out of Atlanta. They had just released a new album called *Next,* and it was up to me to find out what went down during the recording and learn what was interesting about it. To be completely honest, I wasn't very familiar with Sevendust and therefore had to immerse myself in the band's music very quickly.

After that first submission, I was asked to write the column again, then again, until I ultimately became the column's regular writer. Looking back over the last few years, I have been very privileged on a number of fronts. First, to have worked so closely with all the professionals at *Pro Sound News* in carrying out the original vision of the column, which originally meant so much to me as a reader. Second, to have immersed myself in so many different styles and genres of music that I might not have otherwise been exposed to.

As a music enthusiast, I am very aware that my own personal taste might be 180 degrees different from that of the reader; yet in the column I must endeavor to find subjects who appeal to a variety of listeners and recording enthusiasts. This has given me the self-discipline to listen to and appreciate the differences in many music styles, which in turn has greatly expanded my own personal musical horizons.

This book captures artists of many different genres and eras, each at a unique moment in time—during the creation of the music they are passionate about. Some of them—such as Tony Bennett and Pink Floyd—have been making albums for decades and have perfected their approach. Others, such as Kaki King and Ben Kweller, have only made a handful of albums and are inspiring an entirely new generation of artists while striving to take their work to the next level.

As music and recording enthusiasts—no matter what level—we have so much to learn from the artist. It is the artist who must take the recording to the finish line and who is ultimately responsible for the success or failure of the recording. When it comes to working in the studio, it is the artist's ears that need to be satisfied, the artist's artistic vision that needs to be realized, and the artist's voice that ultimately needs to be heard. The producer, the engineer, the recording environment, and the equipment are all but vehicles to help the artist reach these goals.

It is easy to get lost in the sonic forest and miss the root of the creation: the song and performance. To further illustrate this, let me share a recent experience I had while interviewing John Wood, who engineered Nick Drake's masterful recordings. Because there was so little published about how Drake's recordings were captured—the preamps, compressors, and microphones used, for example—I over-zealously swooped in to get the technical scoop behind the recording.

To my surprise, Wood effectively said that none of that really mattered. The room, the microphone choice, and the console were all extremely secondary considerations when you had an exquisite performer like Nick Drake. What was most important to Wood was making Drake comfortable and capturing the moment on tape. This brought home to me an adage that often applies in the design and architecture world: Form follows function. The audio tactics and tools must all serve the performance, never the other way around.

When discussing the technical aspects of a recording, which obviously remain very important, we usually hear from the engineer or producer—rarely do we hear from the artist. However, just as a painter has a perspective on the physical makeup of a canvas and how pigment interacts before finally being applied by a brush, so does a recording artist have an opinion on the technical aspects of how a vocal performance should be delivered or how a drum set should be miked up. While the recording's execution is most often left up to the engineer or producer, it is the artist's work that is ultimately affected. This book is about the relevant perspective an artist has on the recording process—which invariably affects his or her work.

1 Nick Mason and Pink Floyd from the Inside Out

When I spoke to Nick Mason, he had just finished his autobiography on Pink Floyd, *Inside Out*, which documented and recalled his experiences as the drummer for Pink Floyd over three decades. Mason is the only member to have remained with Pink Floyd throughout the complete duration of the group's career. The book, which came out in 2006, is written with a startling degree of detail, and where Mason's amazing memory falls short, he has drawn upon his former bandmates and colleagues to fill in the blanks.

The book itself sheds an enormous amount of light on many of Pink Floyd's early recordings, where little had been documented previously. Pink Floyd's experiences in the late '60s at Abbey Road Studios were primarily overshadowed by the Beatles, who through their mutual label, EMI, afforded Pink Floyd the financial and artistic freedom they needed to experiment and ultimately realize their potential in the recording studio.

Following the group's initial success with singles such as "See Emily Play" and "Arnold Layne" and following the release of their self-titled first album in 1967, Pink Floyd effectively began self-producing their own records. Norman Smith, a George Martin protégé, was the last producer sanctioned by the label to participate (until *The Wall*, many years later); the group then managed their own destiny and, needless to say, vastly expanded their creative frontiers.

I spoke to Nick about his early experiences in Pink Floyd; it is obvious that the group's collective imagination and experimentation were the driving force behind their success, rather than any special kind of recording technique. However, their unique method of composition and artistic expression offered unprecedented challenges for engineers to capture these recordings—even at Abbey Road, the most advanced studio of its time.

Despite Mason's immaculate rock pedigree and enormous success, his manner is very friendly and approachable. I spoke to him just as he began promoting his book to Eastern European countries, a reminder that Pink Floyd's music has resonated on a truly global scale and across many generations.

Courtesy Nick Mason Archive.

Nick Mason, pictured at the dawn of Pink Floyd.

When you were started *Inside Out,* did you realize how big of a job you were getting into? How complex did the project turn out to be for you?

It was much bigger than I anticipated. If I had perhaps thought long and hard about it, I probably wouldn't have started it—it's probably a good thing not to think too hard about what might be ahead. I certainly changed horses in midstream a bit, since the book was going to be the ultimate official biography of the band with every detail in it, perhaps containing long sections from every recording session and every gig we'd ever done. As time went on, it just became more and more obvious that it was more interesting to simply do my version of events and let it spin on a particular speed than to try to cover everyone else's versions of what happened when.

In your book, you talk about your father, who was a documentarian. Do you think this may have influenced your venturing into recording, since he had the gear around?

Yes, I suppose so, but I don't think I ever really thought of it like that. I don't think he influenced me that heavily; it's just one of those things where access to equipment sort of sets you off on a particular road, in the same way I suspect I discovered drumming because I was given a pair of wire brushes and went from there. The fact that there was a tape recorder meant that we could actually record things a lot better than one might normally have done.

So you were the one who brought the Grundig recorder and turned it on while your band was practicing.

Absolutely. And we could actually record in stereo.

In the late '60s, there was a lot of creative experimentation going on in the band. Take "A Saucerful of Secrets," for example; can you talk about how this piece evolved structurally and compositionally?

Well, as far as I remember, we didn't actually try to notate what we were going to do, but we did try and draw up some sort of chart of what was going to happen; there was some sort of graphic representation. I think it was based loosely on having a sort of classical piece in terms of having three different sorts of movements. Then the movements were worked on as individual pieces, then the whole thing was assembled further down the line.

I can't actually remember how we worked out the middle section, which is basically a drum pattern double-tracked and then looped. I don't know why we chose that particular pattern or how we ended up with it. I think the three ideas were meant to lead up to this grand finale, the Hammond organ section. Once we played it live on the Albert Hall organ, and it sounded fantastic.

There are a lot of interesting dynamics in that song, especially when it comes to the drums. You start with soft accent cymbals, then the hard crashing—as Roger plays the gong, then the repetitive pattern, and then the mellow finale.

That was the thing that perhaps made it different and where we found a niche for ourselves—doing pieces that weren't actually full volume from beginning to end. That was the beginning of finding new sounds or new tones—particularly that business of taking the microphone to the very edge of the cymbal on that first section. It was very much something that we discovered in the process.

Do you have any early memories of recording at Sound Techniques in 1967 before you went to Abbey Road? I'm thinking of "Arnold Layne" and "See Emily Play." The drums and bass were so tight, and there was such a great bottom end.

I think we recorded on four-track, and the drums and bass were laid down on two of the tracks, guitar on the third, and then all bumped down to the remaining track to free up three tracks for overdubbing vocals and Farfisa keyboard. The Sound Techniques sessions were much more to do with John Wood and Joe Boyd producing and coming up with the sounds, rather than us. During the Sound Techniques sessions, we didn't have the time that we later found at Abbey Road—we were actually in there to get the single made.

Photograph by Jeff Touzeau.

Joe Boyd today.

I know the *Atom Heart Mother* sessions were challenging for you because you had to play the entire track straight through with Roger without stopping because you couldn't splice.

Well, yes. EMI had a sort of house rule that because these eight-tracks were new and no one had worked with them, nobody could splice the tape. Frankly, everyone was scared of trying to splice it! Looking at it now, after the event, it was really daft. It would have made life a hell of a lot easier for everyone if we could have spliced it. It was a directive from Abbey Road that splicing 2-inch tape was not to be done.

What were some of the challenges in recording *Atom Heart Mother* and how rewarding was it to have finally completed it?

I think it was difficult because we were doing something we didn't know very much about, which was sort of this rather overextended sort of piece, and it involved the orchestra as well. It was difficult for Ron [Geesin], who I don't think had done much work with orchestras. I think most of us feel, listening back to it, that it's a rather flawed album—we could have done a lot better if we had known how to tackle it.

Given the fact that *Atom Heart Mother* was mixed in quad right after its original release, wouldn't this be a great candidate for a 5.1 surround mix? Has anyone at the Floyd camp considered this, or are things focused on the later catalog?

I think we've tended to focus on the later catalog; it's an interesting idea, though. I don't know what condition the original masters would be in, and I don't know to what extent we could clean them up. It would be an interesting project if one could clean up the masters and actually improve things like the drum sound. The drums are very much subject to spill. Actually, what's happened is that they've spilled onto the orchestral sections.

Was this because the mics picked up not only the orchestral players, but also the monitors playing in the live room?

Yeah, and they had to play them loud because of the slightly erratic timing and all of the rest of it. One tends to assume that the purpose of re-mastering is to improve the sound quality, but there might be a case to be made to improve the balance at the same time.

Was *Atom Heart Mother* rewarding to take out on the road?

It was bloody difficult. I think traveling with anything like that is. I mean, you've got a whole bunch of people who really are delightful, but not committed. The whole logistics of traveling with them, recording them, and miking them up was hard. Frankly, I would have said we were pretty relieved when we got back to being a four-piece.

In your live performances during that time, you played things like *The Man Sequence*, which included tracks such as "Beset by Creatures of the Deep" and other songs. Did this framework ever come to fruition like you wanted it to? Clearly, they were early efforts at a more conceptual musical piece.

It was the forerunner of *Dark Side* in many ways; there were a couple of elements to it. But the main thing was the idea of a band really doing the whole show. In the late '60s and early '70s, there were support acts; if it was America, there would be two support acts. The idea of this was that we would do our own show, and it was a seated "concert," not a gig, if you like.

The Man, which was the whole evening, was called something like *The Massed Gadgets of Auxumenies*. The first section was called "The Man," and the second section was called "The Journey." Or vice versa, I can't remember. Basically, it was a mixture of songs, bits of music, and just sort of odd things that were done onstage. For instance, "Alan's Psychedelic Breakfast" was performed live, with actual cooking going on onstage.

Can you tell me more about that? There was a part in your book that discusses when Pink Floyd made furniture onstage.

Yes, that was part of it. I suspect that was "The Man," and it was sequence called "Work." [laughs] And "Work" involved saws…it was a rhythm section with saws, hammers, nails, banging, and so on. And at the end of it, we'd hopefully built a table, and the table was used [laughs] to put a teapot on, then there was the stove [laughs] with a whistling kettle. So there was a sort of mad logic to it.

Can you talk about the Azimuth Coordinator that was built on specification for you by Abbey Road? During this time, were you increasingly using sound effects in the studio and on the road?

Well, we were probably just beginning to mess about with sound effects in the studio, and we met this engineer at Abbey Road—he was a maintenance engineer called Bernard Speight. It was absolutely his concept. It probably existed as an idea, but he said, "Look, I can build you this thing," and he built the original quadraphonic pan pot, a pair of them, and worked out how we'd use them, what speakers we'd need, and all the rest of it. Of course, once we started messing about with it, we realized the potential for running tape and running sound effects, particularly in live shows, around the concert hall.

Courtesy Nick Mason Archive.

Portrait of Nick during the *Piper at the Gates of Dawn* sessions, recorded at Abbey Road in late 1967.

Do you think that your education in architecture gave you a predisposition toward the technology, because it seems like you were pushing the engineers ahead just as much as they were pushing you in terms of technology.

I don't know. What I would say is that it was a very useful grounding. Architecture has a very real mixture of technology and art, so it certainly gave us an idea of how to make things, how to plan things, and how to make graphic representations of what one wanted to do.

Of the people who worked with through your career, can you think of any people who stand out as bright stars who helped you get to the next level either technically or creatively?

I think most of the people we worked with were terrific; it mostly has to do with the timing. Joe [Boyd] was fantastic for the early singles; Norman was good news because he taught us a lot and gave us a pretty free hand in the studios. This was a period when producers were expected to control the band and save money and save time.

Norman played a lot of instruments, right?

Yeah. He was the sort of junior version of George Martin—and that's definitely what he was aiming to be, I think. I'd also cite people like Bob Ezrin, James Guthrie, and Alan Parsons. Frankly, if they weren't any good, we probably would have gotten rid of them, or we *did* get rid of them before they got their name on the album! [laughs]

At what point did you really feel you had free reign to make your own production decisions? This happened quite early on, correct?

I think *Saucer—Saucerful of Secrets*.

EMI was pretty cool about that?

Yeah, because I think the work had been done by the Beatles, who had shown them that if they just allowed the band free rein in the studios, they'd probably get something really good at the end of it. The recording time wasn't quite as expensive as it later became, and the studios were busy, but they could afford to give the time.

Very few live recordings have come out during Pink Floyd's early career, except for *Ummagumma* (the live side) and *Live at Pompeii* in DVD format. But there is a whole host of high-quality bootleg and BBC recordings out there that capture some inspirational performances by Pink Floyd that reveal a completely different dimension to the band. Have you guys ever looked at cleaning up and releasing the BBC Paris Theater performances from 1970 and 1971, for example?

Well, we always look at that sort of thing. But the fact of the matter is that when *Pompeii* was done, we *knew* it was to go out live as a film. So we're very comfortable with how we did it at the time. The problem with things like the BBC and the Paris Theater recordings is they were done as one-off radio shows, and it was never our intention that they would be sort of left to posterity. So we're less enthusiastic about that.

As you spent all this time on the road and in the studio going into the '70s, did you do most of your writing on the road or in the studio? Did you actually write lots of things at Abbey Road?

The answer is that there is no specific answer to that one. There were certainly some, like "Careful with That Axe," done in the studio. There were things like "Saucerful of Secrets," done in the studio, designed in the studio, and carried out there. And then there were songs that generally were written not on the road, but at home by individuals and then brought in as complete or semi-complete pieces.

Courtesy Nick Mason Archive.

Mason during the *Piper* sessions.

Can you tell me a little about *The Household Objects* session that occurred after *The Dark Side of the Moon*? What was the goal of this?

I think it was just a desperate attempt to find some new things to do. It was an experiment, and it was a failed experiment that was consequently ditched, and we moved on. We did spend a lot of time on it, though.

Would you say that "Shine On You Crazy Diamond" was composed in a similar way to, say, "Echoes?"

No, it was a mixture, funnily enough. It was done partially in the studio, and as sections brought in by individuals.

When you look at Pink Floyd's early catalog, the framework appears to be a much more freeform approach of, say, *Ummagumma* or *Atom Heart Mother* than, say, *The Dark Side of the Moon* and *Obscured by Clouds*, when it appears that compositionally things became more structured. Was there a catalyst that led to a more structured approach?

No, I don't think there was. I just think we sort of drifted toward found opportunities or toward things we liked doing. And I think probably when Syd had left, there was more of an interest in, I won't say, *designer* songs, but I think Roger's songwriting was the biggest change. Once he really started writing, the ideas that came out of that were frankly not psychedelic—they were organized intellectual pieces.

What about the period around, say, 1974, when you were writing "Raving and Drooling" and "You Gotta Be Crazy." You were presumably spending a lot less time with one another. Were you still gelling together as a band at that point or was it more individualized?

Hard to sum it up, really. By '74, we were spending less time together because most of us were married and having children—it was about growing older, frankly, as much as anything else. People tended to work a little more individually, and most of us were doing bits of production for other people. There was less of that completely sort of focused "all four of us working to achieve exactly the same end."

Throughout your career, you've been able to maintain strong extracurricular interests, such as motorsport. With such a full career in Pink Floyd, in recording, touring, and promoting, how have you been able to maintain all these interests? For such a prolific musician, you seem very well-rounded in other areas.

I think the answer is that time just made itself available. I'm a firm believer in not trying to combine things so much. The motorsport thing was done in between albums, really. So I actually didn't start until '73, when I actually had some time, because we were always working up until then. But after *Dark Side*, we'd do tours, followed by time off. There was this change from just going in and doing a bit of recording. Suddenly, you'd do whole projects, then have time off again. By the time we were doing *Animals*, we more or less went into the studio and didn't come out until we had done the album, whereas *Dark Side* was done in a very piecemeal way. Once we were into this sort of "project" thing, people tended to need time off in between projects. That's when I found time to go and do other things.

You obviously have a very distinctive drumming style, and I'd be very interested to learn about the kind of care that was taken to get the sound of your drums on tape. I'm thinking of *Dark Side of the Moon*, where your drums just sound perfect.

Well, I think particularly in the early recordings, people took acoustic instruments very seriously. I'm sure they still do, but drum sounds were *the* test of an engineer. Whether it was John Wood or Alan Parsons, they took it very seriously and tended to use the same mic setups of Neumanns for the overheads and AKG D12 for the bass drums. There were very specific ideas of what was best for the drum kit. James Guthrie was great on *The Wall*—I thought he did a great job. It almost became a dying art, you know—engineers who spent so long recording orchestras and had a very clear idea of how to record acoustic instruments.

Courtesy Nick Mason Archive.

Mason pictured during the *Piper* sessions. The overhead mic is an STC 4038.

You spent many, many years doing sessions at Abbey Road, but then made a departure for recording *Animals* by going to Brittania Row. Presumably, you knew the ins and outs of Abbey Road and it was familiar territory for you. Was it a big change?

We'd worked in other studios by the time we went to *Animals*. We'd worked in Air London; we'd worked in France at Chateau D'Herouville for *Obscured by Clouds*. And we'd done film music in Pye in Marble Arch and stuff like that. Abbey Road was great, but it was sort of quite an old-fashioned place in a way, and most of the other studios were more sort of cutting edge and a bit more sort of modern in feel. "Groovy," I think, would have been the word at the time. Brittania Row was certainly a big change because it didn't have anything like the same facilities. But that was perhaps rather good from our point of view—it kept things simple.

In the late '70s, you got into a little producing yourself. You produced The Damned, right?

Yes. *Music for Pleasure*. I also produced Robert Wyatt, a band called Gong with Steve Hillage, and a few other things. The Damned chose me because they couldn't get Syd Barrett. [laughs] I think it was probably better for me than it was for them. They were sort of fighting amongst themselves at the time. Physical and musical differences, perhaps.

Did you enjoy being a producer? How did you fit into that role being on the other side for so long as an artist?

I really liked it. It was really good fun.

Nick, what are you up to now that the book is out?

Well, a lot of more work to do on the book because there is promotion to do on the paperback. It's going to print in the Czech Republic, Romania, and Bulgaria. The rest of the year, I can see a lot more stuff that has to do with that book. To be honest, I really enjoyed writing, and perhaps I'll look to write something else.

Did you anticipate the success the book has had so far?

I'm really pleased with the way it's gone in America particularly. It's been great, and people really seem to be up for it.

2 America—and the Horse They Came in On

In an industry that thrives on trends and varied musical tastes, it is often hard to find something relatively unaffected by constant change. This is true not only with the music itself, but also with the technology on which it is recorded. America is a group that has not only pioneered the singer/songwriter genre with tracks like "A Horse with No Name," "Daisy Jane," and "Sister Golden Hair," but the group has proven that great songwriting and honest performances are two ingredients that hold their own over time.

I vividly recall buying the 7-inch single of "Sister Golden Hair" back when FM was unbridled by corporate control. I listened to the song over and over, admiring the sonics of the acoustic guitar and the tasty slide guitar solos that never seemed to age, despite my wearing the record out. On *Here and Now*, the enduring group has teamed with artistic contemporaries that include My Morning Jacket and Nada Surf, among others.

The group now consists of founding members Gerry Beckley and Dewey Bunnell, who provide the album with a solid backbone of songs that distinctly convey America's familiar sound. Producers Adam Schlesinger and James Iha, musicians in their own right (Fountains of Wayne, Smashing Pumpkins), built on this solid foundation, and the final result was a new vintage of America that is still relevant today. I spoke to Gerry Beckley—guitarist, pianist, vocalist, and songwriter—who modestly brushes aside the notion of being labeled an innovator in the singer/songwriter category.

What have you guys been doing for the last few years?

The group itself has never broken up. This is our 37th year, and we have continued to be a performing band, doing about 100 shows a year all over the world. The hits we had were in most areas around the world, including places like Australia. This has really helped fill in the touring schedule. Having said that, the albums we have done in the recent past have been small independent releases and Internet-based things. *Here and Now* is really is our first studio album in over 10 years and our first major label release in much longer than that.

America, pictured left to right, Dewey Bunnell and Gerry Beckley.

There are so many new things contributing to this album, probably starting with the contributions of Adam and James. It took a couple years of back and forth between Adam and myself. At this point in my career, I try to reach out to the people who I personally admire, in the effort to write, exchange ideas, or whatever. We were all big fans of Fountains of Wayne, and we were so knocked out by their music. I thought, "We really need to hook up with those guys."

How did you actually choose Adam Schlesinger and James Iha as producers for the album?

It started what turned into an almost two-year back and forth—emails, swapping songs and things. It finally turned into, "Why don't we cut a couple of things together?" Then [Adam] explained his partnership with James, and I got James' solo album, *Let It Come Down*. Although I was a big fan of Smashing Pumpkins, his solo album is quite a bit more melodic. Once he was involved, James was really after a timeless America album, and not a "retro" sound. It was also a fantastic opportunity to work with John Holbrook, which was a great decision by Adam and James.

I like to think that this album had a very organic beginning. I like to mention that because so often nowadays there are a couple of people in an office who say, "Wouldn't it be cool if so-and-so did this?" It doesn't mean that it can't work that way, but in this case, it felt right from the outset.

With so many options available to you in the studio now, how do you remain focused and work with only those sounds you really want?

The options have become unlimited, but some processes remain similar. If you want to do acoustic-oriented recordings, you still get a fine acoustic guitar and you put a nice tube mic on it. I'm still sitting here with my fine Gibson, Taylor, or whatever in front of a really nice Neumann mic.

With samples and modeling of audio, you really have every choice available and an unlimited selection of sounds. But it really comes back to "What are you after?" and "Where are you heading?" doesn't it? Because if it's just a matter of choices, we're going to be here all week.

To use a simple analogy, you used to have 11 channels on TV—you could go up and down and back and say, "Right, we're going to watch NBC tonight." Now, with 400 channels, the search never ends—you'd just be going up and down forever. It comes back to "What do you like to watch?" and you plan ahead to watch those shows. If people can navigate and learn their own tastes, you can still be open to recommendations from friends. The same principle can apply in the studio.

What kinds of schedules do each of you have? How do logistics become a challenge in putting together an album like this?

We did the album in four-day spurts and going back on the road. We would have gigs on Thursday, Friday, Saturday, and Sunday, then would work on Monday, Tuesday, and Wednesday. Then we would get on a plane again, do the shows, and come back to record. We never really worked extensively in New York before, and both Dewey and I love New York, so that in itself was really cool.

Gerry, I was astounded by the quality of your new album. Your voices haven't changed at all. What led up to this record?

Well, the group itself had never broken up. This is our 37th year, and we continue to be a performing band and do about 100 shows a year all over the world—mostly in the States, but the hits we had over the years were hits in most major places, including.

Did you guys record at Stratosphere Sound?

Yeah, that's where we did the album. It took a couple years of back and forth with Adam. At this point in my career, I try to reach out to the people I personally admire, just to exchange ideas and things. Dewey and I are both big fans of Fountains of Wayne—at the time we were just knocked out by their album *Welcome Interstate Managers.* I thought, "I've got to hook up with this guy." I just loved his songs. So this started what turned into an almost two-year back and forth of emails and swapping songs. I knew that Adam was also a producer. It turned into, "Why don't we cut a couple of things together?" He explained very early on about the partnership with James, so I went and got James' solo album, *Let It Come Down,* which is very melodic.

It was a case of this organic beginning—I really like to mention that because so often nowadays, there are a couple of people in an office who say, "Wouldn't it be cool if so-and-so did this?" It doesn't mean that it can't work that way, but in this case it really started to feel right. So I went to New York and we cut a couple of things. I kept Dewey in the loop the whole time—Dew knows that I have a studio here at the house and I'm always working. This led to a variety of things; one thing was that an A&R guy with Sony said, "I think I've got a place for this…there's a great new division called Sony Burgundy, and this sounds ideal." He was a big fan of Adam's, too. It became very real when we had a deal; then, the challenge was how to get this recording schedule into what was already an intense touring schedule.

What kind of recording rig do you have at your disposal to do the pre-production work?

At the time, and for many years, I'd been on Digital Performer. I'm a user from 1.*xx* right up until now—my son is a producer here in town, and he's been trying to convert me over to Pro Tools, which he has just done over this last holiday break. For the first time ever, I've been working completely in Pro Tools. I have a beautiful room in the backyard in what used to be a two-car garage, and it has been converted to like an office space. It has a six-foot grand piano and all real instruments. Quite a few of the tracks were actually recorded there, and many of the files were transferred over to Stratosphere.

Here and Now **sounds very acoustic-oriented, which is saying a lot in this age of samples and computer-generated sounds. How do you stay true to this acoustic sound in this day and age of technology advances?**

That particular part of the puzzle has not changed so much. If you want to do recordings of that nature, you get out, find nice-sounding acoustic instruments, and put a nice tube mic on them. A few of my friends still like to record analog—I know Jesse Harris likes to record this way—so you can still do that, too. Obviously, real acoustics, real vocals, and real pianos are important. Real drums are very important. In this case, Brian Young from Fountains of Wayne did the drumming on most of the album.

I know at Stratosphere, knowing Adam, they probably wanted to record you to 2-inch, then dump everything into Pro Tools.

We tried that, but we were having trouble getting it locked. Because we were doing this in four-day spurts and then coming back, we couldn't do it.

Do you and Dewey usually write collaboratively?

I usually write alone. Dewey has been doing more co-writing, I think. He doesn't have a facility, so he'll tend to come over to do his writing if he frees up a week.

So you guys live nearby?

No, he actually lives up in the North of Wisconsin, up in the woods quite a distance away, so we have to coordinate that. But with technology the way it is, we can swap files relatively easily.

Tell me about some of the other cast of characters on the album.

We had Jim James from My Morning Jacket play—in fact, we did a song of his called "Golden." We were fans of My Morning Jacket, and our A&R guy was really hooked on them, so he brought that song into the fold, and we just thought it was ideal. We did one cover by Nada Surf, a song called "Always Love," which Matthew Caws wrote. Matthew and Ira Elliot, the drummer in Nada Surf, came in and helped record it. Ira also happens to be the drummer in Maplewood, and we did one of their songs, called "Indian Summer." These guys came in and played on the songs that they were involved with, which was cool. Despite this, one of the comments we've heard is that the album flows very well from track to track.

It also sounds very much like an America album. On listening to the songs, I assumed that you had written them all, since the style sounds very much like your writing.

James said that he was really after a timeless America effort and not a retro sound. When these people were enthusiastic to be involved, it was not a concern, but something to watch. We didn't want it to become a duet record or be taken over by a bunch of cool young guys. To be honest, it isn't as if we farmed it out, and they produced their tracks, and we produced ours—it was all done by Adam and James. Everything comes into play in creating this—even the sequencing—the back and forth between who wrote what.

What has changed in America's approach to recording and the tools you have utilized in recording?

First of all, the options have become unlimited. It is remarkable how similar the process is in the way that I pointed out earlier. I go back to this singer/songwriter approach, where there are shining examples of people who have always recorded using this process. It's almost like this has come full circle.

You guys were pioneers with this singer/songwriter sound.

Well, you can pick Dylan as the real pioneer if you want, but I pick things like *Rubber Soul*, when the Beatles tended to lean more toward acoustic guitars. They were really doing the singer/songwriter thing on "You've Got to Hide Your Love Away" and tracks like that. It had ceased to be just four guys bashing it out through amps—they were really putting it on the table. I hate to date myself, but that was a turning point for me.

Having said that, all our lives have changed with technology—not just in the recording business. People have 300 or 400 channels on their TVs, iPods, and downloading. The same thing has occurred in recording with Pro Tools, the end of tape and all these other technologies. So you have this dichotomy of, "My God, it's so similar what I'm doing—I'm sitting here with my fine Gibson or Taylor, in front of my Neumann mic," or something like that. That part hasn't changed. But behind the scenes—the process to get it to the listener's ear—the process has really ramped up.

There used to be a closet full of options. Somebody might say, "Hang on, let me go check," and they'd come out and say, "I've got this cool coral electric sitar. Maybe that is a cool sound." Depending on how well stocked your guitar selection was, those were your choices. All of a sudden with samples and modeling, you have every choice. So this whole notion of what's on the table, what are my choices, you really have an unlimited selection, so it really comes back to what are you after and where are you heading.

Why did you include the live album?

Sony was really anxious to find a way to include those titles. At first we balked at that notion because if it comes anywhere near the notion of re-recording them, we're not really in favor of that. There are so many repackaged and re-released versions of these hits. The only reason we included these songs was because we happened to have had a scheduled performance at the XM facility in Washington D.C. They invite groups to come in and re-create start to finish one of their albums, greatest hits included. Which is what we did—we played start to finish our *History* album. It was very well received and an incredibly state-of–the-art recording—that became available for license. Sony heard the broadcast and said, "Wouldn't that be great to get that—we wouldn't have to go and ask Gerry and Dewey to re-record the tracks."

This was a great show.

This is an exciting time for us. The live show has just been getting better and better, decade to decade. Unless you've been following us closely, you wouldn't know about the new material. Our live show is a great way to include this.

How much time and work went into writing these songs? Are you the type who can bang a song out in a day, or do these take weeks?

I do both. I wrote "Chasing the Rainbow" in a very short period of time—it was recorded at different times, and I can hear the difference in EQ between verse one and verse two. I now have a Neumann 149 on which I do all my vocal tracks. For backing vocals, I think we used a Telefunken U47. I use this 149 exclusively through a Universal 6176, which is a combination preamp and compressor. It just gives me really good results—we might mess with the pattern and mic placement a little bit.

I had recorded "Chasing the Rainbow," and the files needed quite a lot of work. I had a fantastic opportunity to work with John Holbrook, the lovely English gentleman. He did the whole album, and it was such a great choice by Adam and James. He had done Natalie Merchant's stuff. It was cool on another level, too, because we worked for years and years with George Martin—George's engineer, Geoff Emerick, is another lovely English gentleman who I stay in touch with—we have lunch or breakfast whenever I can. He lives right here in L.A., and in his house, on his mantle, there are three Grammys: one for *Sgt. Pepper*, *Abbey Road*, and *Band on the Run*. Go figure. Whenever I am in England, I get together with George Martin.

Tell me about your specific technique to mic up a guitar.

I might be lazy, but I just tend to go condenser, close mic—over the neck, but back toward the sound hole. In so many of these EQ presets, you can just see what curve they are working off of; they notch off the lower end and boost the higher frequencies. You want to brighten the guitar—I play onstage with a maple, a Gerry Beckley Taylor (GB signature model). It is a midsize, and it's brighter. As much as I love a good old jumbo, you're really not going to use a lot of that air and resonance onstage.

What about a 12-string? Do you choose a different mic?

No. But I can tell you that my son is doing it, and even with John, they would have an additional ambient mic that they would at least have as an option. Not a lot of difference, but the thing is you want the shimmer of all of those. If a mic is on its own, then a lot of that thicker signature is usable, but when you start to mix a couple of acoustics that won't add, it will get in the way of other instruments, like Wurlitzers and other instruments with similar frequencies.

Did Adam or James try any unique techniques or approaches that you hadn't seen before?

They are very, very talented, but quite different guys. Adam relies on James a great deal. He will look to James to confirm or unseat ideas that he has. "What do you think of this?" James is much quieter but is really involved. For example, he would always be the one to say, "This really needs a raking strummed chord at the start of each bar." Things that I would have overlooked, but on listening back, I am so glad he did. He'll listen to each guitar and really think about which guitar is right for a part—he will inevitably pull out a Casino or a 330. He changes things up just a little bit.

How did mixing and editing go?

Editing was important. Adam and James would say, "We don't need that second or third solo over here." This was really important, and the reason these songs are really strong back to back is because they were really good at keeping the listener's ear. Editing plays a big part in that, and you don't want any superfluous stuff. There was a certain palette of sounds that we stuck to throughout the entire project, but having said that, there were different sounds for vocals among songs. Some were right in your face, and others have a bit of a wash—but they are all from the same color palette.

3 Nada Surf: Beautiful Beats in Brooklyn

Nada Surf's latest album, *Lucky*, plays to the alt-rock trio's greatest strengths: It is complete with infectious pop ballads ("Beautiful Beat"), vulnerable mood pieces ("Are You Lightning?"), and songs with soaring overtones and guitars that hearken back to their formative indie days ("Whose Authority"). I spoke with lead singer and principal writer Matthew Caws to talk about the building blocks of *Lucky* and found that raw talent and a sensible approach to the recording had much more to do with the successful outcome of the record than simply luck.

Nada Surf's *Lucky*, released February 2008.

You've done a lot of records by now. What was different in the overall process with this one?

There are three main differences to this record. One of them, now more than ever, is that we live apart. Daniel lives in Vienna and Madrid, so this led to the most concentrated period of writing and rehearsing that we've ever had—we wrote and played almost every day.

The other thing was that I finally went though all my old cassettes. I have a pretty illogical way of working, which is when I feel like writing something, I turn on the tape recorder and start making stuff up—once in a while this can turn into a whole song, but more often than not, I just do things, then get hungry, go have a sandwich, and move on and never listen to that tape again. I have so many hours and hours of stuff, and it's very hard to go through it because most of it's bad, and I don't want to listen to those tapes.

But there are a lot of fragments that perhaps if you put them together in the right way might make up a unique song.

Yeah. The hope is that there is something I did late at night that I don't remember, and it's actually a real hook. But more often than not, what I write I never hear back. I've been meaning for a couple of albums to finally go through that stuff. It's hard because 70 percent of it is total garbage, 28 percent is garbage enough to be garbage, and then 2 percent is good. So I have to go get that 2 percent.

The other difference was that we really didn't need to be involved in the production this time. Even with the last record, Chris Walla produced most of it, but then we had it mixed by a whole ton of people. It was a very different experience.

Where did you record it this go-round?

We recorded this time at Robert Lang Studios in Richmond Beach, about a half an hour outside of Seattle. We decided against recording in a place like New York because there are just too many distractions. By recording here, we could go home in the evening and not be thinking, "Wow, I really have to concentrate on what I'm doing tomorrow." Also, John Goodmanson is from Seattle, and that's another reason we did it there.

You mentioned you are working under more constrained time because you live apart. How did the basic tracks go down?

The three of us always play together, and we keep everything we can. My favorite place to record is a place called Palindrome that has closed—I think it's now called something like Standard Electrical Recorders. Palindrome was run by Fred Maher, who made our second record, and Michael Beinhorn. That was a great place because the live room was right where the console was; there was no control room. Of course, that makes it a lot harder to monitor, but as an environment, it's really great to record that way without the glass wall and the airlock. Being able to talk to the engineer and the producer through the air is really great—I loved the atmosphere.

There is a house on top of a hill, then the studio is built into the hill. So we lived upstairs in the house, and that's a great thing to be able to do. You don't have to all get together in a car and drive to the studio, but rather just walk down the stairs and there you are.

Photo by Autumn de Wilde.

Nada Surf, pictured left to right: Daniel Lorca, Matthew Caws, and Ira Elliot.

What was it like to work with John Goodmanson?

John mixed a couple of songs on *The Weight Is a Gift*. He mixed "Do It Again" and "What Is Your Secret?" Not only is he a super laidback guy, but he works incredibly fast and has a great ear. Those mixes came together really fast, and the sounds he got were really well balanced, detailed, rich, and heavy. Just from running into him at shows and things, we knew it would be a really good fit. He's really calm and will let everything happen. But he always has an opinion to get you out of whatever rabbit hole you end up in.

Do you find you need someone telling you, "This isn't good enough, push harder," or does he help bring you to another level more naturally?

It kind of happens naturally. He's great to sing with, though—he has a really good ear for knowing when your voice is right for a song, and knowing when to move on or take a break. Some producers can tell what a good take is so much faster than the musician can. That was our experience with Ric Ocasek, who made the first record. With him, we would do several takes of a song, and he always ended up picking the right one even though we would end up debating it for hours. We would be like, "It was take two," and he would be like, "Nope, it's take one." Then a few hours later, we'd realize that he was absolutely right.

John would speak up if a verse or a melody wasn't working, and that's incredibly useful. Also, he was so laidback that I was able to write stuff right in front of him. Normally, I'd be much too self-conscious to do that, but in this case, I'd ask his opinion, change things, and show him what I'd done. That was unusual for me.

Having so many different hands mixing the last album, what was your experience mixing this time, since there was only John and you guys?

I think this was better, but I wouldn't trade that experience. It was so much fun to be able to cut up the record and give certain tracks to certain people. It was great because if we had an all-out power pop song, we'd give it to Ed Stasium because he did all the Ramones things. He was the perfect candidate. Then we gave the single to Chris Shaw, who did it really fast. In this case, though, I really like John's sound, and it was nice to let go of it. There are some tracks that he mixed that we didn't even get a chance to logistically hear and make comments. They came out great, though—I kind of love that because it takes away the temptation to second guess.

How has your approach changed when miking guitars and vocals? Do you have favorites?

Chris Walla and John both used the Coles 4038 on guitars. I've been singing on SM7s forever. The first record was on a Neumann, and then on the second record, Fred Maher stood me in front of eight mics—C12s, the whole deal. I just sounded better on an SM7. In this case, we revisited so we would pick specific mics for each song. One song might have needed a 47 because it was a little darker, for example. I didn't use an SM7 at all for this record, and I wanted to switch it up to give the album some depth.

It's good that you're not married to one microphone. When you started recording *Lucky*, did you come into the studio with any specific sonic reference points?

We're just in our own thing now. I wouldn't want to have such a specific reference, since that could take away from what our own record could be. Sonically, though, my favorite records are *Rocket to Russia*, the third Ramones album, and *Ocean Rain* by Echo & the Bunnymen, but then I also really like all the Teenage Fanclub records because that's just straight guitar pop music, but with a heft and a sheen to it. More sheen than a Cheap Trick record, but more heft than an Elvis Costello record.

I just trusted John: All I really care about is that it has to sound big without being obnoxious; it has to have space without being too reverbed out to the point where it gets small again; it has to have some definition. In the mix, I always think one or two elements should stick out a little further than others, just to give it two planes. If everything is mixed perfectly equally, then you get a sort of flat field. It's better to take some risks and jack up the vocal or the piano or something.

What has changed for you over the years in how you listen and what techniques have you applied to adapt to this?

Unfortunately, one of the things I've learned is actually a bad lesson. You don't really have to be as well prepared as you used to. The first two records, everything was rehearsed to death, and we knew all the little changes. This time, I was having trouble finishing songs, but I didn't want to put off the recording anymore. So I brought my four-track to listen back to all the recordings, and I set up a kind of auxiliary studio and was finishing stuff on the fly. With Pro Tools, you can fly things around a little bit. Not to copy and paste, but to chop things up and make this verse half the length and the chorus twice the length. That's kind of bad because it makes the last minute even later.

Do your musical styles gel so much now from having known each other over the years that it takes you less time to fall into a pocket when either recording or rehearsing?

Yeah. There is one song, "From Now On," that we'd never played together at all. The take that's on tape is probably the third time we ever played it—it was the best one. I always think of the best take as the first time you get it right in rehearsal.

How many extra songs were there that didn't make the album?

We threw out maybe 10 songs that didn't make the album. They were all missing something; either the verses or choruses weren't quite good enough, but we could have finished any or all of them if we had the time. That's one thing that John was really good at—project managing and having the tough talks. He'd say, "We're looking at 23 songs. There isn't even enough time to even think about that, so let's start chopping." He had to be a hard ass about it.

What is different about breaking a record now with things like social media out there? Obviously things like touring remain the same, but what about marketing and distribution?

There is the whole leaking of the album question. We streamed the song on MySpace three months ahead of time, and that does amount to releasing a single in a weird way and gets people to talk about it. Then we streamed the whole record a week ahead of time. That really seems to be the way to go—you can't really force anyone to buy a record anymore because they'll get it for free if they want it for free, and they'll pay for it if they want to pay for it.

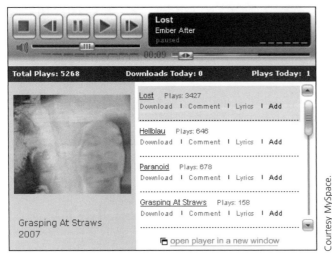

Streaming a song on MySpace.

You just want people to listen to it, right?

Exactly. You just want a bigger number of people who might actually buy it. So it seems to be the right thing to do. There are some bands that make hilarious videos and EPKs, but we're a little old school that way and I'm not an actor—I just like to sing. I would like to do some more guitar video lessons, however. We get asked for tabs a lot, and I don't really know how to write tabs. There are so many made-up chords on this record and our others that I play and I have no idea what they are. Sometimes I'm trying to re-learn my songs, and I can't even figure out how I played them.

Thinking back on your whole career, are there moments that stand out in the studio for you?

Yeah. I remember cutting three tracks on *Let Go* that we did with Juan Garcia at The Magic Shop. I used to intern there, and he was the head intern. I cleaned the counters for a couple years and answered the phones, just one day a week. Juan recorded that stuff, and we just had a day and we did it pretty fast. Later, there was some discussion of, "When are we going to record that song for real?" But I just knew; I was like, "No, they're done, they're perfect, they're great." But I think there was a feeling like they were too easy or something.

So I enjoy those moments when things are easier than they should be or you stumble across the right thing. This time, Phil Wandscher, who plays with Jesse Sykes, played on "Are You Lightning?" He walked in; it was like 10 at night, maybe. He pulled out his guitar, was tuning up, plugged into a little amp—an Ampeg maybe. We were running the song through the live room monitors just so he could get an idea of it. He started playing along, and immediately it was just right. We logically should have brought a tuner into the control room, made him a headphone mix, had him play to the speakers, run cables, and all that stuff, but we said, "Forget it. Stick up a mic and get out of there." So we threw a mic in front of his amp and split. No headphones—he just played with the track that was coming through the monitors, and that was it. We let him go through two or three passes, then he was done. That was really incredible because it felt like he was playing a show, so we dimmed the lights and just got out of there! It was amazing.

How much home recording do you do, and do you have any ambitions to improve?

Not very much—normally the stuff that I do doesn't get on the record. I'd like to get better at recording—I can't even run GarageBand, and I always get latency in the vocals. I move apartments once in a while, and until I know I'm not going to move anymore, it's hard for me to envision building a real place. I do have an Otari 1/2-inch eight-track, and I would like to get that running again. Like everyone who grows up in the city, I dream of having a garage. My happiest moment ever is sitting next to a really good engineer and producer and watching them work or listening to someone mix.

4 A Night on the Town with Los Lobos

Since their 1984 debut, *How Will the Wolf Survive?*, Los Lobos has had a successful, unrelenting run of rock 'n roll, film soundtracks, even traditional Mexican music. The group has worked alongside some of the best producers in the world—folks such as John Leckie, T-Bone Burnett, Mitchell Froom, and Tchad Blake. By touring extensively on their own and with the likes of Bob Dylan and the Grateful Dead, they have also earned a loyal international fan base.

Los Lobos' latest effort, *The Town and the City*, was produced entirely by the group and represents a significant departure from previous records—for one thing, the record has a strong conceptual theme running through it from start to finish. It is also a few shades darker and perhaps more artistically challenging than their previous works. I spoke to keyboard player Steve Berlin, who happens to be a very accomplished producer in his own right, having produced artists such as Jackie Greene, the Fabulous Thunderbirds, and Raul Malo, to name just a few.

Los Lobos, pictured left to right: Conrad Lozano, Steve Berlin, Louie Perez, David Hidalgo, and Cesar Rosas.

29

Where was *The Town and the City* recorded?

Most of the new album was recorded at Cesar's house [Rosas, guitarist/singer]. He converted his garage into a studio, and we've done our last two and a half records there. He had a beautiful, one-of-a-kind broadcast Neve that was just amazing, along with a 2-inch 24-track and some other nice gear he has accumulated. We did the record over about seven months, and at the very end, we went into Sonora Recorders to cut three extra tracks.

How has Cesar's garage evolved over the years with each new record?

In the very beginning, we had two or three ADATs and all the headaches that go along with them. But we made it work—we've done a lot of film soundtrack work there over the years. It has seemed so much easier to go over to Cesar's place and get that stuff done, and it's not so time consuming. We started with ADATs and a Mackie 24 board, which worked fine for the time, but gradually, as time moved along, we got a 24-track 2-inch and slightly nicer gear along the way. The key was getting the Neve because we could do anything we needed to do.

Have you traditionally mixed at Cesar's as well?

We've almost always mixed down somewhere else. It is a garage and wasn't really set up to be a mixing room, though we have mixed a lot of soundtrack stuff there since it's often a "cut to fit" operation if we get the sonics right—in fact, we did a great deal of the movie *Desperado* there.

How does it feel to do the whole album in your own environment and not be worried about watching the clock?

That was really the key for us. We've worked at CRG [Cesar Rosa's Garage] so much over the years that the feeling of not having to worry about the clock isn't really new for us. We're quite used to it—it's nice because the guys can run home, run the kids to school or whatever, and get back to the studio. When we used to record in Hollywood, usually the day was shot if somebody couldn't make it.

You are also a very prolific producer. How are you able to juggle a full-on project with Los Lobos as an artist while handling your other production projects? Is it ever a challenge to balance it all?

Not really. I'm only ever doing one or the other. There isn't enough time to split it. So when it's time to make a Lobos record, it's all hands on deck, including mine. We build a lot of breaks into our touring cycle, though, so if I'm ever going to make a record, it's always in our downtime so I can give that project 100 percent of my concentration as well. Usually the people I produce will have to just wait until I'm done with Lobos, then I go and work for them, but they understand. That's what happens when you're attempting to have a full-time career as a band member and attempting to have a full-time producing career—somebody has to wait somewhere. The people I've been producing have been gracious enough so that it hasn't become a problem. It is harder on my family than anyone else, because I don't see a lot of them.

At what point did you decide you could produce Los Lobos and keep that objectivity? Many people are afraid to produce themselves for fear of losing that objectivity.

The first two Los Lobos records are really the only ones that I can say I produced. In the early days when I had had a little more studio experience and made a couple of records—we're talking like early '80s. After that the guys became pretty conversant with the technology. We became a lot more specific about what we wanted. At that point, we started realizing what we sounded like and what we wanted to sound like. We had a very identified and clear sense of where we wanted to go with this stuff a long time ago. We knew ourselves, and a lot of the stuff that we do is not accepted industry wisdom, and we have broken from the trends. That really works for us, and that's the way we do it. By that point—now we're talking late '80s—I realized that I wasn't doing anything in this band that anyone else was doing. It's been that way ever since—I've always been the first to arrive and the last to leave, but I wouldn't say that I produce these records—everybody gets involved. It's usually the songwriter who drives the ship, and then all of us have a stake and we try to add as much as we can. It is produced by the band—we are all there and throw our weight around a little bit. At the end, it's not done until everybody's happy.

Let's talk about *The Town and the City*. Did you guys consider this album a departure in any way from records you've done previously?

It's definitely a departure in a number of ways. For one thing, it was the first time that we ever really had an overarching, unified concept. We had this notion about an immigrant's journey—it's a story that starts in one place and ends in a different place, and the songs take this individual through a number of different scenarios. That right away is a very different thing for us—we've never done a record that has a single, unifying concept. We've done ones where there might be a musical vocabulary or a set of instruments or an acoustic record, but this record, with its overarching concept, was a very different thing for us. Initially, we had a little bit of trouble getting things started, but once we hit on this idea, it really opened up the gates a little bit and allowed us to move the project forward. To a certain extent after the last record, it presented quite a challenge, and we felt like we were coming in cold and starting from scratch.

It sounds like this thematic approach was very healthy for you.

It was—it was very good. There wasn't the same range of variety of songs on this album because these were the songs that showed up. We've always been holistic about the records we make in that when it's time to make a record, the songs always show up and tell us what kind of record it is going to be. For this one, the songs came in particularly dark—it was kind of dreary in the beginning. We were like, "God, what's going on here?" We tried different stuff, and the songs themselves would kind of steer back into this weird little thing. We finally realized there was this whole thread that was happening.

Photo courtesy Steve Berlin.

Steve Berlin at the recording console.

It's interesting because songs like "The Valley" and "Hold On" strike me as very mesmerizing. They almost remind me of Yusef Lateef's work. Then you get into the "The Road to Gila Bend," when things pick up and become more rock 'n roll.

Well, that song was one that we did at the very end because we cut what we thought was the finished record and put it down for a month. We didn't really listen to it, and once we came back, I think everyone realized that it really was a little slow. We needed to spice the record up a little bit, so "Gila Bend" and "Free Up" came in those last few songs—I really think they made a huge difference for the record and gave it a quantum leap. If those songs weren't there, it *really* would have been a dark record.

The record sounds very diverse, and there a lot of flavors. You are changing timing and other things—it must have been fun to make.

It was a challenging record to make because we were dealing with bleak subject matter. On all our records, we try to bring in all the instruments that we have in our arsenal to bear. We've got all these folklore and percussive instruments, and it's really nice to be able to bust out some of that stuff because it's so unique. A lot of these instruments don't exist anywhere else other than in our collection. We like to mix and match these instruments with other things—for example, on "Valley," there are a couple layers of this thing called a cajón, which literally translates into "box."

There's a guy in L.A. who hand-makes these tuned wooden boxes that have this really beautiful, complex sound—each side has a very different sound. So we use a drum machine, then layer two of these cajóns on top of that. It brings out this interesting, unidentifiable drum kit sound and adds a lot to the track. If you listen closely, it flams a little bit—it's not quite locked in, which kind of works well.

The other thing that we do, which is really part of our sound, I think, is bring in cassettes from those old Fostex eight-track machines. Our primary songwriter cuts his demos on one of these, and they really have an amazing sound—there's nothing quite like them. More often than not, the demo will come in and we'll use something from it, maybe the drum track. In the case of "Valley," we used the drum track, the backward guitar, and that swirling fuzz guitar—that all came from the demo. It's weird because there is such a dynamic sense—if you put the sound up on a graph, it will look strange—but it sounds amazing. The bottom end is incredible, and when you mix this low-fidelity sound with high-fidelity sounds, it can make this amazing sonic palette. And that's been one of our little dark record-making secrets for years. There's a zillion bands doing hi-fi and lo-fi, but this is our own particular recipe for it.

Another thing I've noticed about the record is that it doesn't have a sheen or a gloss to it. It has a nice, raw, simple feel. There is very little reverb on the vocals, for example.

We eschew a lot of that stuff. I can't think of the last time we double-tracked a vocal, for instance. We almost never do that. We like it when it sounds kind of raw, rowdy, and in your face a little bit. That's just partly one of the results when you need to make five guys happy with the mix. I might prefer a little more gloss perhaps, but at the end of the day, you have five people on deck and you say, "If this works for you, I'm good."

How does it feel now that it is all done, looking back?

I always hesitate to say, "It was hard," because I'm making music for a living. Any cop, teacher, fireman, emergency medical technician, on their best day, is having a worse day than me. My job is not hard—I know my job is the easiest job in the world—I get the context and I'm not saying, "Please pity me being in the studio." But it was really challenging. Now that it's done and out, and people have responded so positively to it, I listen to it differently. It really took me a long time to separate the making of it from listening to it as objectively as possible.

For this album, many times I would say, "Gosh, I wish I could get an outside opinion on this, because I really did lose my perspective." I pride myself on being able to separate my player feelings from my producer feelings from my objective "What will the world think?" feelings. As a producer, you really have to be able to step back and look at the big picture. I freely admit that on this record I totally *lost* the big picture. I had no idea if this record was horrible or good. People would ask me, "What do you think of this record?" I would say, "Here, you listen to it—I don't have a clue." It wasn't just glad-handing people—I was trying to get an honest opinion. I've played this thing for a lot of people, and so far everybody loves it. I guess it doesn't suck.

I won't say that our earlier records were as easy as can be, but the challenges some of our earlier records presented were so very different from the challenges presented by this record. We would always come out of these earlier records relatively quickly and relatively in a creative place. For this record, sometimes we had a challenge and we'd be stuck in a ditch for a while—we'd have to wait it out, which isn't the Lobos way. That's not normally the way we deal with stuff.

Maybe it has raised the bar for you guys in some ways?

Exactly. But I will say that I haven't quite solved the whole riddle yet. I still don't know exactly how I feel about the whole thing. It is cool when we've done a lot of in-store signings and I hear it, or I hear it in a coffee shop and I'm very proud of it. But I haven't put it on to listen to it since we finished it. I will, though.

5 Duran Duran: The Best of Both Worlds

One thing you cannot accuse Duran Duran of is being predictable. Throughout the group's illustrious multi-decade career, they have gracefully navigated a diversity of musical styles while never alienating their extremely loyal international fan base. While they earned a reputation very early in their career as a new-romantic, bubblegum pop group, there is no denying they paid their dues very early on, touring extensively throughout Europe. This hard work paid off when they finally went into the studio to record their first album, *Duran Duran*, which featured hits like "Planet Earth" and "Girls on Film." These songs and others are fine examples of how tight their performances were.

If there is a common theme that runs throughout each of Duran Duran's songs, it is that they all sound completely different—from "Planet Earth," to "A View to a Kill," to "Ordinary World." Their recent release, *Red Carpet Massacre*, is no exception to this formula. The group decided to mix things up with legendary hip-hop producer

Photo by Stephanie Pistel.

Duran Duran, left to right: Nick Rhodes, Roger Taylor, Simon Le Bon, and John Taylor.

Photograph by Dirk Noy.

Engineer Jimmy Douglass.

Timbaland [a.k.a. Tim Mosley], combining their massive songwriting talent with a refreshingly different production methodology. I spoke to Nick Rhodes directly following the release of *Red Carpet Massacre*—which, despite being a creatively extraordinary album, was a fundamental departure in terms of how they work to achieve their goals in the studio.

Tell me why the choice of working with Timbaland was significant to the overall objective you guys had.

Actually, what happened was that we had an album finished. It was an album provisionally titled *Reportage* and it was with Andy Taylor—it was much more sort of indie-rock-based and would have sat well alongside albums by bands like The Killers, Bloc Party, and maybe LCD Soundsystem. It went back to sort of our early rock and dance roots. Then when we finished the record, we realized that it was quite political. It was around the time when everywhere you turned was the horror of the Iraq war and the war in Afghanistan. That's what we ended up writing about—and it didn't feel as uplifting as I suppose people would like a Duran Duran album to be. The label said, "Well, it's a great record, but can we just do a couple more tracks and maybe go with a first single?" And we said, "Yeah, fine. As long as it's with Timbaland," because he was the only person we could all agree on who would impart the right vibe for us to work with.

And we had spoken with him before about it. We first met at the MTV awards in 2003, then again at the Brit awards a year later. We sort of talked about working together—he seemed to be keen and had never produced a band. Anyway, we finally pulled it together for September of '06; we were all in New York City. But the four of us arrived—Andy Taylor didn't arrive. Tim was there, and Justin had called a few days earlier, saying, "Hey, I'm in New York. Can I join the sessions for the first day?"

Photo courtesy Roland USA.

Roland V-Drums are a key part of Roger Taylor's drum arsenal.

So we get in the studio in September, and Andy wasn't there, but we just forged ahead. And what we got in five days was three tracks: "Nightrunner," which is the one we did with Justin as well, "Zoom In," and "Skindivers." When we had those three, we all just looked at each other and said, "You know what? This is so exciting; it's a different sound again, and we've really hit on something here."

It was a foundation for new album.

Yeah. To merge the Timbaland beats and Duran Duran just seemed like a very cool idea, and it was really working. So instead of saying, "Let's add these to what we've got," which was the original plan, we just decided to keep working—actually with Nate Hills, who was also on those sessions. As it all happened, we were parting company with Andy, so somehow it all seemed like the right thing to do.

It seems like you were very open-minded about the approach—many bands can be increasingly closed-minded, especially those with so many albums under their belts. How important is it to stay open-minded?

We've produced a lot of albums on our own, we've produced albums with rock producers, and long ago we worked with Nile Rodgers and Bernard Edwards, who were very much from the disco school. And that was very fruitful. So this seemed natural to us. Obviously, the urban producers now do work in a very different way. The biggest obstacle to overcome was the fact that they don't usually work with live instruments that much—which was fine for me, because I'm all keyboards anyway.

But I think when Tim saw all the drums being set up and the bass guitars and the guitars and things . . . I mean, not to say that he hasn't worked with live instruments—of course he has. But generally they do most things with computers and keyboards. So trying to get his head around getting a band sound in there and getting our head around which beats and sounds and stuff that he was creating and we were using was a challenge. And also the fact that we were co-writing. Every track on the album has got a co-writer, some several. That was very different for us. But in a way, it was also incredibly exciting and inspiring. We know what each other can do to some degree, but we do surprise each other sometimes, and often we work together and come up with something that works as a song that we all really like, but bringing people like this on board, they really bring something very different.

I know you worked with Jimmy Douglass, who brings a kind of old-school approach. Can you describe what it was like to work with him?

Jimmy is the missing link between the two in that he has done absolutely everything. We relied on him because the project was dancing around all over the place. There were sessions with Nate in London, back to Timbaland in New York; some things were getting mixed in Miami. He knew where everything was and was able to keep on top of, "Oh, that's a new vocal session that has just come in from here."

It was a lot to deal with, and in some ways, when we used to work on 24-track analog, you'd have to make decisions a lot quicker. You'd say, "Right—that is the bass track." Now, you can record 10 tracks, cut them up, move things around, reverse a couple of bits, stick it all back together, and create something entirely different. But you also end up with sometimes over 100 tracks in Pro Tools.

So on a project like this, just the file management and organization is a project in itself.

Completely. But for Jimmy it was fairly easy, and I think he's used to dealing with that. He has a great chilled vibe when you come in—you know you're going to get what you need out of him. He's got a very good ear himself, and he knows when you've hit on something.

How do you keep technology out of the way and stay focused as a group? How do you keep the good collaborative spirit among the band members without letting all this technology get in the way?

We actually love technology; we embrace a lot of it. But it still has to be about what you can do with the technology, because the technology doesn't write the song. Certainly you can switch on machines now that almost are saying, "Do you want me to write the song for you?" But actually, of course those things are horrible factory-programmed little pieces that don't usually appear on great records. You have to control the machines and find something you like the sound of. For example, I like the Roland V-Synths that I used on pretty much the whole album. I even got Nate into loving the V-Synth when he was here. He obviously uses a lot of soft synths, but I like actually still having hardware.

There is something about being able to touch things and fiddle with them—not just seeing the numbers and dials on the screen. With regard to other stuff, we are always looking for things. Roger used a lot of electronic drums—he used the Roland V-Drums a lot. Simon is always looking for different microphones and effects. The same with John— we had him playing a lot of synth bass on this record. Also, the way that *Red Carpet Massacre* turned out, John has a synth onstage, and he's enjoying it. It is something different.

There is even a part in the set that we did—the show we've worked up for Broadway— which was in three acts. The first act is the whole new album. The second act is us in a 20-minute electro set, where John, Simon, and I have keyboards. Simon's is a vocoder, John plays mostly basslines on it, I play melodies and pads, and Roger has electronic drums. So the four of us are lined up almost as Kraftwerk.

What kinds of things haven't changed in terms of the technology? What gear do you turn to that is still viable for you?

Honestly, I do have all my analog synths, and until this record, I pretty much stayed analog. I have used some analog on *Red Carpet Massacre,* but for the first time, it is mostly digital synths. I realized in working with these producers that they are solely digital. They don't touch analog. A little too complicated means not quick enough, and when you've got thousands and thousands of sounds right at your fingertips, you can find something that is close enough and then maybe just tweak it a little bit if you want.

Because you don't want to miss the idea, right?

Right. That's how they work exactly. Let's get the moment, let's move, let's do it, that sounds great, now we're done.

So they don't go back and refine their sounds?

No, they don't. During the whole sessions, they didn't go back on anything. They make decisions, and that's what I love about it. It was a different way of working—our way would have been to put something in, then come back and replace it with something we liked more.

It's almost a throwback to the days of eight-track analog, when you were forced to make a decision before doing a bounce and moving on.

Completely. That's what I mean. With so much available, the one thing you really do have to do now, to keep it even slightly manageable, is say, "Okay, that's the bass sound, that's the drum loop." Of course you layer and add stuff, but I like the way they do that, so I ended up joining the digital club because it was so much faster. A couple of times when I had a few hours on my own, I would tailor-make an analog sound for a part in a song or something, but for the most part, it's all digital.

I would imagine this way of working also makes you feel like you are accomplishing something, rather than fiddling with sounds for three days and then looking back and thinking, "Have I really done anything?"

Sure. The other thing that I did find when I started playing analog keyboards with the digital sounds is that they just leave the digital effects on everything—I have to say, I usually took the reverb off because I can't bear cheap digital reverb. But they leave the effects on the sounds. So if you suddenly play a very dry analog sound, you really need to pile effects on it before it actually fits in sonically. Otherwise, it sticks out and sounds very strange with everything else because of the sonic zone it is in and the effects.

Taking things down the signal chain a little bit, how sensitive are you to console choice and how much impact do you think this had on the sound?

You'd have to ask Jimmy what desk he mixed on. I think he likes the SSL desks, because he mixed a lot of it in Miami. But we mixed some of it at Metropolis here in London, and certainly a whole lot of it was recorded on Neve desks in London. But a lot of the mix is done in Pro Tools now. It is more a case of them spreading it out over the board, adding some EQ here and there and giving it some space. If I listen to my early roughs, they are not radically different in balance than the actual mixes.

I mean, Jimmy is the master of tweaking things in perfectly and bringing out the things that you really do need to hear, but he does such great roughs in the first place that you still don't know what the song is really going to be like.

If you had to look back on some of your earlier records today—say *Rio* or your first album—how do they hold up to your ears?

You know what? I can honestly say I wouldn't change a thing. The first couple of albums were produced with Colin Thurston. Colin Thurston was an engineer we picked up because he had worked with David Bowie, he'd worked with Iggy Pop, and he produced the Human League's first record. He just had the right credentials, and we met him and liked him. He taught me most of what I know about studio recording. I was very lucky and was able to work with Alex Sadkin, who was incredible, and also Nile, but it was Colin who gave me the understanding of how things really work, how to put together a track, how to balance things, and how to spread things out. He had a very traditional understanding, but at the same time he was a maverick. So he didn't mind when I said to him, "Listen, does it really matter if that goes into the red?"

If it somehow sounded better, he'd say, "Okay, okay. We'll try it." We did a lot of things like tape phasing, which I loved because I'd never seen it before. If I wanted to take a piece of a song and edit it in somewhere else, we'd cut the tape, splice it, and put it together. We created tape loops for things when we wanted something to go around. All this stuff was so much fun and so interesting when you were learning.

Of course, Pro Tools now allows you to make any kind of loops so quickly and fly things in wherever you like. But I remember dropping things in when we were making the song "The Chauffer." I'd found this old nature record, and I wanted to drop in the sounds of this guy talking and these crickets. We literally did it live. I was dropping the needle onto the record when it was already spinning at the right speed, just where I wanted it, because that was the easiest way to do it.

Thinking back on those early records, it occurs to me how tight you guys were. You must have been touring a lot and were obviously very, very well rehearsed. How important is it to come into the studio so well rehearsed?

Then, it was very, very important because that was the way you presented music, and we were playing live. We wanted to get it as tight as we could. Now everybody plays to click tracks; a lot of the things are more programmed, even with Roger's stuff. And Roger is just about the tightest drummer in the world as far as I'm concerned.

I agree—he is unbelievable.

He still is. When we play live with him, he's like a metronome. He locks the band together. But in the studio, people take bits of things and loops—obviously, we do it ourselves to a degree because it makes things sound contemporary. Then when we play it live, we play it live—that is our compromise in that way. We just try to do what sounds right for the record. But back then, we were trying to sound like it was all cut up into pieces, if you see what I'm saying.

When you are playing live these days, which songs from your early repertoire seem to resonate well?

Most of the catalog we can all play completely blindfolded with at least one hand tied behind our back. Actually, that might not be true for the bass and guitar. We've played them all so many times and have played a lot over the last couple of years. It's very comfortable and easy. The ones that go down well with the audience and the ones that are most successful are always "Rio," "Hungry Like the Wolf," "Ordinary World," and actually, "Sunrise" from the last album is proving to be a lot more powerful live than we ever imagined.

It seems like there is a nice camaraderie among you—in the studio, are you really able to let your egos get out of the way and collaborate?

We like to collaborate. The thing is, you do have to accept when somebody else has a better idea than you do, and that goes for all of us. Because the reason we work together as a band is because we like it—we like the sound we create together. Anyone can go and make a solo record—we have done different projects between us over the years. But when we are making a Duran Duran record, the end game is to get the best out of each one of us and to take the strongest idea that any one of us has for a song. And it doesn't matter whether that is a title, a melody, a chord structure, or a groove. Wherever we start, we try and get the best out of it.

With this album, we were lucky enough to be working with some of the world's greatest producers, who also contributed to the songs. There was a hell of a lot of technology and songwriting power in the room while we were making it.

Also, you guys are in a position now where you are probably able to withstand any pressure from record labels—you have artistic freedom to create pretty much whatever you want.

We had a rotten deal when we first signed with EMI in 1981, but the one thing that I personally insisted on was complete artistic control. I suppose it wasn't such a great deal, but they let us have this, and we've never signed a deal where we don't have that.

Thinking back on your recording career, do any special memories stand out for you as spectacular?

There are so many, to be honest. I have a memory like an elephant. I'll tell you what was quite interesting: During the first album, we were going to use Abbey Road. We were very excited because it was the studio where the Beatles recorded half of the greatest pop music ever made. But we just couldn't get the sound we wanted—we couldn't get the drum sound. It was sort of exasperating. We were looking for something quite modern, I think—it was "Planet Earth" we were working on. After about three days in there, we had to leave Abbey Road and go somewhere else because Colin wasn't happy with the drum sound, and it just wasn't working out. It just seemed so ridiculous [starts laughing] to be leaving Abbey Road! I couldn't believe it. But we've worked there seven times since, and we've got a perfectly good drum sound. But it just wasn't working out—sometimes these bizarre things happen.

I also remember recording "Notorious" with Nile in London—I think that was Air Studios. I remember when we hit on that riff. I remember saying, "Wait a minute. How does that work on the piano? You're playing a seventh, right? Then a D minor?" I was just figuring out what it was and converting the guitar to the piano, which I don't usually do an exact facsimile of. But when we were working on that song, it all just suddenly clicked together, and I said, "Where did I do this?" We had the song in about a half an hour, and that was very exciting.

What is up around the bend? What excites you now?

I listen to mostly to what hip hop has turned into, and dance for the last 10 years or so. Recently, I like some of the Kanye West album. I like the last couple of LCD Soundsystem records; I think they are very much in our area. I also like Timbaland and Justin's albums. Of rock stuff, The Klaxons, I think, are probably the most interesting thing I've heard in the last year. I'm looking forward to seeing where that goes. I also like The Kaiser Chiefs.

6 Grant-Lee Phillips' Strange Magic in the Studio

The term "strangelet" refers to pieces of "strange matter" that, according to some scientists, pass through the Earth's ecosystem virtually undetected from time to time. Grant-Lee Phillips' *Strangelet* is anything but alien in nature—its songs are firmly rooted in Phillips' familiar folk roots style, and the album evokes a home-grown feel, making it intimate territory for the listener.

Phillips achieved this intimacy on the record by doing the vast majority of the tracks at his home studio in Los Angeles, which gave him the opportunity to turn on a mic at 2 a.m.—or, for that matter, whenever inspiration happened to strike around the clock. This enabled him to capture that original spark that is perhaps more elusive in a traditional studio setting.

Grant, tell me about your latest album.

The name of the album is *Strangelet*. I recorded the majority of this record on my own in my home studio over the course of about a year—in between touring, shows, and other projects. When it came to the drums, I went up to Seattle and booked a couple of days in a bigger room up there. The drums were actually one of the later parts that were laid down, as were the string parts, which were done on a handful of songs. The string parts were all done at Eric Gorfain's [violinist/arranger] personal studio facility. So the whole album has kind of a home-baked feel about it.

On your last album, you did covers of '80s songs, which was fun. This is your first original album in how long?

This is the first album of my own material in about two years. My last album of original works was cut at the Sound Factory in Hollywood, which is a great room. That was a small, traditional analog situation in which we went straight to tape—we also did that album with every player in the room. Wherever there was a corner to hide another musician, we did so. There were probably about seven of us on the floor for that one.

Did you self-produce this album, and has this traditionally been the case with your albums?

Yes, and this has been the case more and more with my solo albums. Grant Lee Buffalo was a three-piece that lasted on record between '93 and '98. Most of our albums were produced within the band by our bass player, Paul Kimble. It was very much a thing that grew out of a garage-turned-studio, and we brought that to a record-making relationship once we signed our deal.

The final Grant Lee Buffalo album we put out was produced by Paul Fox, which was the first time we reached out to an outside source. The band at that time was down to me and the drummer, so I think we were ready for some input from the outside. But I've written 100 percent of the material that I've put out, and the process of writing and recording has become more and more fused. I've found that the computer is a visually healthy companion to have as I'm putting my songs together. I don't always put my songs right into the computer, but it has enabled me to get what I am hearing in my head much more quickly—then I can develop the song and start showing it to other musicians. I've found there are so many different ways to go about it. You do one record, then on the next one, you want to take a different angle on it.

What is different about how you are writing now, and how has technology changed this?

My philosophy has been to sing first and write second, and having a tape recorder rolling when I sit down with a guitar and throw ideas out there. That is probably the healthiest thing.

Would you consider the flavor of the songs different on this one?

I find that the spirit of the writing tends to go in cycles. There are certain things that this album has in common with some of my earlier albums—even ones that I made a decade ago. I think it's because I had that secret hideaway that I can go to and develop the material without feeling like anyone was looking over my shoulder. Perhaps that is the key benefit of having a home studio, more than anything. Hopefully you can go out there in the middle of the night and chip away at a song.

The other thing is that we've moved past the idea that first you work on the song, then you demo it to death, and finally one day you go in and do it for real. These days, it's very probable that the initial spark, the seedlings of the song, may actually turn out to appear in one form or another on the master. I've always placed a premium on that spontaneity factor, and now that home recording has become so good, it's a lot less likely for it to sound dumbed down or demo-like.

Has this way of recording saved you time or enabled you to get into other kinds of projects?

My career has become increasingly varied and interesting. On a given day, I might be writing a song for a soundtrack for a film or television show, or on tour with a friend—I did a fun tour back in December with Aimee Mann and a number of other artists she assembled. Meanwhile, I am sometimes called in to play the town troubadour on *Gilmore Girls,* which is kind of a strolling musical character that I've been involved with playing for about six or seven seasons. So it's really varied.

Any areas that are really catching you as a sweet spot?

It's all sort of like that—it's all pretty fresh. I think about a year ago at this time I was scoring a television program. That was an interesting process to wake up at the crack of dawn and have to create music very quickly, on the spot and on a deadline. I think that often brings out some good work—you learn some tricks and you find a flow that you can hopefully apply to your own work, where you are not necessarily working under the clock, but you want to capture something and keep it. That was a show called *What About Brian.*

On *Strangelet,* were there any difficult areas that you had to overcome?

In terms of the recording, there was a lot of trial and error in recording the new album. Doing a mix and getting accustomed to what it sounds like in the real world as opposed to my little room can be a challenge. I think that's a natural thing for anyone doing home recordings. As far as my signal chain, it's not too involved. Most everything goes through an Avalon compressor and into Digital Performer running on my Mac G5. I got turned onto Digital Performer through the Sundance Film Lab, which is this amazing program I was lucky to be involved in. It's basically a program that stimulates and mentors budding composers—that happened to be the software I was using up there. I've really warmed up to it. I've made other albums where it was exclusively in Pro Tools, but there are many bells and whistles in Digital Performer.

Digital Performer is similar to Logic in that everything is already there in the box, and it is so easy to use in that respect.

When I got into doing some of the film scoring, I realized that I would be under the gun time-wise, so I invested in outside plug-ins like Ivory, the piano soft synth, and the Native Instruments B3, and other things that would allow me to get the sound that I would prefer to get in those days when I didn't have a day to move a piano or an organ in. I needed the authenticity but didn't have the time or the space to deal with the real instruments. My music has typically featured real instruments—I've often preferred the sound of a single guitar to something that fills up every molecule of air on the track.

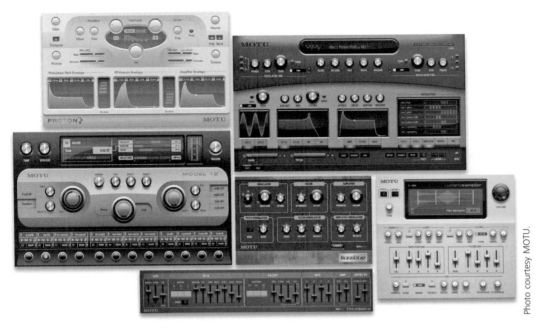

Digital Performer is Grant's workhorse platform.

Did you need a second engineer or did you actually do all the engineering yourself?

Everything at home was done on my own—it was pretty erratic and involved a lot of running around. I've gotten to a place where with one hand and one arm I can hold the microphone down to the guitar and up to my vocal [laughs], then I can spin around, and within arm's length it's all there. It literally becomes an extension of the songwriting at that point.

Did you experience any difficulty in room monitoring? What was it like moving the project from room to room, and how long was it before you could trust what you were hearing?

That's something that I was able to fine-tune little by little, but having said that, I also had help on the outside. The drums were recorded by a guy named Jon Ervie at Jupiter Studios, one of the engineers that works there regularly—he got a great drum sound right away.

What was the sequence in laying down the instruments?

I would often begin with the guitar and vocal, then build in the loops, complete with fills. I didn't want to get too lost in programming and creating the loops, but I did want a template against which all the other instruments would feel comfortable. Bill Rieflin, who played drums on the album, suggested we go up to Jupiter Studios in Seattle, which has a bigger room.

Grant-Lee Phillips' *Strangelet,* released March 2007.

Tell me about some of the other musicians you brought in.

For the strings, I used a quartet that I've worked with on a few occasions, now called the Section Quartet—they are based out of Los Angeles. Eric Gorfain is the violinist and the arranger in the quartet that I have worked with—we've toured together, recorded together. He and I sat down with the songs, and he came up with great arrangements. That was something that was put in near the end. In some cases I had a template that I had written using string patches, with which I was able to express what I was looking for.

Did this add dimension to the record? What did this really bring to light?

The songs the quartet played on have a lot of subtlety, a fair amount of dissonance, and there is a soft coloring to them. They tend to bring out all of the mysterious qualities of guitar and piano chords that can be heightened with strings. We've done some live shows together where it is just me and the quartet—sometimes no guitar and just a voice and a quartet. This allows me to delve into something other than the rock-and-roll outfit of guitar, bass drums.

How did the vocals go down?

I did all the vocals on the album—it is layered at times. Most likely on choruses, and sometimes I go in for the octave double and things like that. I've got a pretty good range.

And the guitars?

As far as guitars go, they were pretty varied. I played a number of Gibson acoustic guitars, including a big J200. I also played a baritone ukulele, which I miked up with a Neumann TLM 103—the baritone ukulele almost sounds like you've capoed up a nylon string guitar. It has a soft, plucky kind of sound, and when you couple that with a '60s Wurlitzer, you get this interesting third sound.

What about mixing? Was this done at home as well?

The album was mixed by Husky Hoskulds, an amazing engineer and mixer who I worked with on my last original album, *Virginia Creeper*. He's mixed and engineered everyone from Norah Jones to Elvis Costello to Allain Toussaint. We transferred everything from DP into Sequoia mixing software and mixed at his home facility.

When mixing with Husky, I began to hear everything in a different light. All of those little things that might have slipped past you during tracking—for example, if something was slightly out of phase—became immediately apparent. At the same time, he had been given all the reference mixes and had a good sense of how it could work out even if it required some cleaning up. We're of like mind and spirit and appreciate all the little barbs that can go into a recording. Technically, he's quite capable, but at the same time in an aesthetic sense can appreciate having captured a moment as well.

Sequencing the record is the final touch where you really get to hear the finished album in its context. What was sequencing this record like, and were you pleased with the end result?

I've gotten pretty good at sequencing because for me it's kind of like putting together one long song. Oftentimes, you run into certain challenges where you want a certain song up near the front and you don't want to bury it—it's a song that beckons to be heard. Those are more arbitrary considerations, I think. Probably within three or four tries I found the right sequence, though. There is a kind of arc that occurs when you stand back and listen to the album: Sometimes you find it accidentally, as I quite often do. For me, there is a lyrical story that begins in a state of conflict—and I'm speaking specifically on this album—then weaves its way through a turn of events, then finally arrives at a state of hope or redemption.

You take a very literary approach. Obviously, you are both a writer and a musician, so you understand where the story is going based on the theme, so you sequence based on that.

I just go with my gut on that type of thing, but I suppose being a writer, it's difficult not making sense with it. Gavin Lurssen over at the Mastering Lab mastered the album. I'm very hands-on throughout the process, since the genesis of my album is right here in my room under my own roof. I follow it all the way through to calling the printer and asking for a matte varnish on the Digipak! I'm very involved.

7 Recording Roger Waters' Post–Pink Floyd Masterpiece

As a founding member of Pink Floyd, Roger Waters asserted his leadership within the band well before *The Wall*. Indeed, even as early as *The Piper at the Gates of Dawn*, he was seen by others—including Norman Smith, Pink Floyd's first producer—as their "captain." Following Syd Barrett's departure, Waters' creative intellect became the driving force of the band, while David Gilmour, Nick Mason, and Richard Wright provided an invaluable musical context.

Even before *The Dark Side of the Moon*, Waters' lyrical prowess was manifested in such songs as *Ummagumma*'s "Grantchester Meadows"—a poetic tribute to the natural beauty of his native Cambridge, England. Waters was a key contributor to the Floyd's early experimental albums, such as *Atom Heart Mother*, where he gained his first experiences working with choral sections and orchestras, and *Meddle*, on which the group painfully pieced together 23 separate musical pieces to create the legendary "Echoes." Waters was an early tinkerer with Moog and Putney VCS3 synthesizers, the latter of which famously created the wind noise audible on *Wish You Were Here*, and now *Ça Ira*.

When Waters left Pink Floyd after *The Final Cut* was released in 1983, he went on to create highly successful conceptual albums, such as *The Pros and Cons of Hitch Hiking*, *Radio K.A.O.S.*, and *Amused to Death*. After the historic reunion with his former bandmates for the Live 8 concert in 2005, Waters released what is arguably his life's masterpiece—*Ça Ira*. *Ça Ira* tells the story of the French Revolution through song and through a cast of characters Waters adopted from a libretto he happened upon.

When I met Roger in 2006, he was extremely enthusiastic and animated about *Ça Ira*—it was clear that he had challenged himself yet again with a subject that was both intellectually stimulating and artistically rewarding. The scope of his undertaking—both from a writing and a recording perspective—was staggering and would take several years to complete.

Roger Waters' *Ça Ira*, released in September 2005.

Ça Ira is an emotionally moving piece—on hearing it, I was very touched at how powerful it is both musically and lyrically. Can you describe the moment that you became transfixed with the idea of writing it?

Wow, that's extraordinary for you to say that. I think I became transfixed with it when I saw the last page of the libretto. I think I've got it here—in fact, I have got it—in fact, I'll show it to you. [Roger briskly walks off seeking the document, and after a few moments walks back in, a smile on his face and a document in hand.] This is not the original, but it's my working copy. Here you can see the translations that I had to do when I started writing the introduction. This is the last page. Do you speak French?

A little. My ancestors were Royalists who were pushed out of Paris during the Revolution.

Well, the translation here is that, "If we're not taken in the misery of luxury, in forgetfulness of others, and in certitudes of our forefathers, in the solitary dream, in the envy of the powerful, in respect for the strong and in fear of ourselves." When I read those words, I still get a chill. This first page is amazing as well—basically, the translation is this: One day, a sparrow was sitting a bush, and someone hit it with a stick. A priest, from no matter which religion, said, "You're right,"—not to the bird, but to the stick. *Un guerrier,* a soldier, from whatever *maison,* or side, put the features of the bird on a shield. A judge, from whatever institution, decreed that the sparrow should not sing in the bushes. One day, the soldiers, the priests, the judges changed. *Pas de tout,* not all of them, but enough. The birds sang in the bushes—it was the revolution. The revolution is a story with sticks and birds and bushes.

Photograph by Jeff Touzeau.

Roger Waters holding a copy of the original libretto that inspired *Ça Ira*.

The strength of this message must have carried you through the recording process of the album, which was doubtless long and painful.

Yeah. They in some sense have claimed some kind of inspiration as well, and that's why when they turned up on my doorstep with this, it already had my interest.

Can you explain how *Ça Ira* landed on François Mitterrand's desk and what your reaction was after you heard that he listened to it?

It was scary, but very interesting. If you look at the DVD, Philippe [Constantin], our friend, had a friend who worked in the Palais de l'Élysée, called Sophie Boucher, Sophie the Butcher. She was working for Jacques Atteli, later to be disgraced in a Deutsche Bank scandal or whatever.

She listened to it, played it to Jacques Atteli; Jacques Atteli took it to François Mitterrand. He listened to it and wrote a letter to Pierre Bercher of Chanel fame, but at the time his day job was as a director for the Paris Opera. Mitterrand wrote him a letter and said, "This piece must be part of the bicentennial celebration," because he really liked it. Because of that there was a lot of talk, and there was talk of it becoming the inaugural piece of L'Opéra de la Bastille. Particularly because another old friend of theirs was a man called Fernandez who had been the director of the Théâtre Bohème. He became the first theatrical director of L'Opéra de la Bastille.

Anyway, that all floundered because they took on a new musical director called Chung who was Korean, who spoke no French, no English. This was only a demo that I made in my home studio. There was no manuscript, notation, nothing.

Since this piece dragged out for so long and there were seemingly so many obstacles, were you ever worried that this might be your unfinished masterpiece? How did you maintain your determination to get it finished?

The evolution was natural, but nevertheless hard. It took a big turn when I agreed to translate it—or to write an English version is a more accurate way of putting it. Because, as you see here, I got a literal translation done by somebody else. But as soon as I had it in English and had written my English version, I realized that it wasn't satisfying to me in narrative terms. So I discussed it with Étienne [Roda-Gil]—I said, "I'm going to have to write some more stuff. If I do, will you translate it into French?" [Roger changes character. Holding his head down low, pretending to hold a cigarette and making his voice gruff and low, he imitates how Étienne spoke.] "You know me, Roger. I say this to you now. I think it's better in English!" [laughs]

He's so clearly still alive in your mind.

Oh yeah, I miss him so. So then I started to write prologues and added a few scenes here and there—partly because of that, partly to enhance the narrative, and partly because I wanted to give the singers, who had become my friends, something to sing. There was nothing really new for Bryn [Terfel], but for Paul [Groves] and Ying [Huang], I wrote really good new tunes for both of them to get their teeth into. So that was very cool to be able to do that. So the English thing made a big difference, and it also enabled me to get a little bit more politically involved in it.

It also made the whole thing a bigger job for you and the scope increased, right?

The last process, the very end of the thing, was I sat down one day and I wrote over a period of two days nine little bits of sort of Shakespearean—not quite black verse, because there is more rhyming in my verse than in Shakespeare's. I put them into the piece as spoken text. This was at the very end of the thing, and I even went so far as to have conversation with actors.

We spoke to Tim Curry and Christopher Plummer, who was doing *King Lear* in New York at the time. I liked the quality of his voice. Then eventually I decided it couldn't have spoken text—it had to be songs and set to music. They are the bits that are like, "And high above something in the brook's melancholy proclaim a schism between God and Satan even the churchmen...," and the bit that goes about that says, "But soft...," which is my kind of joke about it being more Shakespearean: "but soft as ever in the ebb and flow, sweet reason deft and incorrupt, the toiling of the humankind, illuminates man's plight. Should he embrace the root base tilt...the carousel or at least hear that other voice and entertain the choice between the darkness and the light." I was on a roll. I just scribbled this shit out, and I wrote nine or ten of these in two days. And that was kind of easy, but setting it to music was incredibly difficult. The thing was sort of finished, and I had to notch these things in and rework everything.

The lyric, "A story about everything under the sun," is really resonant to me. It reminds me of Thackeray's *Vanity Fair*—you are dealing with an enormous subject matter, and this lyric kind of encapsulates this fact. Even down to the detail of letters that Louis XVI wrote.

The letter is here in the manuscript. This isn't a copy of the real letter, but Étienne always claimed that this was the actual text of a letter that Louis XVI wrote—it would be nice to find it. But Étienne often played games, and I'm not sure if that's true. But I wrote the thing to the French version [Roger starts singing in French]; it's sort of better in French. I sort of disagree with Étienne in a way because to express the ideas in English takes more syllables, so it's hard.

Three of your close collaborators on the project died before their time. How does it feel to be the one to take the project to the finish line, so to speak?

[Long pause] It's sort of difficult for me—I feel very emotional about it. When we do this in Rome, it is going to be very hard. I am conducting the "Overture" [starts to laugh].

And are you nervous about that?

Yeah, of course I am. I've never, ever taken beta blockers, but that could be the first night.

Photo by Jimmy Ienner, Jr.

How did you work out the various narrative voices on the album who articulate the story?

Well, in the original libretto there is a big part for the storyteller. There is a very strong sense of a detached narrator through the piece who keeps coming in. But sometimes he sings in duet with, like, the priest.

You use the metaphor of the bird a lot throughout the storyline. Can you describe the different ways the bird takes shape throughout the storyline?

We would need to resurrect Étienne to give you a proper answer to this question, but as I understand it, the reason that Étienne and Nadine [Roda-Gil; Étienne's wife] used the bird as their metaphor for the proletariat and for human beings in general is because the bird is very fragile but has this potential to be very free. The idea of bird flight and bird song are all very freeing images. But as I say, it's also a very fragile thing. So I think that's why they used the bird as a metaphor, because human beings could be seen as similar in that we are kind of fragile but we also…. I think Étienne felt that human beings have the potential to soar once they discover the light side of their nature and embrace it, rather than the dark side.

"Honest Bird, Simple Bird" is probably one of my favorite pieces on the album. It moves from a single, simple melody to the very powerful and richly orchestrated "I Want to Be King" section. Is this one of the more poignant pieces for you?

Strangely enough, no, it's not. But I'm very glad it is for you. I have all those kinds of favorite bits of the opera that I really like, but that was one of the first pieces that I orchestrated, and I often worried slightly that since it starts in C major the melody was slightly too obvious, and people might accuse me of it being too poppy. So I'm very glad to hear that's not the way it comes across to you, and I think the way Ying sings it is really, really beautiful. When the kids are singing I want to be king, queen, and all of that stuff, I always imagined troops of child acrobats jumping through hoops. There's a lot of hoopla going on [laughs], which is why that sort of motif at the end is meant to be very circus-like.

This is all very visual for you.

Very, yeah.

"In Paris There's a Rumble Under the Ground" almost reminds me of Mozart's "Requiem" because it has all of these sad minor chords. It's almost spooky. What is behind that one?

Well, this is in response to the fact that the pope at the time had a look at the French Revolution and decided that the Declaration of the Rights of Man was a very bad thing. So he issued an edict saying that it was actually a sin to declare human rights—and what people should be paying attention to is that there is a holy connection between Louis XVI and God that nobody must interfere with. That's why that piece is slightly—well, not slightly, but very—satirical, particularly the way I've recorded it with the crowd repeating the priest's lines and so forth. But obviously, the writing is meant to be in that rich choral tradition of the religious music of the 17th and 18th centuries. I was always a big fan of Fauré and Berlioz. So I know the "Requiem" very well; I was always a big fan of this.

This was a really huge work for you. It seems like in the past, your greatest work was achieved when you reached for something huge—take *The Dark Side of the Moon* or *The Wall*. What new challenges did *Ça Ira* represent for you both conceptually and musically?

It is true that I was taking some risks, but the biggest stretch was the technical stretch of coming to grips with the way a symphony orchestra works. I think I always had a pretty good handle on the way choral music works, but I didn't know much about orchestral instruments—what their ranges were and so on and so forth. So quite often when I'd finished some orchestration I would go to Rick [Wentworth], who worked on it with me, and he would say, "I think that's really beautiful, but you know an oboe can't play that line—it doesn't go that high or that low or whatever." "Okay, give it to a bassoon."

I also had to make sense of notation and manuscript. I had never even bothered to look at a piece of manuscript paper, so I had to learn to read and write, which I did—albeit very slowly. I'm not claiming that I now sight read, but I now know all the basic stuff about notation. I sort of knew an awful lot about it anyway, because of the work that I'd done in music before, but it was all done by ear. Of course you learn about keys when you're playing the guitar willy-nilly, but an orchestra is much more complex.

You are mainly used to recording rock 'n roll, which requires a completely different approach to recording orchestral instruments. What sort of things had to be taken into account from a recording perspective?

I'm not sure how far I should go into this, but we spent one week with a team of people who were brought in by the record label because they wanted a marquee name on the record when it came out. So we spent an abortive four or five days with a producer and an engineer who had come in from New York, and it was an absolute disaster. He either didn't get it or was just in it for the money, couldn't be bothered or whatever. I said, "This is not working—I am not hearing this." They would say, "It's fine—we've got everything covered."

Photo by Jimmy Ienner, Jr.

Roger Waters monitoring on headphones during the *Ça Ira* recording sessions.

I sort of believed them, then I pulled the multi-tracks—we were working on Sony 48-track—after they had gone, and we realized that we may just as well have had a pair of stereo mics over the conductor's head for all the separation there was. Unfortunately, I had to can that first attempt. The record company, to their eternal credit, picked up half the tab. And I'm talking about a big tab. It cost us 300 grand to record that, so they picked up 150 and I picked up 150, and we started again. So we started again with Rick Wentworth conducting and with Simon Rhodes, who I've known before. He is probably the top classical engineer in England.

Had you worked with Rick before?

No, but I knew him and knew people who he had worked with before. And we got so close doing the orchestrations. We absolutely hit it off and did a fantastic job conducting the orchestra for the recordings, and most of the time I was out on the floor with him, and we would just divide our time. We would work very, very closely, and it was great. It was obvious from the first sessions that we did that it had been absolutely the right decision to start again.

Simon Rhodes, classical engineer at Abbey Road Studios and engineer on *Ça Ira*.

For such an accomplished writer and musician, you come from a fairly technical background. I know that you have had a home studio and that you worked out some elaborate demos before you went in to record the album. Can you tell me a little about your setup for recording the demos?

The setup when I started was archaic. When I made the demos, I was recording analog onto a Studer 24-track just using a grand piano in the billiard room. The piano was miked with two Neumann U 67s. I always recorded piano with a pair of U 67s, and I always sing through a U 48. I have my own U 48, which is like a bar of gold to me—I treasure that mic. I do all my vocals on it, and I've had it for 20 years.

You mean a U 47?

No U 48. I think it's a U 48....maybe it's a U 47! I beg your pardon, it's a U 47. It's much bigger than a U 67, and it's got that chrome bit that goes across the top, and there's a big old tube and all of that. It's a fabulous machine. I also worked with an old E-MU 3. The best sample it had was bombs going off and shells arriving—the sample was called "Armageddon." I also had a brass sample and a Salinas string synthesizer, which at the time was state of the art. I also used a LinnDrum, particularly for the West Indian piece.

I think I saw the loop on the DVD that was released with *Ça Ira*.

Yeah, you can hear the loop that I had made on the DVD. I made my demo with those things, and then when Rick and I were notating, we were working on an Atari with Notator, which I didn't get at all. But very soon after that, Emagic came out with Logic. We just went straight over to Logic, and I haven't looked back since. I keep upgrading my Logic—am on six point something or other, which is always a pain because it means the stuff you have been working on before doesn't work. It's always hard to get it all translated into the updated versions. But I think Logic is such a brilliant system, and I now do all my rock 'n roll writing in Logic.

It's amazing you find time to dabble in all this stuff, considering your schedule.

Well, I don't. My great friend and collaborator and dear engineer who worked with me for the last 20 years, Nick Griffiths, dabbled in it. He tragically died of liver cancer last year. He was the guy who led me through all these systems. He would come to me with suggestions on how I should upgrade or design all my systems, and I miss him deeply. I also miss his input and have not managed to replace him.

Not many people know this, but you actually recorded the coins on *The Dark Side of the Moon*'s "Money," right?

Yeah, that's right. I had a Revox A77.

What about all the sound effects for *Ça Ira*? You have so many wonderful sound effects—you have dogs barking, horses, the thunder, and rain. Did you go through sample libraries for all that stuff?

No, I didn't do that personally. I worked with a guy called David Novak, and he had a henchman called David something else. So I worked with the two of them at a sound studio on 54th Street—I think it is called Sound One. We sat in a little room there and put it together. They did Foley sessions, and I didn't attend. We had recordings of them chopping melons in half and all that crap for guillotine noises. One thing that is interesting, though, about the *Ça Ira* sound effects is the wind. The wind is all generated by a Putney VCS3, which was in 1965. It just predates the Moog by a few months. I've still got one of the original VCS3s—it was an old thing in a kind of wooden case. It stood for Voltage Control Synthesizer 3, I think, because it had three oscillators that were VCOs. But it makes great wind.

So using this thing to record the wind must have been your suggestion.

Oh yeah! It's my machine, and I had to fly it in from America. Noboby's got one of these things. It's what makes all the noises on *Wish You Were Here* as well. I've been using that thing year after year after year. I love it [laughs].

Ça Ira wasn't the first time you worked with choral work. You had also used orchestration and choral singers on *Atom Heart Mother* and *The Wall*—on "The Trial." Did these experiences give you any kind of basis to work from?

They would have done if I'd been in the studio at all for "The Trial," "Comfortably Numb," or any of those sessions. All of those sessions were done in New York with

Control room inside Miraval Studios in France, where Pink Floyd recorded overdubs on *The Wall*.

neither me nor anyone else in the band there. Michael Kamen did those sessions on his own. We sent him the multi-tracks from the South of France, where we were living at the time, and he produced the scores. He probably didn't even send us any MIDI—thinking back, there probably wasn't any MIDI. He just made the recording. We trusted him to do it—they came back and they were brilliant.

On *The Dark Side of the Moon*, you were obviously forced to economize on track counts—even though you had a couple of tape machines at your disposal. But on *Ça Ira*, there was no limit. Is it good to have limitless tracks now?

Well, we chose to work on a 48-track Sony machine because Simon Rhodes was determined to go analog. He is based at Abbey Road in London—an amazing, amazing engineer. You can sort of mike everything, and he did a great job. I didn't get involved in that at all, really—I was busy making sure the noise they were making was the right noise at every point. The only thing I can say is that I would say, "I can't hear enough of the clarinet playing that solo." So he would move a microphone a bit closer to the second clarinet or whoever, just to make absolutely certain that we got it during the mix.

What about the mastering? When the album is finally done and mixed, how involved are you during this phase?

I never get involved in mastering. I sit there through every second of the mix. Simon would do a good mix of the orchestra, then I would sit in the middle of the room, particularly when we are making the 5.1, and say, "The color of that's wrong," then mainly change the perspectives of the singers. In Simon's original mix, the singers were much more in your face. I said, "Simon, we've got to pretend we are in an auditorium and try to make the singers sit on the stage somewhere in front of us—with an orchestra or behind it, but not right in our ears." I wanted it to sound like a performance of the piece.

Now that you have the final masterpiece in your hands, can you recount any other stumbling blocks you faced along the way?

The false start was a bit of a hiccup. There could have been a bump if Étienne hadn't been such a great guy. There could have been a bump when I said, "I want to start adding to this in English. Would you then be prepared to help me translate what I've written?" A lot of artists might say [imitates French accent], "No, it's my work, you don't touch that." But Étienne went [again, with French accent], "Roger, come on. You know what I think. I think that it is better in English what you have done."

This album is fantastic melodically, but quite frankly, what really drew me in were the lyrics. I would be very interested to hear what your literary influences are. Do you have any favorite writers?

I hope you are taping this. Here is the first verse of a poem I wrote after I read Cormac McCarthy's *All the Pretty Horses* for the first time. This is how I feel about literature, and this is specifically about that moment when you are reading a book and you are getting to the end of it, and you keep putting it down because you don't want to finish it because the experience of reading it is so exquisite.

The poem goes like this, if I can remember it: "There is a magic in some books that sucks a man into connections with the spirits hard to touch that join him to his kind. A man will eke the reading out, guard it like a canteen in the desert heat, but sometimes needs a strike and then the final drop full of sweet, the last page turns: the end." I only quote that to you because it expresses how I feel about the power of literature and the power of words. So that's one guy, Cormac McCarthy, who I am somewhat devoted to. I'm not a great reader—I read quite a little bit of trash. I love Elmore Leonard. I get incredibly enthusiastic, then suddenly I fall into gaps. What was the last thing I read that grabbed me? Ford Madox Ford.

The Good Soldier?

The Good Soldier and *Parade's End,* for instance. I was just dumbfounded by the brilliance. At the moment I'm reading *Independence Day,* which is very good. I read the new Ian McEwan novel, which is called *Saturday.* Aldous Huxley's *Brave New World* is such an important book in my life.

Dealing with the subject of the French Revolution for so long, is must be nice to have the record behind you—kind of like a big exhale.

Yes, I am happy to move on from that, but I will always be deeply attached to it because of my three friends who died. The whole thing is very mixed up in life and death and struggle and love for me, rather than any lasting attachment to the politics of the late 18th century in France.

8 The Bongos and Echoes of *Drums Along the Hudson*

I always felt a connection to the Bongos, since they hailed from Hoboken, New Jersey—a stone's throw away from the small suburban town where I grew up and was in a band myself. Their music was different—Richard Barone's compositions were melodic and complex—even though it seemed like they all had a three-chord foundation. The Bongos' rhythms were hypnotic and mesmerizing. When they played live, unrestrained and untethered, they had an electricity and spirit about them I have never seen in any other band since.

Although they weren't known at a national level until their later influential MTV video, "Numbers with Wings," they were instrumental in creating the music scene in Hoboken that is thriving to this day. While it's safe to say that most American music fans never noticed when the Bongos quietly disbanded, I noticed—and was crushed and saddened. Richard Barone went on to become a solo artist and a producer, and 2007 saw the Bongos re-forming to create both a new studio track ("Bulrushes 2007") and a few shows. When I spoke to Richard, he was excited to have remastered their debut, *Drums Along the Hudson*. He also had just finished a new book—*Frontman: Surviving the Rock Star Myth* (Backbeat Books, 2007)—and a collaboration with legendary Bowie and T. Rex producer, Tony Visconti. He sounded as energetic and optimistic as ever.

What led to the remastering of *Drums Along the Hudson*?

Actually, it was Moby who inspired me to take it to this level. We had made a deal with the record company to reissue the original album—we had planned on doing an exact copy of the original. But the day the contracts arrived, Moby wrote an email to me and said, "I just listened to *Drums Along the Hudson*. What a remarkable album." I wrote back, "Wow, your timing is perfect because we just got the contracts to reissue it today. Why don't you produce a bonus track?" He said, "Sure." So that's what started this whole ball rolling and what made it more than just the usual reissue in that we added material to it. It became a 27-track album!

The Bongos' *Drums Along the Hudson,* re-released in June 2007.

Did that surprise you, or were you already friendly with Moby?

We were already friends, and I had worked with him. He had performed in a show I produced at Central Park last year called "The (Not So) Great American Songbook." At that time, he told me that the first song he ever performed in public was "The Bulrushes" from that album. I hadn't really thought that much about reissuing the album at that time, but a year or so later when this all came about and he popped up the same day the contracts were arriving, that's when I started thinking about expanding the album. There was new material, including the first show we ever did.

Which tracks are on the new album?

The first 15 of the original album. More than half of them were done in the U.K. at John Foxx's place, called Jacobs Studios, in Surrey. The original engineer was Ken Thomas, who engineered a lot of records for Mike Thorne, including the first Wire album and many other pop and punk records that had come out. I thought, "I really liked those; we have to work with him." The main point of doing the reissue for us was that it never really sounded the way it did in the studio when we released it on vinyl originally.

What were the limitations, and why didn't it sound like you had originally intended?

The drums had a much deeper sound than what you heard on the first vinyl record. Today's mastering is really like a whole new world. When we first cut the record, according to Greg Calbi, the grooves couldn't really handle the low end we had on the tom toms. The drums in general ended up sounding much tinnier than I wanted, and the sound that we got at Jacobs—where we got a really deep drum sound—never made it to the reproductions.

How do you know if that's the monitors at Jacobs, for example, or just a translation of what transpires between the bounces between the 2-inch and the 1/4-inch? Could this deep sound have been from the monitoring environment there?

Possibly, but it doesn't matter because that's the sound that we left there with, and one thing has to be the final sound. When you master, that's what you have to go for, and it's always tricky. I've worked with Bob Ludwig quite a lot, and it's hard to sometimes get that sound again that you had in the studio. It could be a combination of the monitors, the amplifiers, and that room. But in a good studio, what you hear you should bring home, basically. On *Drums Along the Hudson,* we never got anywhere near the power of what we had done. Take a song like "Three Wise Men," which is all tom toms. It just got really reduced down to a third of what the drum sound should be—until now.

When it originally came out, you were probably okay with it and just kind of forgot about it.

To me, it sounded close enough to the representation—it was the limitation of vinyl, and this was as far as we could get it. And you know what? I liked it a lot.

Well, it worked on me and probably a ton of other Bongos fans.

It's been a favorite for a lot of people, and my own. We produced it ourselves with Ken Thomas, and we had a lot of control over what we wanted to do. I kind of assumed at that age and at that time that this was as good as we could get it to sound in the reproduction. Until now, when I rediscovered the master tapes in my own house. I have the original 2-inch tapes, but I also have the original 1/4 mixdown of the album from England. That had been copied when they made other copies in America to produce the records. Everyone was using safeties, and no one was going back to the tapes that had all our edits in them—a little rough, but it still had a more pure sound. That's what we used for this, and it opened up a whole new world for me. It sounded so much closer to what I wanted it to be.

So you had no need to pull the multi-tracks, and you just pulled the final mixes?

Yes. The multi-tracks are mostly in my possession, but we didn't need to because we really worked on these mixes, and I was really happy with the balances.

Did you fly them into Pro Tools?

I think Steve [Addabbo] used Pro Tools. I brought in the tapes and ran them from the analog machine to convert them into digital. We had to bake the tapes overnight—when we baked the tapes, the leader that they use in England had red stripes instead of a plain white leader. The red ink became like glue, so all the intros were ripped apart. All the songs' endings and beginnings were ripped out, and we had to find other sources for intros and endings for all the songs. We used anything we had, but I only wanted to use the smallest increments of these things.

Steve Addabbo and Richard Barone, pictured at Shelter Island Sound, NYC.

Why did you choose to work with Steve Addabbo on this?

I knew Steve for many years socially—New York City really is a small town. One of the really funny things about this project was that some of the equipment he had at Shelter Island Sound was originally at Celestial Sounds in New York, where we recorded "Mambo Sun," "In the Congo," and "Hunting." I was practically a teenager at the time, and that studio has since closed down.

Steve worked there at the time, but I didn't know him then. I walked around and saw all this old familiar equipment, and I realized that this was where we recorded quite a few songs from this album originally. That was very interesting to me.

That is like serendipity.

It was. We were going through the same console, and some of the other equipment, including the tape machines, were from Celestial.

Was there any old equipment that you had to source just to get the project done right? You are crossing a fairly large time gap here in reissuing this album.

One thing we did not find was dbx, and we had to work around this. Three of the tracks had dbx—that's what they used at Celestial. It was a pain because Steve had to get rid of the sibilance and the hiss. Plus, the level is lower. He had to really bring up the gain without bringing up the noise. We could not find any software that would help us with this, and he ended up applying EQ and compression in different ways. It ended up sounding fantastic, though.

Did you have the temptation to add anything or do any overdubs to these old songs?

No, because I really liked it. When I heard the resulting sound, I realized that this is what I really wanted in the first place. I was very happy with it. Also, I knew we would be adding all the bonus tracks.

What exactly did Moby end up doing on the new record?

We re-cut the "Bulrushes"—there is a completely new version called "Bulrushes 2007"—and we went into the studio with the original three Bongos. Moby played 12-string guitar, piano, Juno-106, and acoustic guitar. I just sang and played my electric. It has more textures, more steady grooves. The Bongos never cut to a click track—this was a much steadier groove. Also, adding the piano to the guitar added another poly-rhythm in there—there is a nice offbeat.

Photograph courtesy Brian T. Silak.

Left to right: Moby and the Bongos—Rob Norris, Richard Barone, and Frank Giannini.

Did you record to 2-inch?

We recorded directly into Logic, and we knew there would be another challenge, which was to match the sound of the rest of the album. We didn't want to make it sound artificially analog, though. We tried all kinds of techniques, and in fact we even put it to tape at one point and said, "That's not it."

Where did you lay down the new track?

I had been producing a project at a studio called Dubway, which is about a block from Shelter Island. I grabbed one more day there since Shelter was already booked. We went in there and did all the tracking, overdubbing, and vocals in one day. Then, Moby took it to his home studio to mix, and I added final touches at the Magic Shop with Jason Marcucci from Dubway. That was a fun session, too.

What was it like with Moby in the studio?

I was very impressed with Moby. He works fast, and this matches my own style—he likes to capture a moment and move on. It's more about the performance with him. My instinct was that he would be a real tech head, working with samples and stuff, but it was just the opposite. He was really into the performance and the group playing together as much as possible and getting it to sound like a real band. This is exactly what the Bongos always strived to achieve. But from the beginning, we told him, "You're producing this." I was just singing and playing the guitar. He had a great attitude, and we had a very pleasant day. The recording was done in a day, and the mixing was also done in a day.

And what was it like to play with the Bongos again in the studio?

What was funny to me was that it had been over 20 years since we were in the studio together, and it felt like it was the next day in the studio. It was very natural, and we worked very well together. We instantly meshed anyway when we first met, and this was just a continuation of that. It was as if no time passed at all, and it was a really nice experience. The Bongos never really ended since we never broke up, so this put more of a closing on the Bongos story in my mind.

What did the Bongos record to originally on *Drums Along the Hudson*? Were they all done in 2-inch 16-track?

It was done in all different formats. The eight tracks we did in England were all 24-track. The first things we did at Mix-O-Lydian in Boonton, New Jersey, "Glow in the Dark" and "Telephoto Lens," might have been eight-track. Don Sternecker was just starting—he kept growing and was soon doing 16. By the time I came to work at Mix-O-Lydian later, it was all 24-track.

Once the restoration and repairs were complete for the remastered version, did everything else go smoothly?

In a way—this was a major project for all of us. After we repaired the intros—and that was Steve and I trying to find maybe one hit of another drum from another version of the song from another source—it sounded really good. But then there were two songs from a show in London we wanted to add that were recorded at the Rainbow in 1981, among a total of 11 new live tracks we wanted to add. The first two were from London, which were sonically much brighter. We had to adjust the sound so it would fit with the rest of the album.

Then Rob, the bass player, had saved the cassette of our first live show from the Showplace in Dover, New Jersey. It was a really rough live cassette taken from the board, and the two channels were phasing, so we had to make it mono—and it sounded great. So the live tracks are *Drums Along the Hudson* songs, but just evolving since we were just creating that album.

Photograph by Jeff Touzeau.

Steve Addabbo, mastering engineer, and Richard Barone listen to a mix on *Drums Along the Hudson*.

It seems like Steve Addabbo helped you tackle a very difficult project.

Part of the mastering process is that you have to go into a different frame of mind; it's almost like you become a doctor. I've worked with some of the best, including Bob Ludwig, mostly for my albums. I think of him as Doctor Ludwig. I say, "Here's my pain; what can you do to help me?" I was impressed with how Steve Addabbo could go into that mode even though he is more of a traditional producer/engineer himself. Overall, it took about a year to get the Moby track finished and to get the rest of this material gathered and mastered, including the live stuff. I'm really happy with this record—I had never been entirely happy with it before in this way. All the guys are really excited about it, and it was a nice experience all around.

Now that the Bongos release is out, what is on your own plate?

My new album is coming in September of this year by Tony Visconti. It's a really special record because I always wanted to work with Visconti. We created it together—we wrote all the songs together and did it all in Logic. I didn't have any songs written—I came to him with ideas for songs, and we wrote them together. I'm a Logic user—for me, it has a very creative interface and feels really comfortable. Tony uses Drum Corps so sometimes we use that; other times we'll have someone come in and lay a drum track down. If we really like a loop and it's something really intricate that we've created, we'll use that.

How often do you use the stuff from your demos in the final recording? Is there such thing as a demo for you anymore?

Usually I do demo. My last studio album was so meticulously demoed, it was almost impossible to re-create the sounds in the studio. So when I started worked with Tony, I said, "Let's just start this thing in Logic, and there are no demos." That's how we approached this album. It was a clean slate, and we started from nothing. I would literally bring in one word for a song, and then we would write and record the song right there on the spot. This was the first time I ever tried this, and I've always wanted to work that way because sometimes I have demoed myself into a corner.

It's key for us to be able to use MIDI and real audio in a program—it's just so easy to do this in Logic to make a beat or something. Tony is really into the beats and sometimes brings in samples from other sessions he's done. He chops up these beats and creates a great loop for me, then I will write a song on top of that.

9 Jackie Greene: A Natural Bluesman from California

Jackie Greene's album *American Myth* is definitely a guitarist's guitar album, laced with a variety of deeply rooted blues-based tracks—some screech and holler, while others are silkily plucked on his '62 Martin D-18. Throughout *American Myth*, multi-instrumentalist Greene displays a wide range of guitar-playing styles, taking cues from blues heroes such as Mississippi John Hurt, Muddy Waters, and Willie Dixon.

Greene was drawn to the blues; from the classic bluesmen of the Mississippi Delta to Led Zeppelin, it became part of his blood. As a result, his recordings sound very natural—almost effortless. Throughout his career so far, Greene has made a point to surround himself with the best players he could find. Among these players on the new album is Val McCallum, an amazing slide player whose interplay with Greene throughout the record creates an album of astonishing textures and emotions.

Greene has a perfect storytelling voice—perhaps akin to Kris Kristofferson, only softer and a little more rock 'n roll. Producer Steve Berlin did a fantastic job producing Greene on *American Myth*, preserving the intimacy each song conveys. In a separate interview I did with Berlin, he said that the session was magical and reminded him of Rod Stewart's *Every Picture Tells a Story*, in the sense that all the performers seemed to find a natural pocket while dynamically responding to one another.

What originally attracted you to guitar? Why not another instrument?

Well, I've been playing guitar for a long time, since I was a kid. When you're a teenager in high school, and even before, that's what you want to play: guitar. Nobody wants to be a clarinet player, right? I always had dreams of being a big guitar player like Jimmy Page. I probably started playing the guitar for the same reasons everybody else does, because of my guitar heroes back then.

What about the blues? What specifically drew you to this genre as a boy in California, of all places?

Well, I was really into Zeppelin, and a lot of their stuff is really blues-based. In fact, a lot of it is pretty much straight-up blues. I kind of went backwards from there and got into the blues players; they kind of go hand in hand. Same with the Stones; you go back and you're like, "Who is this Willie Dixon cat who wrote these songs?" Then it was Howlin' Wolf, Muddy Waters—it's like, "What is all this stuff?" You put it all together, and there you are.

How did you intimately discover all of the early blues masters, like Howlin' Wolf and Robert Johnson? How did this alter your own playing?

I was about 15 or so, and I remember one summer our TV broke at my mom's house, and there was nothin' to do. So I went into the basement and I found an old turntable and I pulled out this box that had a bunch of vinyl in it of my mom's and my father's—records from when they were younger. There was a Ray Charles record, a Mississippi John Hurt record, some Doc Watson records; there was Led Zeppelin, the Beatles, and the Stones. So I hooked up this turntable, figured out how to use it, and I played these vinyl records.

I remember being blown away by the sound because I'd never heard Ray Charles before, or any of these people. I grew up in a really small town called Cameron Park, about 40 miles from Sacramento, and there was no record store, no radio station—there was nothing. It was out of boredom that I discovered this stuff—the TV didn't work! Once I made that discovery, I started asking my friends if I could go through their parents' collections and I started finding this whole world of music that I never knew existed.

Which one of these artists really got you?

That would have to be Ray Charles.

Tell me about your first guitar.

The first guitar I bought with my own money was when I was 13 or 14. There was a little music store in Cameron Park called Cameron Park Music. I can't remember the owner's name, but it was a really crappy guitar, a Strat knockoff. One summer, I went in and put $5 down, then $10 down, and by the end of the summer, I had this guitar. It was maybe like a $150 guitar, just a piece of junk. I played that guitar forever.

Then did you begin to imitate or learn some of these records you had gotten access to?

Yeah, my friend had a piece-of-junk five-watt Crate amp, and by then I was also really into the Allman Brothers, Skynyrd, and that whole Southern rock thing, still all blues-based.

There seems to be a great synergy on the record between you, Val, and all the other musicians. Is it hard to find people who you are especially compatible with in the studio?

It was easy with Val because he's just so good. He could hit it off with anybody—he's like a chameleon and can make himself fit with anybody's playing. That's what attracts me to him as a player. No matter what he plays or where he plays it, his tone is always great and he always plays really well. He's *way* better than me, and I learned a lot from him during those [*American Myth*] sessions. I think we naturally played well together because we like the same music and seem to fit in the same space. The guitars that we play complement each other really well.

One thing that is great on *American Myth* is the guitar playing covers such a wide range of emotions. During certain songs the playing is sweet and soft, and at other times it is rippin' and roaring. How easy is it to "change skins" like that?

That's one of the things that keeps it interesting for me as a songwriter as well as for listeners. There's definitely a conscious decision to make things sound diverse. I don't want a record to stay in one spot and get boring both sonically and emotionally. I want it to go places, to go up and down—listeners can get very bored very easily these days. If we sense that a vibe of a tune is similar to another song, we say, "Let's do something different with it." Maybe we'll suggest to Val that he pick up a different guitar.

Now that you presumably have access to a much wider variety of guitars since you started, what kind of guitar do you find yourself picking up most frequently?

Well, now I have about 15 guitars. I have a few favorites, but I play them all equally. I have a '70s Les Paul gold top with these mini-humbuckers, which sound great. I used to play a Tele all the time, but the guitar player in my band plays a Tele a lot, and I like to play what he's not playing. If he's playing a Tele, I'll often play an Epiphone Casino, which I love. It's an inexpensive new one, but it sounds great. It's weird, because it's a little bit lo-fi.

Which guitar do you usually pick up when you are writing? Do you favor a certain guitar?

Not necessarily. I don't gravitate toward a certain guitar when I'm writing. Sometimes I don't even have an instrument with me; I just write what's in my head, and then I'll come to an instrument later, and it doesn't really matter which one I pick up. I don't really worry about what the guitar sound should be like until we go to the studio. In fact, I kind of want the song to just live by itself on paper for a while.

Did you have to work really hard to gain your competency in guitar playing? Or was it just fun and you finally got to a level where you could play stuff?

It's all sort of fun. I never sat at home and practiced scales. In fact, I don't know anything about that. In fact, I don't read music. There's no way in hell I could ever read music. For me, the best way was to listen to people you like and learn to play along. It keeps your spirits up. I don't play things note for note, I always played my own interpretations of them, which drives some people crazy.

What kind of amps do you favor?

Well, I am glad you asked, because I have just bought my favorite amp in the whole world! Vox made these hand-wired AC-30s—they made like 250 of them in like 2002 or so. I played one at a show once, and I tried to buy it off the dude who was doing the backline. He kept saying, "Ah, no, no." I finally found one in a music store, and I bought it on the spot; I've been using it ever since. It's the most expensive amp I've ever bought, but it sounds great. That's what I play now; everything goes through that. I used to play through a '63 Super.

I used to have a black-faced Super, but I sold it before they became collector's items. Now I could never afford to buy one!

Oh, those are great amps. The guitar player in my band has one also—he has an early '60s Super. They have a great sound; the vibrato on it is great. Before that, I played a Bassman for a while, before I actually cared about having reverb or a vibrato.

So what other fretted instruments do you have around your house? Do you have a different guitar in each room? What's the first thing you pick up when you're loafing around?

Well, last night I was playing that Les Paul. I just got an advanced Jumbo Gibson acoustic guitar, which sounds great. It has this huge neck on it, which is abnormally wide. It's kind of strange to learn how to play because it's so large, but it sounds really great.

Pretty much all the acoustics I have are Gibsons; they are easily my favorite guitars. I do have an old '62 Martin D-18, though, that I do a lot of recording with. I record with three different acoustics: I have the '62 D-18; a Gibson Nick Lucas, which has a smaller body but the tone is nice and even; then I have an old Gibson LG1, another smaller one. Then I have a Gibson J185, a bigger one. They all sound great in their own way.

You have a dobro as well, right?

Yeah, I have two. One of them is really interesting; it's a pre-Gibson dobro, a metal-body one with a lipstick pickup in it—really funky-sounding. I used to bring it out and play it, but it's been really finicky lately; the electronics are funny.

Was the dobro an easy instrument for you to pick up?

I'm still learning a lot of it. You reach a point where you think you're a halfway decent slide player, then you hear Derek Trucks and you think, "Oh, shit!"

The slide work on your new album is just amazing.

That's Val—all the slide is Val. I tried to do it, but I was like, "Val, you're a hundred times better than me; why don't you do it?" I have no ego when it comes to making records. I just want the best person for the part; if it's not me, that's fine. Val pretty much fit the bill—he's one of the best guitar players I think I've ever heard; he's really on it.

Are you more comfortable playing live or in the studio?

It's about equal. I like the fact that when you are in the studio you can really stretch out without worrying about whether it's going to sound bad—you can do it again if you want to.

Do you play with a lot of gizmos or effects in your signal chain?

I think stomp boxes are fine. I used to have an old green tube screamer and that was it. I change it up now a lot. With the new Vox, I get a really nice overdrive by itself, so all you really need is a boost. So I have a Sex Drive, that Charlie Sexton boost thing. That is about it, except on some songs I do use a fuzz pedal. I also have a thing called a Red Snapper, which is an overdrive pedal. It is kind of like a Tube Screamer and almost like a safety net. So it really comes down to a fuzz and a boost.

What are some of the more unusual guitars you used on *American Myth*?

I have a couple old junky Silvertones that I play all over that record. I bought them in the junkshop for about $50 each, and they sound really great. I also have a piece-of-junk Danelectro baritone guitar that I rely on all the time, and it sounds so great. In fact, I used it all over Hollywood.

Now that you are experiencing wider success, have you had a chance to play alongside any of your own guitar heroes?

Yeah, I did a tour with Buddy Guy, and I got to play keyboards with him in his band for like six or seven shows. That was pretty cool. I also played harmonica with Susan Tedeschi a lot of times. I'm really not a great instrumentalist, though. I think people invite me up more out of fun than anything else. I don't really think I'm that good—I just try and fit in wherever I can. It's funny, because the guys that are really good are *really* good. I know that, and I know that I'm years behind them.

Who are some guitarists out there now who have a certain feel or touch that you just love?

Well, Derek Trucks in my opinion is the best guitar player right now. Just listen to his slide playing; it's just like a great singer. The way he plays slide is like how a really good singer sings. His intonation is perfect—he can go anywhere on that fretboard and stay in tune. It's like, "How the hell does he do that?" That might just be due to the fact that I don't play slide and that it's so far off for me. I'll tell you who is really good. David Hidalgo from Los Lobos. Here's a guy who can play guitar, violin, accordion, the keyboards, and the drums, plus he sings. And he does it all well—he is an incredible musician.

You grew up in California. Was it ever difficult to get into a blues scene around there?

Yeah, the thing is, there's a blues scene almost anywhere you go. It's like these blues jams, and that's what everybody does. Every Stevie Ray Vaughn-abee. You hook up the Strat and you just wail. But as far as a legitimate thing, the blues thing doesn't exist in this town too much. There are some cats here who are pretty hard core, just blues guys, but this is more of an indie-rock town, actually. There are a lot of indie-rock bands, and a lot of them are great.

How long does it usually take you to write a song? Is it very quick or is it usually drawn out?

It's both. Sometimes it takes as long to listen to it as it does to write it. There are songs on that record, like "Hollywood," that I wrote fairly quickly. I got this groove in my head, and I looked at it as almost more of a rap, the way the rhyming scheme goes. I just wrote it all down at once—there were originally 12 verses, and I just cut out most of them and kept the ones that I thought would keep the vibe of what I wanted. Each verse is sort of a different character.

I also love the intro to that. The piano introduction is great.

That's me and Val just sitting there, and Steve Berlin, the producer, is holding a crappy microphone beside us. We played it back, and it worked well as the introduction of "Hollywood."

10 Ben Kweller: Recording Something Good, Something Great

Brooklyn-based pop craftsman and multi-instrumentalist Ben Kweller plays and sings everything on his new self-titled album, which delivers emotionally revealing and artistically convincing performances throughout. Teaming up with producer Gil Norton, who has also worked with groups such as Counting Crows, The Pixies, and Echo & the Bunnymen, Kweller creates a sonically cohesive album that stays true to his rock 'n roll roots. The end result is immediate and sincere, *sans* all the posturing so often associated with the so-called indie scene.

The album delivers blow after blow until the final knockout punch, "This Is War." Norton's minimalist approach on the production, which features primarily bass, guitar, drums, and organ, brings out the strengths of Kweller's arrangements and his natural abilities on each instrument. For Kweller, this record was a technical departure from previous ones in that it was done entirely in Pro Tools at NYC's The Magic Shop.

While Kweller's work has an inventive, DIY edge to it, his roots are squarely based in classic rock, having been raised on music such as Steve Miller, Fleetwood Mac, and the Electric Light Orchestra. Indeed, he tried to get Jeff Lynne to produce his latest album, but alas, Mr. Lynne had his hands full with other projects and could not accommodate Kweller's request.

On Kweller's self-titled album, melody and emotion are king. His lyrics, which are self-effacing and highly personal, create the framework for the album, and Kweller's brilliant arrangements and instrumentation fill in the blanks. Ben had a tremendously approachable familiarity about him, and speaking to him was like catching up with an old friend.

A lot of people probably don't realize that you played all the instruments on this album. At what point did you decide to perform all the instruments on the album? How did you go about doing this?

It all happened in a slow, natural sort of way before I came to the realization that I would be going into the studio all by myself. For about a year and a half, I'd been on the road with my last album, *On My Way*, while writing songs on the road.

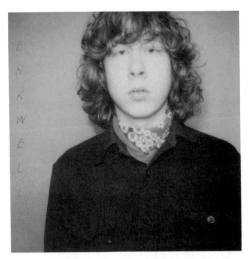

Ben Kweller's self-titled album, released September 2006.

When I got home, I'd go to my friend Roger's house by myself and just make demos of my new songs. I played all the instruments just because I knew how to, not because that's what I was going for. It was strictly out of convenience.

When it came time to make the real album, ATO sent the tapes out to the producers, a typical step in the sequence of events. After I met with the producers, Gil Norton was the only one who said, "Man, I can't believe you played all the instruments on your demos. You've got to do this on the album!" He explained there's just something that happens when your hi-hat is carrying exactly the same rhythm as the strumming on the acoustic guitar.

Did having this multi-instrumental approach influence your producer choice? What other challenges did it present over the long run?

[Playing all the instruments myself] was one of the non-challenges, the *easy* part. I have it all in my head, so I can just go in and lay down the drums, pick up the bass, then the guitar—it's boom, boom, boom. The real challenge is that because you are alone, there's no one to bounce ideas off of. But I have to say, having Gil there was equal to having a hundred of the best musicians ever listening. If I went in by myself with an engineer friend of mine, I'd probably still be in there today because I wouldn't know when it was "done."

Is guitar your first instrument? How easy or difficult was it for you to pick up all these other instruments besides the guitar?

My dad's a drummer, and actually drums were my first instrument as a kid. Whenever my dad would come home from work, he'd plug in his Telecaster, and I'd get behind the drums, and we'd play Beatles songs, Hendrix songs, and everything in between. This was really how I grew up, from the time I was seven years old until I was an early teenager. My dad and I used to jam every day.

Then I gradually moved over to the piano. Someone taught me "Heart and Soul," like every other American kid, and I used those chords to write my first songs. One thing led to another, and then the guitar happened.

For some reason, I never dove into the synth world. I learned on your basic, mainly acoustic instruments: guitar, harmonica, and piano. There's something about the way that I write songs that is very raw and human, and I think these instruments evoke this better. I've never been able to embrace drum machines and samples because I think it would disagree with what I'm trying to get across emotionally.

Tell me what you think of the record sonically. Did you have any preconceptions or sonic references going into the project?

My last album was really raw: 16-track 2-inch, no overdubs, everything live in the room with the band—a total vintage approach. For this album, we just really wanted to blow it up, take more time, and get it sounding really big and beautiful.

Sonically, I wanted to make something really big, like Tom Petty's *Full Moon Fever* or Jeff Lynne's work from the mid-'80s. I actually contacted Jeff Lynne early on, and he said he liked the demos but that he was too busy building a studio. That was a bummer because that was really my dream for the album. Once I met Gil, though, it was a match made in heaven.

This was my first album done completely in Pro Tools, done on Gil's suggestion. I told him how much I love tape, but he has been using Pro Tools for a long time and convinced me that it's not really *what* you record on—it's more about the microphones and the mic preamps. So we ended up tracking right into Pro Tools and mixing down to 1/2-inch tape.

What is your typical approach to choosing a studio and what were the considerations for this album?

I did my last two albums at Seer Sound, which is my favorite studio in New York. I knew I wanted to do another album in New York, but I'm really affected by my surroundings and wanted to try something new. I went to a bunch of different places, and I liked that The Magic Shop had a single studio, so we'd be the only people there for six weeks—we could take it over.

The basic process for basic tracks was that would get the tempo, put up a click track, then I would go into the live room and lay down a rough guitar vocal or a piano vocal. The basics were fairly easy, and the majority of the songs went really quickly.

[The Magic Shop] has two grand pianos, one black and one white—the white piano was really out of tune. They were going to tune it up, but I told them to leave it out of tune and just tune the black one. Both pianos were up against each other, like a yin and yang. In addition to these, they had a really great upright piano. Every song really has those three pianos together, and that's kind of a signature sound on the album. For example, the key hook in "Nothing Happening" is those three pianos: one upright, an in-tune grand, and an out-of-tune grand.

Photo by Andy Willsher.

Ben Kweller.

Let's talk about how a typical song might evolve. Do lyrics or melody come easily for you? Let's take "Thirteen," for example.

"Thirteen," which is originally about this really old acoustic guitar I have, is one of my favorites, and it wasn't even going to be on the album. I was already two weeks into the project with Gil, and I kind of rewrote it over a period of three days in the studio—it was the longest amount of time we spent on any song. I wrote lyric after lyric and cut out each verse until there were like 25 different pieces of paper, which I mixed and matched to get it right.

I decided not to put a chorus in there because it seemed to cheapen the whole thing. I ended up using three verse sections, a break, and three other verse sections—a weird structure for me, but one I've been gravitating toward lately. "Penny on the Train Track" uses the same approach if you look at it: You get three, a break, then three more.

On "Thirteen" there is a fantastic, soulful harmonica. Why did you include a harmonica track versus, say, a piano?

The harmonica solo on that track took a long time to get right. Originally it was going to be a piano solo, but the recording was so sparse that I thought a harmonica with that lonesome reverb would be perfect. One night I just kept working in the live room with my engineer while Gil went out to dinner. After a few glasses of red wine, I kept working and working, and I finally got it. That's one of the best-recorded performances I've ever done.

One of the things I really like about the album is that it does not have too much "sheen" on it—sonically, it is not overproduced in the least. The vocals are a good example of your minimalist approach.

I prefer a dry vocal because I think my voice has a lot of character to it already. For me, it's all about the words—I'm really trying to connect to people's hearts. Out of the 50 or so songs in my discography, only four or five have reverb.

When it came to gear choices, I let Gil run the show. I didn't question any of his technical choices. I do have a mic preference, though, which has always been a Neumann U 47. On this album, however, we used a U 87, which had a nice crunch to it and sounded just right.

Photo courtesy Sennheiser USA.

The classic Neumann U 87 microphone, which Kweller used on lead vocals.

How have these songs translated for you on the road?

I'm really digging playing these songs live. Right when the album came out I was touring as a five-piece, sometimes as a six-piece. On the next tour, which begins in February, I'm going out as a trio, which is something I haven't done in my solo career. It'll be really fun to strip everything down because it was kind of a big production last time around. The instrumentation will just be bass, drums, and guitar or piano.

11 Clap Your Hands Say Yeah: Grass Roots Rock 'n Roll in Brooklyn

Two-thousand five was the year for Clap Your Hands Say Yeah. The Brooklyn, NY–based group's self-titled debut album, financed entirely by the members of the band, startled the independent music community, leaving a long trail of ecstatic music reviewers in its wake. Much to the disappointment of many an A&R rep, Clap Your Hands Say Yeah remains independent, controlling its own destiny and selling out shows wherever they set foot.

In these days in which the music industry has become more and more unpredictable—and seemingly unstable—Clap Your Hands Say Yeah is a case study of success for independents. Over the last couple of decades, remaining independent has always been the tougher row to hoe. Tying up the business side of releasing music—record promotion, public relations, distribution, and marketing—can be much more difficult when you don't have the massive budgets and leverage of a multi-national record label behind you.

Using the Internet and word of mouth and following a relentless tour cycle made it easier for Clap Your Hands Say Yeah—though they admit having a great record helped just a little bit. I caught up with the group just as its record topped CMJ's new music charts and they launched their first Japanese and European tour.

Now that you are touring in the U.K., how do you find the audience there? Are they receptive to your music?

It's pretty similar to the U.S. We were lucky enough to get an enthusiastic welcome on the first tour of the United States, and it translated over to Europe pretty well. So far the reception has been great. I think we're coming back to the U.S. around March.

There are few successful bands that can say they are truly independent, but you guys have done really well. Has all of this happened very quickly for you?

Yes, it has been pretty fast. As far as I'm concerned, the idea of being independent and remaining independent is always keeping in the back of your mind how you started in the first place. To say that it skyrocketed only appears to be the case externally. Not only have we been working on all this for some time, but it is skyrocketing from certain people's

Clap Your Hands Say Yeah, following the release of their debut album.

perspectives, which is to say that more people are listening. But as far as I'm concerned, it is still always an independent relationship between the music and the musician.

Where did you do the basic tracks and overdubs?

We did six or seven of the basic tracks at Machines with Magnets in Providence, Rhode Island. Then we started mixing and doing overdubs at Fireproof Recording [in Brooklyn]. Then it turned out that we wanted to tack on some more songs to make a full-length album, so we also did some tracking at Fireproof. We tracked about four more songs at Fireproof.

Photograph by Jeff Touzeau.

Adam Lasus' Fireproof Recording.

What was it like working with Adam Lasus at Fireproof?

He's a nice guy. It was my first time in any proper studio, so I was just getting adjusted and working at an instinctual level. I was there pretty much the whole time, during the entire process from tracking to mixing.

Adam was great—very accommodating and very open to suggestions, which I am pretty strong about because I have a pretty good idea of how I like it to sound. The important thing about working with somebody like that is to make it through the translation, I think. Fireproof was big enough that if you wanted to lean on a room mic for a big sound, you could. It was a great kit that Adam had that Sean borrowed.

From an engineering perspective, the record sounds unconventional. What unusual techniques did you guys employ while you were recording it?

Some of the basic techniques might have involved leaning on room mics a little more, à la Pixies albums like *Surfer Rosa* on a couple of tracks. For me, though, it was always a matter of sound, more than saying, "Let's use this for EQ or this for a compressor." We had a limited amount of time, and that might have had a lot to do with how the overall sound of the album came about.

The album has a great live feel to it. How important was it for you to achieve this?

Some of my favorite albums I look to are like Velvet Underground's *White Light/White Heat* and some of Bob Dylan's albums, where you can just tell that everybody is sittin' around trying to figure it out as they go along. The idea of spontaneity is a strong one, and I think we've started off on this album concerned about trying to preserve a certain degree of spontaneity based on the fact that everybody was learning as they went along.

Do you have very much time to write on the road?

I don't have much time to write at this point, but I have enough material to cover the next couple of albums if we go that far.

What were you doing before you joined Clap Your Hands Say Yeah?

I live in Philadelphia. I was renovating a house in Philadelphia, doing carpentry and construction kind of stuff. I would go home at night and work on songs. Everybody else was doing design work generally, up in New York. Tyler was doing computer web design type stuff, for example.

Tell me about some of the sonic reference points you had in mind when you were creating the album.

I remember bringing some early albums from like the Rolling Stones, trying to convey certain points about compression on some of the songs. The idea that you had to make sure that you compressed the hell out of certain things to enhance the sound—say the tambourine, for example. I'm not sure whether I played *Scary Monsters* or *Low* [David Bowie] for Adam, but in the song "Scary Monsters," I think it's [Tony] Visconti who worked on that with him, and I'm not sure what they used to make his voice flutter in such a way. They might have run it back through an amplifier or something like that.

It is important as far as instrumentation and color are concerned to have certain precedents to rely on, but not get too close to them. That's a whole part of the translation, especially with someone you just don't know and who has no idea about what you're bringing to him. So I brought some of the demos that I was working on, which was kind of the groundwork for the songs themselves. It was pretty speedy the way it shaped up because I had a pretty clear idea initially. There are a lot of things that were drawn on to make it work.

What is your schedule like now? Are you just playing date after date after date?

Pretty much. We started in Japan, came over to Paris. Now we're in London, and we're legitimately starting the tour tomorrow in Belfast.

Did you know that your record is number one on the CMJ chart? That's got to make you feel good.

I didn't know that.

What other music influences do you have?

David Bowie and the Rolling Stones would be more subconscious influences. The ones I listen to are Doug Sahm, Townes Van Zandt, the Minutemen, Hüsker Dü, The Pixies, Wire, The Band, Willie Nelson, Velvet Underground, stuff like that.

How is the next record shaping up? How do you see it shaping up sonically compared to the last one?

The things I'd like to keep the same are how wide open the album sounds. I like that live quality to an album, and I think that is something to hold to. I also always favor room microphones rather than close mics for certain things because they always tend to enhance a certain aspect of recording. I'm not exactly sure what will be on the second album, and I haven't picked out what songs will be on it yet.

Tell me about the interesting backing vocals that appear on the album.

We used a variety of mics. We tried different ones for each one of the songs and for the backup vocals as well; we tried a bunch of different stuff. [For the backing vocals], I had the idea before the song was tracked, and sometimes I recognized a certain hole in the song and just sort of filled it spontaneously.

How are you dealing with all the business aspects of being a working, successful band?

I'm adjusting to it. Actually, it's a little disconcerting because it happened a bit fast, which is to say, you found yourself a lot busier than you used to. And also, I was used to working on songs all the time, and now I'm just working with the guys and trying to execute on stage. It's a different game. I don't have much time to write at this point, but I have enough for the next couple albums if it goes so far. [The song-writing process] starts off in Philly, where I live, because I put together a tiny studio just to kind of get down ideas. When I hear something in my head, I bring it up to the guys and just run through it in the practice space. Everybody is talented and creative enough to take the suggestions and run with them.

12 Sevendust's *Next* Big Thing

When Sevendust released *Next,* its fifth album, it debuted on Billboard's Top 200 Albums chart at number 20. Straight off the heels of a record deal that didn't work for them, Sevendust wanted to rethink the way they had been making albums. Specifically, the idea of punching the clock in the recording studio was no longer appealing and brought about an undue amount of stress and conflict.

With about 80 percent of the writing complete on the album, Sevendust holed up in a house-turned-studio outside their hometown of Atlanta, Georgia, where they set out to lay down the tracks. Although it was liberating to break away from the traditional studio setting, it was also risky, because there was no on-site studio tech or engineer who was intimately familiar with the gear. Recording *Next* was somewhat of a struggle, yet it turned out to be successful both as a learning experience for the band and as a final recording project the band could be proud of. I spoke to guitarist John Connolly during the record's publicity tour, just as *Next* continued to gain momentum and move up the charts.

Are you keeping busy?

Yeah, we're actually going to get to play a few shows over the next days. That's a nice change because we've been flying around doing a lot of press and a lot of promos. It's time to go, time to keep busy.

How do you feel about *Next* debuting on the Billboard Top 20? That has to feel good.

Definitely. I couldn't be happier about it. We got ourselves out of a bad situation we were in with our old label, and things are working out. It's a lot more work on the band than we are used to, but we welcome the change. At least we know what is happening.

When you were writing this record, you didn't have an attachment to a label. Did this make things more liberating for you?

All labels always try to throw their two cents in, and I think our old label really lost sight of what this band was really all about a long time ago. It was very liberating not having the little bird chirping on your shoulder, chirping in your ear, saying you should sound like the White Stripes or whatever. It's nice not to have any of that crap going on.

Tell me about where you recorded it. Was it a risk to record it in a house versus a proper studio?

It was a complete risk, but at the same time, Maury and myself had actually got into working with some smaller bands around the Atlanta and Georgia scene. We love being in the studio. As much as I love being on the road, I'm a studio rat when it comes right down to it. I'm the guy who wants to sit there and blow things up to see if it will make a cool sound. This was our first shot at really being able to self-produce the band. We've got co-production credits on every record, but in all fairness, we've never gotten recognized for what we actually did. To be quite honest with you, it wasn't a whole lot different on this record than it was with all the others—we had to engineer this one as well.

Tell me more about the house—did it live up to your expectations?

The house is owned by a couple. It is the same house where Creed recorded the *Weathered* record. The equipment was good, but we had to modify some stuff. It had a control room and a drum room, but I know from experience that a drum room either sounds really good or doesn't. This room actually took a lot of work—it was just a strange room. It had a wood floor and looked like it would work well, but we ended up just fighting with it.

We basically unhooked their Pro Tools rig and hooked ours in. We used the Pro Control just for monitoring and pulling faders up and down, but we basically kept everything in the box. We basically just ran through some nice preamps and didn't get too fancy with it.

Did you mix this in the house or did you go somewhere else?

We went and mixed it at The Tree for two reasons. Number one, we have a comfort zone with that room. Our engineer, Sean Grove, actually works out of that room. But also, we've done demo stuff in that room—we did drums and bass to *Animosity* in that room. It just kind of made sense. Being in a house, it's hard to tell where you are at. You are dealing with so many variables that are unfamiliar—we had to listen to a lot of CDs to get back to our point of reference. We'd sit there and look at each other, saying, "I think it sounds good, or at least it sounds good in this room, but I'm not used to this room."

There is always that question mark.

Exactly. That's why we took it back to a room we were very comfortable with. We pulled everything up and we were like, "Okay, cool, that's what we did!" We spent about a day a song at The Tree. We moved along at a pretty decent clip because I've been involved in mixing sessions with guys who did two songs a day, then I've been involved in mixing sessions with guys who did a song every four or five days.

It can be a real fine line, but the reason we moved along at a relatively quick pace was because as we were tracking the record, management was asking, "Can we get a few songs just to drop it on some people's desk and get some feedback?" So we said, "All right, cool." So we probably spent two or three hours per song one day just rough-mixing everything. We had such positive feedback from what we had done in two and a half hours that we said, "We shouldn't over-polish this or over-think this—we should just do a better-sounding version of what we did with the roughs."

Were there technical issues or other obstacles you ran into at the house?

Absolutely. We had a list of, like, 12 things we had to accomplish by the end of the day, and I think we got 1 of the 12 done; it was just one of those things. You walk into somebody's house, and they've got gear—you think it works. You've got these banks of patch bays in the walls, and you're trying to figure out where they come out on the other side of the house. We had to get the owner over to the house to kind of show us the method to his madness. It's a decent home studio, but he's got a certain system of working. Our system is obviously a little bit different, so for the first two days we realized that we put ourselves in a really unfamiliar situation. How is this going to turn out? You just don't know, and there are a lot of question marks.

How are things working with Sonny [Mayo, who has since been replaced]?

Everything has been great. Getting him in was just a breath of fresh air. We're excited about everything, but he has a different level of excitement than we do. He fits like a glove, and he's been a friend of ours since we did the first tour as Sevendust.

There is a lot of emotion on this album. Does that really strain you at the end of a day in the studio?

Absolutely. The upside was that we did it by ourselves, on our own schedule, at our own pace. But the downside was that we set a pretty tight schedule. We had a lot of work that we wanted to get done in a very short amount of time, and only because it was all on our dime. We didn't have a deal at the time, so we went to the bank and got a loan to do the record. It was like, "We need to get in here and get to work," so we pretty much worked for, like, six weeks straight. We only had probably 75 to 80 percent of the lyrics finished when we started, and there were always two or three rooms at a time working—whether it was Sonny writing guitar parts or one of us writing lyrics while Vinnie [Hornsby] was cutting bass. There were a lot of moving parts.

Even though the album has a really hard edge to it, there are some really beautiful melodies sitting beneath all your guitars. Can you tell me about recording the vocals?

We used a Neumann M 149 on LJ [Lajon Witherspoon, vocalist]. We tried a 47, an 87, and an old 49 that sounded great, but it was really, really dark. The 149 was the winner. It was a hands-down thing—everybody who walked in the room picked the same mic. We got two of them, and we used them for all three of us, which is pretty unusual for all of us to be on the same mic. Occasionally, we put LJ on a 58 to sing the part again. We've never doubled him before, but a triple was great.

Photograph courtesy Sennheiser USA.

Sevendust relied on the Neumann M 149 tube for vocal work on *Next*.

On *Next*, the guitars sound massive and there is a fantastic stereo spread. How did you achieve this?

We used two 57s on one of the top speakers on the cabinet running in stereo—those two mics would come in on a fader, and then we had a 421. There was just something about those 421s. I have always been a fan of 421s; it's just that meat. We were in between 6 inches and 12 inches off the cabinet at all times with that mic. It's hard to beat the midrange of a 57, though.

How far did you go out on the 421? It doesn't sound too tight, and you really captured the room.

We were in between six inches and a foot off the cabinet at all times with the mics. That was the same room that we struggled with the drums in. On the flipside, it did something on the guitars that was really cool. It was odd with the drums, but great for the guitars.

How did you record the bass? Did you go direct?

We recorded the bass with two DIs and then we used a re-amp. We miked up a cabinet, then brought it back into the board. We had an SVT head that had issues, and when it came time to get a replacement, there was nothing that was really beating the DIs, so we said we'd fix that later. Then afterwards, we put the bass in. It's basically just an SVT through an old 8×10 cabinet.

What was Sean's contribution as engineer? Where were his strong suits?

He is gifted at getting us to sound like us. He's done the last two demos for us, and we've known him for years and years. We actually produced a song with him—"Face to Face," the last single off the album *Seasons*. We've always wanted to use him as engineer, but anytime you get into a producer situation, there is always an in-house guy he wants to be faithful to. Sean is an unsung hero from Atlanta who just gets it. He knows how we want our band to sound, he's a fan of the same things we're a fan of, and he's brutally honest. He had just as much involvement in the production end of it as the engineering part of it.

He's got the mics he likes to use, I've got mine, and we kind of meet in the middle. I kind of let him be my ears after 10 hours and I can't hear anymore! "I don't know, is it good? I can't tell! I've got to get out of here for a minute." [laughs] He had a ton of involvement at every level, and if he wasn't excited, we had more work to do.

How do things look for you now from your vantage point of having just completed this record?

Things look great. It's a completely different way than we have ever approached producing and releasing a record. We have a totally different relationship with our label, and this is something we are going to benefit from together. We listen to each other. Traditionally, our label would take all the money, front-load the hell out of it, try to get the highest Billboard position you could get, then a month later, we'd be looking for the record, wondering, "Where the hell did it go?" This time we said, "Let's come out strong and let's try to build on that." And so far, so good. Radio is coming on board, and we're getting ready to hit the road in November with Mudvayne for a month.

13 Travis: Scottish Craftsmen at Work in the Studio

I've been following Travis since their first release, *The Man Who*. Their career has seemed to follow a unique trajectory, falling squarely between other traditional and independent rock acts. All the while, they have remained true to their own sound, letting music fans find them rather than actively seeking out commercial success.

The formula seems to have paid off in kind. Travis stormed the U.S. album charts with their release *The Boy with No Name*, after which they completed a largely sold-out U.S. tour. *The Boy with No Name* is the fourth album by the Scottish quartet, who has in the past received repeat accolades from the U.K.'s prestigious Brit Awards, including Best Band.

When I saw the band at New York's Webster Hall, it was very apparent that they were really a *band*. They shared a natural chemistry with each other onstage that is the result of knowing and playing with each other since their teenage years. For a band as successful as Travis, recording and touring schedules can be mentally trying, but it was very clear that they truly enjoyed themselves onstage. This feeling also translates to their recordings, especially on recent tracks such as "Selfish Jean."

Although *The Boy with No Name* was recorded with no fewer than five producers at a host of different studios over the course of about two years, it is a very cohesive piece of work that draws the listener further and further in with each play. Reuniting with producers Nigel Godrich and Mike Hedges, Travis once again proves they are expert dynamic performers, moving effortlessly from gentle ballads to driving rock 'n rollers. I caught up with bass player Dougie Payne while the band was in Boston for their North American tour.

How did you choose the facility where you recorded *The Boy with No Name*?

We recorded it in pretty much every studio in London. It was recorded over an extremely long period of time, like two years, and it was down to who we were recording with a lot of the time. For example, we did some recording at Nigel [Godrich]'s place called The Hospital, where he's got all his gear set up. We recorded a lot of it at RAK, where we recorded with Brian Eno. We also worked with Mike Hedges at

Wessex Studios and at a newish studio called British Gold. While we were there, we got down "Selfish Jean" and "Eyes Wide Open" in two days.

Frankly, we recorded anywhere they would have us and were not precious about it—we just wanted to get the songs down. As far as we're concerned, a studio is a studio—it's down to you to being good. That said, you tend to feel comfortable in places you've been more often.

Are there any studios you feel more at home in?

Not really. You feel comfortable in places that you've been more often. We did our first album at RAK 10 years ago, and for us it's a bit like a second home—we feel very comfortable there. I don't think about it too much, though—it's just down to the band.

What was it like to work with Mike Hedges and Nigel Godrich?

Mike is a lovely presence in the studio and a very nice man. He's incredible at vocals—that is his forte. We worked with Mike on *The Man Who,* so we felt very comfortable with him. He owns the desk that was used on *The Dark Side of the Moon,* and it sounds really nice. Nigel, on the other hand, loves to tinker with things—he's like a guy in a shed. His strengths are that he is really inventive, very creative, and he just has this instinctive knowledge of how to make what's there 10 times better. I don't know how he does it.

You guys have been together for a long time now and you've really held true to your own sound. Does it still feel natural to you?

We make a certain kind of noise when we play together—it's never really been second-guessed or overly thought. The way we work is very natural and organic—any development or advance has been just because we're growing up a little bit. Maybe we're getting a bit better at being in the studio and knowing what we want and how to get the sounds we're looking for. We're still the same people, and it's the same band, so it's a very natural progression. It's a bit like growing up with friends.

One thing I find very interesting about Travis is that you guys seem to play with great sensitivity when it comes to playing a particular segment loudly or softly.

As far as dynamics are concerned, the initial impetus is to be sensitive to the song—that's what it really boils down to. We are very aware of the fact that the song is the most important thing because without that, there's not really any point in playing quietly or loudly. It's about what's best for the song. I think Neil [Primrose, drummer]'s playing is amazing on this record.

How was your bass recorded on this record?

I used the same 1972 Fender Jazz bass I've been using, going through Ashton amps—a British company that makes great amps. I also use DI as well. I love the bass because it's really about melody. I am mostly playing one note at a time—it's the perfect instrument because you get to weave little melodies all around.

How do you think you guys have grown in the studio record to record? In what ways have you learned?

You're always learning. For this record, we went back to recording on tape for the first time since *The Invisible Band,* which was brilliant. Pro Tools is very convenient because you get loads of shots if you can't get it together. You have a million tracks and all that, but analog is better for capturing a whole performance, and I think we've all decided that we will just use tape in the future. We are lucky to be a band that can actually play live—we can play together in a room. And we pick up songs really quickly, so there's nothing stopping us from going with tape.

Also, that 45 seconds it takes to rewind the tape and put on another roll is crucial. It gives you the time you need to let the dust settle after the performance so you can just process the information. It makes the next take just a little bit better. With Pro Tools there's no rewind time, so you're just bashing on through. This can result in you losing a little bit of the sensitivity for that magical, electrical feeling.

You guys now have the luxury of building up the songs any way you want—either during writing or pre-production or in the studio. Do you prefer to do arrangements together in the studio, or are they constructed in advance?

We spend time working them out, generally speaking. If there are demos, we often scrap them and bring an acoustic guitar to a corner to get an idea. But to get the parts we will all just sit and play together to see what fits. That is the exciting part—when you get a good little tune, you can't wait to get your hands on it. Generally, we work pretty quickly—if we sit through an afternoon, by the end of that afternoon we'll probably be ready to record.

It must be exciting for you as a backing vocalist because you actually get to sing alongside Fran, who has a fantastic voice. Do you actually work out the harmony parts with him before you guys roll tape?

Generally, what happens is we'll get an idea while we're playing, then we'll sit and listen and work out the harmonies, and then we'll do them together. Ever since I was 17, I've loved singing with Fran. It's one of my favorite things.

Can you shed any light on how they are miking Fran up while he is doing vocals? I ask because it sounds like many times the mic is right on him, literally right next to his mouth.

The main thing is he is right up against the pop shield and he always sings into a Neumann 67. It's all vintage mics, obviously—really expensive ones. He just puts his face up to the mic and does it!

How are all the new tracks translating live? What songs are standing out with the audience?

Great. The tour is going well. We've had a go at playing just about the whole record except for "New Amsterdam." On any given night, we'll play six or seven songs off the new album, and they're going across really well considering they are relatively new. "Selfish Jean," "My Eyes," and "Eyes Wide Open" are going down really well—we've been opening up our set with "Selfish Jean." It's very nice because the songs kind of take on a life of their own—you see people singing along and starting to learn the words.

An interesting thing about *The Boy with No Name* is that it really sounds like an album. This is surprising to me at least sonically, because you recorded it at so many different locations and you had so many producers. What are your thoughts?

We had 40 songs or so recorded. We knew half of them were really good, so we mixed 20 of them and then went away and listened to all of that. After a couple of weeks, we just emailed each other our perspectives, and it was a little bit of an anxious moment—we each could have been completely on different pages when we came back, which would have been disastrous, but weirdly, we had eight or nine songs in common on all four lists. That was surprising and really nice because we all knew that these songs would sound like a record together. It was just a matter of fitting in another two or three tunes to make it so it would flow nicely.

It would be easy to say, "Okay, nobody listens to albums anymore; let's just put a bunch of songs out." But we are of a generation where albums were important—we're all 33 or 34. Albums changed our lives. For me, there were certain albums that would take you to a completely different place—they were exotic and like foreign countries to me. We still kind of view the record as being a bit sacred—the LP as it was—so we came up with a running order that feels like a proper album.

You seem like a tight group of guys. Has all the success in the studio affected you? Do you all get along pretty well?

We get along pretty well—there are always a couple of moments, but it is bound to be that way with any family. We like playing together, and over the course of making this record we got back to the enjoyment of playing. We love making music—that is key to getting the enjoyment back in the process and making songs.

Can you remember any special moments in making this album?

We'd just finished recording "My Eyes"—it was really good and we were really pleased with it, then Nigel came in. We proudly said, "Hey, what do you think of this?" He said, "It's good, but I think you should put this bit at the start, do this, and move these other things around." We said, "Okay, go ahead and do it." We left him with the song for an hour to move things around and see what he could do. We came back, and it was so unbelievable. He sprinkled his magic on it, and it just sounded amazing—suddenly, the song was so good that it made me feel really weird! [laughs]

You're dealing with big-time producers on a frequent basis. Do you ever worry about them taking over a project or changing your vision?

Not really. There have been a couple of moments—usually with mixes—where you kind of go, "Oh, that's not right." Because as I said earlier, it's all about us playing together. When you leave what you've just recorded in the hands of someone else to mix, that can be a little bit frightening. Then sometimes you get it back and just think, "Oh, that's not right."

How did you handle mixing this record? How much time did you leave between tracking and mixing?

We mixed rough mixes as we went, but then we went in with Michael Brauer at Quad Studios in New York and took the 20 songs we decided would be the main contenders and mixed the whole lot.

How are the older songs translating live?

It's interesting because the new songs always re-energize the old stuff. The older stuff can really come alive again. Eight or nine years of playing "Why Does it Always Rain On Me"—they're still fun to play.

14 Guster Keeps It Together with *Ganging Up on the Sun*

Guster's *Ganging Up on the Sun* is their follow up to the highly successful *Keep It Together*, released in 2003. Since its last recording, the group has evolved to a four-piece, adding Nashville-based multi-instrumentalist Joe Pisapia. The new record was completed in two parts: The first batch of songs was recorded in Nashville, and the second batch in New York.

Ganging Up on the Sun is a departure for Guster in more ways than one—in addition to increasing its lineup, the group also decided to record in classic, "big room" studios, including Nashville's Sound Emporium and Allaire Studios in upstate New York. Despite the enormous facilities at these locations, Joe described them as "intimate"— and the views at Allaire as "awe-inspiring." I had a chance to speak with him as the band was placing the finishing touches on mixes for the new record.

Tell me about the recording of this new album. I understand you guys recorded it in "big" studios—was this a change?

The title we are working with is *Ganging Up on the Sun*. It's lifted from some lyrics about the darkness catching up with the light, I guess. We started this record a year ago, and half of it we did at my place in Nashville, and half we did at Allaire in New York. We've been doing it in between touring; we did some last winter and some this fall, so it's been in kind of two chunks. We also did a spring and a late fall tour, just to keep our road chops up. Then we took some time off just for writing and stuff, and before we went in for the second round, we wrote some more songs just to have more options, I guess.

How does the writing process occur? Does the music come out of jam sessions?

We try to write on the road; it doesn't happen very often, but if we are near my home in Nashville, for example, we'll just go and set up the instruments for a day or two to jam and come up with ideas. If someone has an idea, we'll try it out at a sound check. We want to develop a little more discipline to do more writing while we're on the road so we don't have to take chunks of downtime while we're in the studio.

Photograph by Taylor Crothers.

Guster.

I co-wrote one of the songs with the guys on the last record, and we ended up recording it together. It was funny, because I had just done a record of my own in my apartment studio at the time, and I was so psyched to go up to Bearsville and be in a big studio with all this great gear. The ironic thing is that we went up there, and the song we wrote was real organic—it was like an acoustic number with a banjo, so we ended up bringing the Pro Tools rig into the house where everyone was staying and sitting around the fireplace and doing it live there. So after going all the way up to Bearsville, I was back at what I was kind of doing at home!

You recently made an evolution from being a three-piece band to a four-piece. What was involved in this and what led you to this decision?

For years I had a band with my brother called Joe, Marc's Brother, which was a three-piece. After 10 years of being in a band, there is a pretty deep entrenchment of personality and communication that goes on in the whole "trinity" thing. I totally understood that, and I always wished that somebody could just come in and help us out. So with Guster, I tried to be that guy.

At first I was just helping them [Guster] out on half of the songs, and then we reworked all of them. We did the writing and producing together; we were like a new band. We self-produced the first half that we did in Nashville, and then we did the second half with Ron Aniello. In Nashville, we worked with Jason Lehning, who came in an engineering capacity but ended up being a good sounding board and co-producer as well. He settled the disputes a lot of the time and helped us play good cop/bad cop with each other.

Tell me about the different places you cut this record and what the differences were.

We cut the tracks in Nashville at a classic old place called Sound Emporium. This was perfect for us because it has really big rooms but they aren't really reverberant. It was an intimate environment, but huge, with really high ceilings. When we got there, we were experimenting and putting the mics out, like, 40 feet away, and it was as if they were 10 feet away. They also have tie-in lines to a B room, which is very splashy and really live-sounding, so we did some tie-ins to that room. We then finished up at my place, Ivy League Studios, which is basically just the upstairs at my house.

Once you got going, were you able to just run through the tracks, or did you stop and revisit them occasionally?

Before we ended up in New York, we went back to the drawing board to do more writing because between us and the label, we felt like we wanted to round out the album a little. After we did 14 tracks at my house, we knew what we wanted, and we knew what we were missing. So then we tracked at Avatar in Manhattan with Shakir King engineering. He did a great job, and it was great to look over his shoulder; the drum room at Avatar sounds amazing!

Finally, I went up to Allaire. The rest of the band had been there before, but I had never been. I have always had a dream studio up in the wilderness, but that place [sighs]...it was kind of a weird feeling because usually in your dreams the sky is the limit. But that place exceeded anything I could actually dream up. I would say it would be the perfect place to take your girl for a weekend, but when the romance thing got a little boring, you could open up the closet and break out the vintage guitars! [laughs] We did all the overdubs up there, and now we are mixing at a place called the Mix Room, working with Ben Grosse, who is doing a great job.

Photograph by Jeff Touzeau.

Interior shot of Allaire Studios' Neve room.

Would you characterize the recording process as being rather loose or regimented?

A lot of the stuff I tracked on bass, some guitar, and then for overdubs, we just all grabbed whatever. I played some piano, a B3, a banjo, and a dulcimer. Wherever we found ourselves when we were jamming and writing, coming up with ideas, it was like, "Switch chairs!" Whoever came up with a part in rehearsal ended up doing it in the studio. At my house, there was a non-intimidating atmosphere; we felt like we had plenty of time to try things, throw paint at the wall, erase stuff, start over again, do other versions, and try to get the best vibe. Then at Allaire it was nice because we only had to do six songs. It seems like after we indulged ourselves so much on the first half, we wanted the second half to be simpler. We had gotten a lot of the experimenting out of our system.

What do you see as the fundamental differences between this album and the last album? How did you approach each album differently?

I would say the last record is sort of like an entrance ramp to this one, in a way. I think we took things a little further than that record, even though that record was kind of a departure for us. We kind of stretched out the instrumentation a little bit more. The label is really excited about this song called "One Man Wrecking Machine." When we wrote that one, they were totally psyched and thought they had something they could bring to their world. I think that's going to be the one that hopefully we all get sick of!

How does the mixing go and how intuitive are the mixes. since presumably you're gelling pretty well as a band?

We're averaging a song a day. Our mixes on the first batch were pretty focused. We had a pretty good template, and our arrangements were pretty much set. The first mixes were almost easier than some of the new stuff because we didn't spend as much time doing really thorough roughs on them. In Guster, everyone has a lot of strong opinions on arrangements, sonics; once we start, there are a lot of cooks in the kitchen! Everybody kind of knows what they want to hear.

15 Elf Power: Back to the Studio

Elf Power's album, *Back to the Web*, which came out in 2006, was their first record since signing with Rykodisc, following an extensive catalog of independent releases dating back to 1993. Since then, the Athens, Georgia–based group has steadily increased their loyal fan base both here and abroad, while making great strides forward from a songwriting, recording, and performance perspective. *Back to the Web* is a gentle, moody, and dramatic album full of beautiful imagery and sparse acoustic instrumentation—one that seems to flow effortlessly from one track to the next.

Andrew Rieger is a perfect example of the fact that having little to no knowledge of recording technology is perfectly okay—in fact, for some, worrying about these things can just get in the way of the songwriting process, which is counterproductive. However, there is always a recording geek within a given collection of musicians, and in the case of Elf Power, this is no exception. On *Back to the Web*, Reiger provided the compositions, and bass player Derek Almstead lent his ears and engineering expertise to help the songs rise to the occasion.

Elf Power's journey in the world of recording has its roots in the most basic, low-fi four-track setup, but now the band leverages the power of the computer—specifically Nuendo and WaveLab, the two software platforms on which *Back to the Web* was baked, following some initial tracking on an analog deck. The record was entirely self-produced at Almstead's home studio in Athens, Georgia, an approach that helped achieve a highly creative, yet inexpensive, result. I spoke to Andrew Rieger, lead singer, guitarist, and principal writer, about *Back to the Web* and Elf Power's upcoming U.S. and European tour.

When did you begin the process of writing *Back to the Web*?

I guess it was about a year and a half ago that I started writing the songs and I began to put them down on a digital eight-track and an SM-57 I had at home. I bought a 12-string acoustic, and I was listening to a lot of Middle Eastern music and gypsy music. I found that you can kind of emulate the string sounds of that kind of music with a 12-string. A lot of the songs were influenced by listening to that type of music as well as just writing with the 12-string. I would just do demos on my eight-track, just playing chords and singing nonsensical words to come up with the vocal melodies. Then later on, I would go back and listen to it and come up with the real words, but grabbing little phrases that came out of the nonsense words that I came up with off the top of my head, and incorporate those into the real lyrics.

Elf Power's *Back to the Web* lineup, left to right: Derek Almstead, Andrew Rieger, Laura Carter, John Fernandes, Josh Lott, and Jimmy Hughes.

It sounds like everything fits on this album—you don't hear layers that don't belong. For lack of a better word, it sounds organic and like everything belongs. What is behind this natural sound?

A lot of the basic tracks we would record live, with drums, guitar, and bass and other basic instrumentation—this led to a more organic feeling for us. Our records in the past have typically been done by recording the drums first, then layering each instrument on top—so this time we got a little more of a live feel. This time we achieved a nice live feel by playing together. We actually recorded some of it onto 2-inch, then we would go back, put it on the computer, and do a lot of the psychedelic flourishes and vocals in Nuendo. So it was definitely a hybrid mix of analog and digital.

Elf Power's *Back to the Web* was released in April of 2006.

Where did you actually record it?

We did it in our bass player Derek's home studio. This was the first time doing that, and it was really great—a relaxing way to record it. He's worked on a bunch of good records over the years from bands in Athens, so we had a lot of confidence in him. It was just a more relaxed way to do it and not have to worry about paying a lot of money for studio time.

Are there any mics that you like to sing into based on your experience?

When I'm recording demos at home, I just end up using an SM57, and sometimes that stuff ends up getting used on the record. We'll put it through some effects and spruce it up a bit, though. I don't really have a favorite mic, and I leave that up to the engineer— I'm kind of naïve and leave all that up to the engineer.

How was the process of recording this album different than recording some of your previous ones?

All our records have been different, and we've had many different experiences recording—our first record was done on a four-track by me, and we have slowly gotten more advanced in our recordings as we have gone along. Our second album we did on eight-track cassette, and our third album we did with Dave Fridmann [Flaming Lips co-producer] at a big fancy studio in New York. He was great to work with, but the experience of being on the clock, being under the gun, and knowing you only have a certain amount of time and money to get the job done was definitely not enjoyable. And even though the album that we did with him is an album that our fans liked a lot, we didn't really enjoy the experience.

Since then, we've really just gone back to recording in mostly home-studio setups in Athens. With the way technology has advanced over the past few years, you can get as good of a sound from a good home-recording setup as a big fancy studio—if you just spend the time. The way that I see it, it's the best of both worlds. You can still achieve that low-fi charm, but with programs like Nuendo, you can give them an extra sheen.

For the feel of the record, I was definitely riding on the 12-string acoustic. It just felt so natural, and I wanted to use it on every song—I didn't feel like it would get monotonous, but rather lent a good, cohesive feeling to it. We miked it up with an Earthworks, and it just sounded great.

John [Fernandes] played the violin and the clarinet, and Laura [Carter] played the accordion. I really felt like the violin and the accordion were going to be dominant instruments that I wanted to use, because they would add to that gypsy kind of feeling. So I recorded the demos and gave them to John and Laura, and the three of us just got together a bunch of times and played the songs acoustic, and they came up with the arrangements. Heather [McIntosh], who plays the cello, lives in New York and just came down for a weekend. She's such an intuitive player—she just came up with wonderful melodies right off the top of her head. I guess the arrangements resulted from a mixture of these acoustic rehearsals and just kind of going for it.

We also brought in a new drummer, Josh Lott. It worked out great—he has a very powerful style, but he keeps it all simple, which is what I like in a drummer. We got together, played a few songs, and it just gelled together.

How do you guys feel about home recording? Did you find it necessary to go into a commercial studio to track any of this?

We recorded the entire *Back to the Web* album in a home studio that our bass player Derek has. This was the first time doing that, since we did our last few records in professional studios. It was really great and a very relaxing way to go about it for a change. Derek is a great engineer, and he's worked on many good records from bands here in Athens, so we had confidence in him right from the start. The obvious benefit was that we didn't have to worry about paying a lot of money for studio time and all that.

The space was just a big, open room on the second floor of a large two-story house in Athens. The control room was in the same room as the studio—sometimes we would record stuff out in the hallway, but most times everyone would be in the main room. I used to get shy about my vocal performances, but I'm pretty confident these days, and I was very comfortable having Derek recording me right there in the same room.

Have you played any of these songs live? How are they translating?

We did a tour last fall where we were kind of in the middle of recording it. We did play a bunch of the new songs live while finishing up the album in December, but this will be the first tour that we do for the record. We're doing a month around America, then we're going to Europe for a couple weeks, making for a busy couple of months. The European tour kicks off with the All Tomorrow's Parties festival on May 21st. We've already toured across Europe a couple of times, and we seem to do especially well in Spain and Scandinavia. The new songs work great live—all our fans who have heard the songs without hearing the record have been really enthusiastic.

How did you choose the order of the songs for *Back to the Web*? Did this involve some difficult decision-making?

I feel like we really nailed the sequencing. It took a long time, and we tried a lot of different combinations on the song order, as well as using weird little segues of sounds to bridge the songs together. I think it really paid off, and it does have a really nice flow to it. Derek ended up mastering the entire record in WaveLab, and we couldn't be happier with the result.

16 Fields: Recording on the Emerald Isle

Fields brings truth to the notion that at any given time, somewhere in the world, someone is producing a bedroom masterpiece. Most of the songs on *Seven from the Village,* the band's first EP, were conceived and roughed out in Nick Peill's home studio, which was modest by any stretch. After a U.K.-based record label got hold of Peill's demo, they immediately identified the spark and potential in the songs and wanted to get an album out to market without delay.

The EP created a firestorm of interest, and Peill had to quickly put together a "real" band. He assembled musicians by word of mouth, asking a friend of a friend whether he knew anyone who played. Eventually, Peill assembled a patchwork group of relatively new acquaintances—but a group that gelled nonetheless. Before long, and following an extensive touring schedule, it was clear that a new, proper album was needed to reflect the band's true sound that had evolved.

They recruited producer Michael Beinhorn, holed up in a basement studio in Ireland, and got to work, embarking on their first professional recording-studio experience. Although it was difficult, their hard work and strong material persevered. I spoke to Nick while they were touring through middle America to highly enthusiastic audiences.

How did this album evolve with the demos, and what were your original visions for the songs?

Basically, I started piecing some ideas together at home using Cubase on a PC. I pretty much just put down the bones of the tracks using acoustic guitar, some keyboards, then programming drums within the computer. That was a little bit before the band got together. Basically, the tracks that make up the mini-album are a halfway step between those home demos and the band learning how to record in a proper studio.

"Song for the Fields," the first track, was sort of half of my home demo. The stuff with drum machines is what I would have done at home before getting together with the band. Then we went out on the road and did a lot of touring. The songs grew the more and more we played them. By the time we started working with Michael [Beinhorn], we almost disregarded those demos and started again from scratch doing full studio recordings.

Photo by Jenny Lewis.

Fields—Nick Peill pictured center.

The seven-song EP is a combination of my home demos; there are a couple of different things we did in a studio in London with Dan Grech-Marguerat.

The guitars sound great. How did you record them?

We rented in a whole load of different vintage amps—we probably used everything from AC-30s, Fenders, and Marshalls. All kinds of different combos. We basically had a whole collection—some of them were Michael's, and some of them we borrowed from local guitar stores.

What about the vocals?

Myself, Þórunn, and Henry [Spenner] did all the vocals. We used different mics for each person. Some mics suited my voice more than the others, and vice versa. We tried out a whole bunch of them and picked the ones that suited us best. We did them pretty swiftly, and we spent a little time making sure the sound and texture were right.

You said many of these tracks evolved by yourself in your home studio. How did the band actually get together?

There was a point where I recorded a whole bunch of demos, and I eventually wanted to play stuff live, so I just asked friends and friends of friends if they would play. We socialized a little bit, then had rehearsals to see what would work. The first few people that I thought of, everyone was available, and it just worked out—that was about 18 months ago. All five of us were on that EP.

That's amazing to me, because for five people who had just gotten together, it sounds very focused. Usually when you have that many musicians, it can be difficult to get a cohesive end result.

I think we all share the same vision. It was sort of like a learning curve for us—it was the first time all five of us had gone into the studio together. We applied the things that we learned on that recording to the album that we did with Michael. The full-length album was a step up from the mini-album.

What was it like working with Michael? Was it a good fit for you, and how was the chemistry between the six of you in the studio?

It was good—Michael has a very good ear for recording sounds, which was a main draw of working with him. He was also very open to experimenting with different sounds and textures. It was quite an intense experience, but also a very enjoyable one.

How hard did you have to work on arrangements while you were there? Did everything seem to fall into place?

The arrangements were sorted. It was more that we had technical problems with equipment breaking down. We were working in a place that was like a basement studio, and it suffered from dampness somewhat—the acoustic guitars and the drum kit took on a bit of moisture, and we had to kind of dry them off, so that slowed down the process. Also, we hired in so much equipment that there was almost too much of a choice—it was a good experience for us, though.

You guys were probably working on a limited budget and a limited amount of time, so the performances probably had to be pretty tight, too.

I guess that is the case for any recording—you would like more time. We did run out of time on some things, but it is not necessarily a bad thing to be forced to get stuff done. Otherwise, you might experiment forever in some songs.

I really enjoyed some of your programming on the EP. Can you tell me on how many tracks you programmed the drums on the new album, versus laying down real drums?

We didn't get to do as much programming on the full-length album. There are electronic elements in the keyboard and tweaking on the guitars to synths and things like that.

Did you record the drums to a click track?

Yes, we worked that to a click. Luckily, our drummer was fairly on the money, so it was no problem playing to clicks, thank goodness. Michael put so many mics on the drums. There were mics on every available inch of the kit, and the room was miked up with about six or seven different mics as well. Probably on the drums there were 28 mics. He plays with a standard kit—two toms. We overdubbed the cymbals afterward.

Did you do bass and drums simultaneously or did you overdub the bass later?

We did bass and drums with acoustic and vocal guides, and then we redid the bass after the drums. I think we redid all the acoustic guides too, from what I recall.

How did you like working with Pro Tools?

I like working with Pro Tools and the flexibility it gives you in terms of how many tracks you can put down, and how you can pluck around with everything once you record it.

How would you compare your recording experience in Dublin to when you recorded the EP in London?

It definitely wasn't as fancy—in Dublin it was all about the sound of the room. It was quite a claustrophobic and intense atmosphere, and this definitely impacted the overall mood of the album. We mixed it back in London at SoHo Studios with Elliot James and did a few more overdubs there as well. Mixing was a really enjoyable part of the process, and we were able to sweeten up the vocals using things like vintage space echoes.

Mixing can be tricky, and it varied from track to track. Some tracks were harder to balance. You start pushing the vocals up, then you can't hear the guitars, so you push them up, and you're back at square one. So it's a bit of a balancing act, but for the most part it is pretty straightforward.

How do you feel about the album, having all the time now to look back?

I think you get the best perspective on the album when you have a deadline to get it done by. Generally speaking, at that point there are things that we still want to do with it, and you never feel 100-percent happy with something at the point when you have to finish it. But looking back, yeah, I think we did a good job on it. It gives a good snapshot of where the band was at that point in time.

Did you bring any specific sonic reference points to this album, or were there any particular influences you think stand out?

There were things like certain My Bloody Valentine or Sonic Youth kind of guitars. There is a Californian singer named Linda Perhacs—she made albums in the early '70s and had a very distinctive kind of vocal sound. We listened to lots of things but didn't try to copy anything directly.

What areas would you like to see the next record move toward sonically?

We are thinking of adding more of the electronic element into the next recording. It kind of depends on the material—we have a whole bunch of things we are working on, but we would like to see a bit more of that. We did a session in London where we tried purely electronic versions of some of the album tracks for our own enjoyment, and that was an interesting process to go through.

17 Ivy: Converging Talent at New York's Stratosphere Sound

Andy Chase, a multi-instrumentalist and composer in the group Ivy, is no stranger to the recording studio. He is a partner in Stratosphere Sound, along with James Iha, formerly of Smashing Pumpkins, and Adam Schlesinger of Fountains of Wayne. Stratosphere Sound is a top-flight, Francis Manzella–designed studio in the heart of New York City, which has since attracted folks such as Ryan Adams, America, and many others.

Ivy's record, *Guestroom,* was a collection of their favorite cover songs. Doing an album of covers enabled them to discover their own arrangements and interpretations of songs that were important to them for one reason or another. It was also a vacation of sorts away from the pressure of writing all new material, and at the same time a challenge to reinvent classic tracks such as The Cure's "Let's Go to Bed" and even the Ronettes' "Be My Baby," which had an otherworldly feel.

I want to focus on Ivy's *Guestroom,* but also the studio you have created, Stratosphere Sound. Can you walk me through the setup, then we'll get into specifics on how you engineered the album and some of the ideas you had?

Well, just imagine the space was just storage lockers, and it was 30 feet high. You'd walk in, and it was this huge, cavernous space that went on for 8,000 square feet that way. We just thought how much we wanted to put up a dividing wall, and then we bunkered down for 10 months.

How much experience did you have building studios?

I'd had a studio for eight years—really since I was right out of school. And that studio was literally built by me and some friends—we learned how to drill into drywall and put up the studs. I was what they called the lackey. My friend, who is also a musician, would do carpentry work on the side—I just kind of helped him. Our old studio was a step...I wouldn't even call it a step down from this. It was like an escalator *all the way* down from this. So Stratosphere Sound was an enormous step up—obviously, financially, technologically, on every level it was bigger.

I'm assuming there was much greater risk involved in building it as well.

Higher stakes, higher everything. I bought out my partners at the old studio because I was talking to James Iha, my one partner, and Adam, who is in Ivy, my other partner. At the time, I was thinking about buying out my old partners and re-forming with these guys—maybe we could find a new place. The first thing we did when I bought out my partners is we found this board, which is really the centerpiece of the whole studio.

Where did you find this board [a Neve 8086]? It's beautiful.

It was in upstate New York...I can't remember the name of the studio.

Early '70s?

This is a '78. And it's just like your classic gorgeous Neve with GML Automation. It's been heavily, heavily modified by Dan Zellman. These boards were really no-frills—it seems like they weren't back then, but compared to what you'd even get with a Mackie today, you know that Mackie's more flexible than the way this board was designed in the late '70s.

So you're talking mainly functional modifications?

Well, there are lots of modifications that you can do to update it so that it is every bit as flexible as any board you'd buy today.

How deeply involved were you in speccing out the board and getting it fitted electronically?

I'm not that hands-on with that kind of thing. If a module would go down, I would just call Dan Zellman. He's one of the premier Neve guys on the East Coast, and he happens to be in New York, which is convenient. And he has totally modified this board so that it's incredibly flexible and can pretty much do anything you want to do today. It's been totally re-capped as well. By his own admission, it's one of the best-sounding Neves that he has come across.

So we've got a good marriage between old vintage stuff and new solid-state tube. We consider ourselves retro-heads, but we also are fully blown with things like Focusrites. You'll have a Focusrite next to the old Beatle-esque mic preamps. We also have a full-blown Pro Tools rig, 16-track 2-inch tape machine for those purists who like to do bass and drums on that.

So you are tracking directly to 2-inch for the most part, and you dump into Pro Tools to mix?

I always track to 2-inch. Not even just to mix. The tracks get recorded and may only spend their life for five minutes on multi-track tape. And as soon as the band takes a break and has Chinese food upstairs, we're transferring it into Pro Tools through our converters, our ADD converters.

How hands-on are you at managing the studio?

We have a studio manager who runs the place, and I'd say that the lion's share of the business has been coming by what we call in-house stuff—projects that I bring in that are my projects.

What bands?

Tahiti 80, some Japanese bands that I have worked with, Mexican bands.... I seem to be a little like the United Nations producer: France, Spain, Mexico, and Japan.

How are you finding all this stuff? Are they finding you?

You know, really Tahiti 80 started it. They had a massive, massive hit on their first record in Japan. I guess I already had a profile from my work in Ivy, but it was more like kind of indie-underground in Japan. But the Tahiti 80 record was one of the biggest records in Japan when it came out. So that led to a lot of work from higher-profile Japanese artists who wanted to work with me. You need your one big break to kind of jumpstart things.

It's really comfortable in here. It doesn't seem too clinical or clean, like many other upscale studios around town.

Well, we gave the designer Fran Manzella a mandate, which was that sonically, it had to be every bit as competitive with studios that were, you know, twice as expensive as this. But we wanted to kind of keep the vibe a little funky, and we didn't want to go too nuts on all the finishings because to us that's what also can make it very corporate. The word "corporate" came up a lot as something we wanted to try to find whatever the antithesis would be.

So this is kind of like the guts here. We've got our 16-track, 2-inch, Munchy Crunchy Intermittent—you know, MCI? We pretty much run everything on the Studer over here, just to capture the sound, and then it goes into Pro Tools.

How quickly do you typically dump it into Pro Tools?

It could be as quick as a guy comes in and does two guitar parts, and I would say, "You know, between those two, I could comp together a good one." And he goes to the bathroom or something, and by the time he's back, it's dumped into Pro Tools. As long as we capture on the multi-track, it can immediately go in.

That's an old Ludwig kit, huh?

It's an old late '50s, early '60s, I think. I started off as a keyboard player and a frustrated drummer. I think I was maybe technically a little better on the drums, but mostly because I was a composer, I was writing on the keyboards.

So that's obviously your best vehicle for composing?

It was at first, but then I met Dominique [Durand], the lead singer in Ivy, and then we fell in love, and she thought that keyboards weren't cool—all her favorite bands were guitar bands. So I immediately sold all my keyboards and bought a guitar.

Guestroom **is a very electronic-based record.**

On the album that you have, the last five songs were songs that we have done over the course of our career.

And the first few songs were new studio songs, correct?

For that, we took three weeks here and we just recorded those five, which was a blast. It's so much fun when you're not working on your own songs. There's a psychological, liberating element like you're disconnected from anything…any kind of over-analytical kind of approach that you usually have with your own music.

What is the origin of all this gear?

Most of the stuff in here is just all the gear that we have amassed between the three partners since we were kids. That CP-70 was my first keyboard that my parents bought for me. I've been waiting for a studio big enough so I could take it from my parents' garage and bring it up here.

That's good you didn't sell stuff. A lot of people tend to get rid of so much gear along the way, including their first instruments.

Here we have a huge loading dock, which is good because we have a lot of foreign bands come in, so they come with tons of gear and wheel it all in.

What on earth would they need? You have your Vox AC30s, your Matchless combos.... I guess folks just want to track with their own equipment, huh?

As people get more and more familiar with the studio, they bring less and less. But the first time, if they've never been here before, it's kind of like a security blanket. They want to bring their own toms.

You mentioned that most of your projects have been coming from the inside. Are there any other projects that come in from the outside that have caught your ear?

Yes, I'd say most—70 percent—of our projects have come from the inside. I mean, studios have been just dropping left and right. We've been fortunate that most of the work, since we've opened a year ago, has originated through projects we had something to do with. For example, the first projects since then have been Ivy doing the *Shallow Hal* score, then a Mexican band I did, then Tahiti 80, which took us to Christmas. Then Adam did a whole bunch of stuff here; Adam and James have Scratchie Records and did their first big signing with Scratchie Records here.

How do you keep everything afloat? You are playing in a band and co-managing a recording studio. You must have a great work ethic.

People say that, but there are periods when we feel overwhelmed. There are other times when we are hanging out with our kids and doing stuff like going on vacation. So it seems balanced to us. It doesn't seem that crazy.

Do you often have both rooms working in tandem? Or are there typically separate projects going on?

Yep. For example, these guys have hooked up both rooms, so they are here doing both edits and mixing. There's Pro Tools in both rooms, so you just walk out with your drive and swap files.

We have tied all the rooms into each other. If you want to do a piano track in the little room or a John Bonham-esque drum track in the live room, you can do it because the rooms are all tied into one another. The only thing we don't have is a video screen where you can see each other, but the talkback systems still work.

Do you do all of your work at Stratosphere, or do you have a studio at home as well?

I have a studio at home, and I work there a lot, too. And frankly, the studio gets booked so often that I have no choice but to work there. I'm not an early person, so the idea of coming in at 8 to 11, when I might be able to come in, is just not practical.

How are you able to juggle all this…touring, writing, producing, running a studio? How do you keep a balance?

It seems to always work out, and it's stuff you love to do, so it's that much easier. It's a great life, you know. Everything you're doing, you enjoy doing. Working in your studio, touring…and it's cyclical. You won't tour for a year, so you focus your energies on something else, and then that gets released, and you're touring again. From somebody else's perspective, they might not understand it. They might just see, "Oh, they're touring all the time; they're this all the time," but it seems pretty balanced.

When do you do your writing? When you are on tour?

No, no. The singer in Ivy is my wife, and she's French, so we go to her parents' country house up in Normandy—we take a two- or three-week vacation. I'll bring my guitar, and she gets to see her family. I go there and I end up writing songs that appear on our releases, so I'm almost superstitious now about going there to write. When you need to come up with a bulk of songs, not one or two—you need to bunker down and come up with 10, 15, 20 ideas—you need to go somewhere.

Do you push yourself, or do the tunes seem to just come?

The songs just seem to come.

Was it fun to choose songs recorded by other artists on *Guestroom*? How did you find the songs you wanted to record?

Some of them we had known for years that we wanted to do if we ever had the opportunity to do a covers record. Over the years we've had reason to do one every now and then. Our first EP that we ever released was a cover of an Adam Cohen song from his Orange Juice days, called "I Guess I'm Just a Little Too Sensitive." Dominique worshipped him when she was a little girl, and when we talked about putting out this EP, she said, "I want to cover this song." She played it for us, and the production was so badly dated that we just couldn't get around that. We had to listen to it a few times. When you kind of strip down all the heavy reverb and chorus and flange...

The melody rang through.

The melody was awesome. And we just deconstructed it and worked it from the ground up.

One of the first things I noticed about *Guestroom* is that it is a really good "headphones" album. I was listening to it on my PowerBook, and it seemed very spacious.

Well, my favorite records have been headphone albums. And in a way, for me, that is the litmus test. If it takes you to another world in headphones, then it's done and it's served its purpose. And if it doesn't, it still needs work. Those are my favorite records—that do something a little bit more than you realize by listening on a pair of speakers.

On this album, you deconstructed the originals and rebuilt them. How did you handle the arrangements?

We really take each song as it comes and...like "Let's Go to Bed"—that was an obvious song we knew we were going to do because the running joke was when we were on tour,

Adam would start sound-checking his bass, the house guy would go, "All right, give me some bass," and he would start with the Cure riff. And for years, that's what he would play. It became this running joke. We'd all end up jamming. Sometimes we'd do the reggae version, sometimes I'd sing it, sometimes Dominique would sing it, so when we were talking about doing a covers album, c'mon—it's got to be The Cure.

What a great opening track. The bass sounds great on that. What was the signal chain?

I recorded the bass direct, digitally. I think I compressed it going in with a Teletronix LA-2A, and somehow it ended up distorting pretty heavily, just through the Teletronix. It was too hot, and it was kind of crapping out, but it crapped out in a very sweet, sonically pleasing way. So it has some grit to it. It's not a clean sound, like digital sound.

I never would have guessed you recorded it direct. It sounds like you had a cabinet blasting.

No, it's really the LA-2A. Then we put some delay on it. If you take off the delay and you really study it solo, you can hear that it's not going through an amp.

How many of the tracks off *Guestroom* were done live versus building them up by sequencing, programming, et cetera?

Obviously, "Let's Go to Bed" was all programmed. And really, we put down this keyboard part, which actually sounds like a guitar, which is a really key part. It's kind of a guitar sample played on a keyboard. I added a Wurlitzer part to it, and Adam put the bass line down, and we had this pulsing kick drum. Kind of like a heartbeat. We got to the point where I knew we needed something aggressive, but I don't think Ivy is really the right call to come up with something really aggressive and edgy, rhythmically speaking with our programming, so I called Pedro, who is the bass player and key programmer in Tahiti 80. I asked him if he wanted to help us, and so I just sent him the tracks. He's got a Pro Tools system in France, and that's what he came up with. So he single-handedly came up with the whole drum beat, and that kind of set the song in motion.

"Kite" [the second track] is driven by a fabulous melody, with a driving beat and gentle acoustic guitars. On the chorus melody, Dominique's vocal kind of soars. How did you get her voice to sound so expansive? During the first part of the song, her voice is kind of minimalist. But then in the chorus, it just gets wider.

I like to do that a lot on choruses, where you feel like a chorus kind of explodes—not in a Nirvana-esque way, but in a lush, pop way. You know, where it just kind of spreads out when you get to the chorus. So typically I will take a double-track or two double-tracks of the vocal and split them in, so that it thickens up her voice. And many times,

I'll still keep the same effect on her lead vocal, but when the double-track vocals come in, they've got lots of delay and kind of an analog or tape delay with filtering and just a sense of twisting and turning. Not just a repetitive digital delay, but something that just kind of morphs into something else. That will be on the background vocals, and that's just enough to kind of spread out the whole feeling of her voice, like with this angelic quality that comes on. But you still get the tight crispness of the lead vocal where nothing has been put on it.

The drums sound really tight and crisp as well. I'd be interested to know your mic setup and distances used.

Yeah, that's our touring drummer, Marty, and he came in and played on "Kite." We set up our Ludwig kit. We have an old, beautiful kit that just sounds unbelievable. I like to close-mike stuff, and I like to record it in a pretty dry room. I am more of a fan of starting with something that on tape might be closer to The Sea and Cake style—you know, the band from Chicago—or more classical, maybe like Fleetwood Mac. You know, bands like that, where it's really, really dry. So the mics are really close—421s on the toms. Sometimes I might do a 421 and a 414 on the tom and a 414 on the bottom. Sometimes I don't like the way the bottom end responds on the low tom. D112 on the kick and a '57 on the snare, pretty close for the proximity effects. You get kind of a fat sound. B&Ks on the cymbals. The problem with the B&Ks sometimes is that when you are really trying to get a big, fat, bashy sound on the overheads, they are a little too tight and pristine-sounding. So if we're going for something less polite, then I'll swap those out and put maybe U 87s or something with a bigger diaphragm up there.

Photo courtesy Sennheiser.

Chase relies on the tried-and-true Sennheiser 421 when recording toms and even vocals.

Do you usually record Dominique's voice dry, or are you EQing going in?

I've been recording her voice for so many years that I almost do things before she's even sung because I just know. I know the song, I've heard her sing it a couple times practicing it, I know which mic I'm probably going to pick, and based on that mic, I know the whole chain already. So it's nice having worked with the same people for so long. When we're going for your basic meat-and-potatoes voice sound, I use a Telefunken U47, and I like to put her really, really, close to it. Like, really close—as close as I can get with a windscreen in between. Maybe even two inches from the mic.

For vocals, I am also a big fan of the 421s. I'd say half of the Tahiti 80 record was recorded with him through that. But you really have to crank the mic pre to kind of…if the mic pre is too low, and you have a singer singing through it, it's kind of lame-sounding, unexciting. But if you go too hot on the mic pre, it's really electric, and you get this really present but focused compact vocal sound. The girl in the Cardigans, that's all she sings with.

Do you give Dominique much guidance on how loud or soft to sing? She seems to have a very soft voice, almost whispery.

You know, I'll give her some directions, but she seems to have a pretty good handle on what she needs to do. She sings very softly, and I find that putting her up real close on there gets a nice low-end bump and more crispness to her voice. I'll usually put that through a 1073 and immediately put it though a high-pass filter. Sometimes I cut everything off at 160k.

Other than that, no EQ coming in?

No. I listen in the track, and if it's sounding like there'll be a lot of EQing that will be needed at the mixing stage, you can already hear it since the song is well underway. So if her voice is sounding muddy, I might even just change the mic, but if I've tried all the mics and it keeps going back to the U47, but it's a little dark, then I will probably boost her anywhere from 3k to sometimes as high as 7.

Your version of "Be My Baby" sounds 180 degrees different from the original in that the Ronettes' version kind of sounds hopeful and dense, while yours sounds kind of lonely and more sparse.

Well, that song is so famous. We weren't huge fans of that song, and it wasn't something that we had been dying to do. Our publisher at the time wanted some of their artists to do a compilation, so they just happened to ask us toward the end, and all the choice songs that we would have gravitated to first had been taken, so of course there's "Be My Baby," and it's like, "Who wants to cover that?" We took a lot of creative liberties with that song. We just changed the arrangement, left out a verse....

Who handles the male background vocals?

Typically in Ivy, it's me. Sometimes Adam does, but 90 percent of the backgrounds are me. For some reason I sound like Dominique, like when I'm high. So it's fallen on me to do a lot of harmonies.

On the Serge Gainsbourg cover you did, your French is perfect. You obviously must speak French now, right?

[Laughs] Enough to get by, but what people don't see is that there's a big piece of paper in front of you with the whole thing spelled out phonetically. Also, I have the luxury of punching enough times, too, so...

"Say Goodbye": Is that a Roland TR-808 I hear as the drum track?

You know where that came from? The Alesis DM Pro. People underestimate the flexibility of that unit. It has banks in there running through all the old Roland classic sounds—the 808s, et cetera. With a little EQing, you can push it even further.

What other sound modules do you reach for? Do you like the Korg Trinity or other samples or...

I'm not a huge fan of the Korg Trinity. Sometimes I find that the keyboard sounds are so high-fidelity and realistic that there's this shimmery gloss to it that I don't think is appropriate for the type of music we play. I like the DM Pro stuff; my only gripe is that it often comes out sounding, for lack of a better word, just a little MIDI—a little cold and right out of a box. A lot of times what I'll do is record it to cassette tape. And I'll make sure I pick a cassette tape that's not a high bias, but a crappy old used tape that always has dropouts and stuff. And I'll record it at a low volume so there's some tape hiss, too. The idea is to record it to cassette tape to make it smaller and loosen the fidelity, then re-import that back into Pro Tools and line it up with the original, because obviously the tape moves and warbles. And then what you end up getting is something that's a little bit more vintage-sounding. And it takes the edge off the MIDI sounds when they're sounding too polished. I do that all the time. So my cassette deck still gets used a lot, but not the DAT.

Was mastering *Guestroom* difficult, since you were pulling tracks from so many different parts of your career?

It was actually really interesting because, going back to the song we mentioned, "[I Guess I'm Just a Little] Too Sensitive," that was '94. The first cover we did. I didn't want to start with the master of that; I wanted to go back and find the two-track mix, pre-mastering. Which I did. So when we brought all that stuff to Blotto at Sony Mastering, this is in 2002, going back from '94. Eight years later. You know how long eight years is—technologically speaking, like 50 years. So the difference in mastering was just unbelievable. Like how much louder they could get. How much more high-fidelity. Go put on our original EP *Lately* and listen to "Too Sensitive," then quickly go put in *Guestroom* and listen to "Too Sensitive," and if you're an audiophile, you'll hear a real difference. And all that is attributed to the difference in mastering today versus where we were in '94.

What was it like scoring *Shallow Hal*? Had you scored music prior to this?

No, I mean we had lots and lots of songs used in films and TV shows, but they were just pulled off our records. I think the nature of the music that Ivy has always done—we've always felt that was a form for us that we knew we could feel comfortable with. It wasn't based on any experience, only instinct. We had a feeling that if we were given the opportunity, it would be something that we could do.

How difficult was it to pick up the necessary technical aspects of scoring?

We got all the equipment we needed, set it up here, and I think the first week was a little intimidating, you know, getting around the technical aspects of how to sync to picture and all that stuff. It was a complete and utter blast. We loved every minute of it. Plus, you don't have to write lyrics [laughs], and the songs only have to be 30 seconds long.

How did you get involved with James Iha, and how is the partnership going?

The connection is James and Adam's best friend growing up, Jeremy, were both living in Chicago and started a label with D'Arcy and some other people called Scratchie Records. So Jeremy, Adam's childhood friend, called Adam up, who lived in New York, and said, "We're starting this label. Do you want to be a part of it?" So through joining the label, Adam and James became friends, and James was coming to New York at that period, when they were working on the label and Ivy was in the studio working on our album, which was to be *Apartment Life*.

This was at The Place?

This was at the old Place, before. So James would come by and hang out, and at that point we kind of got to know each other superficially. He ended up making comments on the tracking, and ended up contributing to the record. Playing some solos, singing some vocals, there was just a great vibe there. Coincidentally, it was at the period where I was thinking of buying out my partners and looking for new partners, so I talked about that with Adam and James, and things just kind of progressed.

The Place ultimately burned down, right? Were you able to salvage any equipment from the fire?

Right. The fire didn't affect our space per se. The flames didn't lap up at our equipment. We were on the third floor. We suffered severe smoke damage and damage to the studio structure and everything else because the firemen just busted through everything to put out the fire.

And you were overseas at this time, right?

I had a baby and we had just started what was to be *Long Distance* there, and we decided we just couldn't. Dominique was just too tired, our baby was only a month old, she was crying all the time, and we were sleep deprived. We said, "Let's just take a little vacation." We'll start on the record in a couple months. So we took off and we went to Martha's Vineyard. The night we arrived at Martha's Vineyard, I got a frantic message on my cell phone that said, "You gotta come right back; there's been a fire at the studio, in the building." The long and the short of it is that the building was destroyed enough so that they didn't prepare, and they used this clause in the New York State lease that says in a catastrophic fire, a landlord can terminate all leases. So that's what he did. He terminated our leases. We had 15 days to get everything out of there.

I can't imagine how you could just pick up the pieces and move on to build Stratosphere.

Well, we almost gave up. At first we were optimistic. You know, the space was really small where we were. The only reason that we didn't start a studio somewhere else at the time was because we wanted to run the course of our lease up, because we still had a year and a half. So it was already set up, soundproofed. In that sense, we knew we would leave eventually, but things at that point in New York—I mean, real estate was just going through the roof. So when we were evicted, at first we were optimistic. We'll just find another space.

Then everything seemed to come together. I mean, you still pinch yourself and can't believe it happened. I had just moved around the corner, down the street. And Adam had just moved in across the street from us. Like when we wake up in the morning and talk on the phone, we can look out our windows and wave to each other, just like something out of a sitcom. We were looking for a studio and having serious talks between the three of us about, "Well, maybe we should sell our board, sell our gear—there's just no way we could have a space here." Then we got a call, because Billboard apparently wrote a piece on the demise of Stratosphere, the unfortunate fire, our plight, and the search for our space. And then there's a girl who works at Billboard who's kind of an acquaintance of James and Adams. She called us up and said, "My father owns a lot of real estate in Manhattan. Maybe you guys could talk to him." So we met with him, and he was about as accommodating as you could get. He said, "Well, I've got buildings at this location, that location, and that location." He mentioned that there was one here, which was three blocks from where we lived, so we were like, "Well, okay, how about that one?" We kept waiting for the big catch. He was like, "How much space do you want, ideally, in a perfect world?" We were like, "Three-thousand square feet." [And he said,] "How much do you want to spend?" We just came up with a figure, and he was like, "Okay." He's kind of an amateur musician. Semi-retired and successful. I don't know, I'm just guessing, but maybe he just thought it would be cool to have musicians there.

Maybe he was excited on your behalf, helping you start again and all.

I think he might have liked knowing that he was helping us out; I think he also liked knowing that he was going to have a really nice recording studio in what was really a storage facility of his. We offered him 10 free hours per month for him and his friends to come in and jam and make their recordings.

Has he taken advantage of this?

They haven't, but it's racking up. It's getting kind of scary [laughs]; it's been years! They're going to drive us out of business when he finally decides to camp in here for four months. It was one of those arrangements that just had a good feeling to it.

Since you were constructing it yourselves from the ground up, you were able to customize the space to suit your needs.

Yeah, we really were. Obviously, we took a business loan to make this stuff happen and worked with budgets, contractors, and banks, really operating at a level that I had never done before.

You were handling all the management of the studio....

Yeah, that's a little strange, you know, wearing different hats. We're a little used to it because in Ivy, we self-manage. So we're used to switching hats from artist to management, and knowing maybe how to do it in a way that is not so distasteful to other people.

We kind of got through it and we didn't make too many huge mistakes, and I think the overall vision of the studio was to try to generate as much of the business as we could ourselves. James producing bands from Scratchie, bringing them in here; Adam producing; me, all of us, just trying to bring in the work. We have other people, a staff here, who is very well connected with the New York scene, and between all of us collectively, we're friends with the majority of the New York–based bands. So far, knock on wood, I think that compared to the state of affairs of a lot of other studios, we've been okay.

What's next with Ivy and Stratosphere? Next six months?

[Loud sounds, like fireworks, begin blasting repeatedly in background.]

I think with Ivy, we're just letting the covers record run its course. It is kind of serving its purpose. We just wanted to get something out to remind people that we haven't gone away while we bunker down and make our next record, which can take years. And we were talking about doing a covers record for a long time, so we kind of satiated that part of us. At this point we're just starting to write songs for the next record. We talked to our label network, and we're tentatively scheduled to have something by the summer.

18 | This Way, That Way, and Scofield's Way

John Scofield has always been an innovator in contemporary jazz guitar, having released nearly three dozen albums over the span of his career and performed for sell-out audiences around the world. Having played alongside a wide range of jazz greats that includes Miles Davis, Charles Mingus, Pat Metheny, Bill Frisell, and others, his style and improvisational capabilities are instantly recognizable.

On his latest collection of tunes, titled *This Meets That*, Sco displays his usual diversity and technical mastery on a variety of material, such as a brilliant, eclectic rendition of "The House of the Rising Sun" with his old friend, Bill Frisell. Throughout the album, Scofield is featured playing as a trio with his "A-Team": bassist Steve Swallow and drummer Bill Stewart. The album was recorded and mixed entirely at Avatar Studios in New York City.

Photo courtesy Nick Suttle.

What are your impressions in hindsight now that the record is finished?

I think it came out really well. It's hard to listen to your own stuff and judge it, but I do think this record is good. You get so involved in making a record that you know it all by heart, so it's like, "Here's that clam I made," or whatever. We've been playing the tunes in the trio, playing them on gigs for a couple of years.

How does it feel to be back in a trio again? This isn't your first time playing with Bill Stewart and Steve Swallow.

I've played with these guys for many, many years. Steve Swallow I've known and played with since the '70s, Bill Stewart since 1990. They are two of my closest friends and absolute favorite musicians. It feels like home, you know?

You've done several dozen albums over the years and have been recording since the '70s. In your mind, what is different now from both a practical and a technical perspective?

The Pro Tools thing has been huge. Overdubbing has always been fairly simple on traditional multitracks, but editing is a whole different ballgame now. Splicing would be this really dangerous thing that you would do; now you can make just about any splice work. I remember when digital first came out—the first major revolution was that you could edit each track in a different place. That was the first major kind of revolution, but even then that was hard and took a lot of time. Now in Pro Tools we do it so any edit point can work.

Pro Tools is scary to me because if you know what you want to sound like but you haven't mastered it on your instrument, you can go back, and just by moving stuff around rhythmically and pitch-wise, you can make yourself sound like the improviser you wish you were in jazz solos, so that changes everything. You don't need to know the music as well—you can make mistakes and edit. That hasn't changed the way I rehearse and practice for a recording session, but it does mean you can fix little booboos.

Can't this approach potentially diminish a jazz recording, since it's presumably about improvising, taking risks, and sometimes failing to reach that perfect note?

For me, my love of jazz music and my experience has been hearing the greats of jazz improvise on their instruments, while taking big risks and being able to pull off these amazing things. On all the old records, this performance element has been faithfully captured. But now, I think the temptation to fix all your little mistakes in programs like Pro Tools takes away from the art form in a way. That said, you still have to go in and come up with something that is good. You still have to have musical ears and play your instrument well.

How hard is it for you to find that pocket in the studio versus when your band is playing live?

Most of us are more used to playing live, but over the years I've gotten used to playing in the studio, and I realize it's just different. The great thing in live performance is that in a few hours, you warm up in a way I think you never do in the studio—especially for people who play jazz and are at a high level in their instruments. The audience is also there to give you that boost, and that is so important.

In the studio, the only really great thing is that you have no outside interference to break your concentration. You just go in and try to create this perfect performance, and you hopefully have this great sound situation where you can really hear everything perfectly through the cans. You're in a great sonic environment where you can go back and have the immediate reward of hearing the performance in a beautiful playback situation where you really hear the instruments the way they are supposed to be heard, rather than in a lousy concert hall with a P.A. system and maybe some really awful acoustics.

John, on this album you took a more active role in the arrangement. How did that present a new challenge for you?

When I write a tune, I write it on my guitar, but I hear more orchestral parts behind it. On this album, I arranged some of it for horns. I checked it with a keyboard and a guitar, but you never know until you play it with the real players. It's really fun to try to paint a picture with many instruments, rather than just with a trio. Once in a while, someone will say, "I think this would sound better in another register," but that's what they do. They are all used to working with really good arrangers and having high-quality notes in front of them. These are studio guys—if the arrangement is no good, they would say something. Then again, they're getting a check at the end of the day, so what do they care?

That said, a performer can play the notes and still not feel it and fit in with the groove. The idea is to play it with a certain feel for the other people around you so you can get a very good blend. These guys are really great at doing that—their intonation and rhythm are perfect, and they are able to play with dynamics. They are able to add to the performance in really subtle ways; maybe they shade a note this way or that way and then do it in a whole section. Or the trumpet player will do this little thing on the note, then we'll all do it. This kind of thing can impact how we all play. Whatever note is written, they'll still have their own interpretation, and this is what makes it different than playing it through a sequencer.

Where did you record this?

We recorded this album at Avatar Studios in New York City, where I've recorded all my records for the last 20-something years. It's the best place in New York that has a good-sounding room and which can accommodate large ensembles. We wanted the room to be big enough so we could all fit in there comfortably—if the room is small, that's going to be boxy-sounding, right?

We recorded this in Studio C, where there is a main room and two booths—actually, the booths are more like small rooms unto themselves. They have floor-to-ceiling glass doors so you are isolated, but you really have full visual contact with everybody. We ended up putting the drums in the big room, and we had the guitar in one iso booth and the bass in the other. There is probably a slight amount of leakage of guitar into the drums, but it sounded great. We overdubbed the horns the next day.

How did you approach production, and what was it like to work with James Farber as engineer again?

I've used producers on a lot of records, but I produced this one myself and was obviously also the artist. In this case I knew what I wanted to do, and I knew the sound that James could get for our group. I knew I wanted to expand our sound with horns; that was a little like, "We're not sure what it's going to sound like 'til we get there." Sonically, I knew I wanted James Farber and the sound that he gets—I really rely on him and wanted to get his sonic vision on the CD. James Farber is a giant in this field and has recorded a bunch of albums with me, starting in the '80s.

You achieved a fantastic drum sound—there is so much space you can really hear. What was your approach?

Getting a great drum sound always starts with having a drummer who really gets a beautiful sound on the instrument. James Farber did a spectacular job of capturing that sound on this record. All the drums are miked. The overhead mics are a key ingredient—everything goes through them, and that's the basis of the drum sound. James Farber makes the microphone selections for everything. On my guitar, I will usually have two close microphones—both different kinds. I can't even remember what we used on this record.

Your guitar has a nice edge to it. Can you tell me a little about your setup?

I used my same Ibanez AS200 guitar that I have used for years. I have two of them that I brought in, and I'm not even sure which is which on the different tracks. One is from 1982; the other is from 1986. I also played a Telecaster on one tune. I played through this incredible amplifier—there is a guy in New York City named Artie Smith who provides amps and drums for musicians on recording sessions in New York City. I used a 1959 Fender Twin amp, called the High-Powered TWIN. It was a tweed, before the blackfaces. As far as stompboxes, I use a boomerang phase sampler, and I might have used my rack distortion on some. Otherwise, it's pretty straight ahead.

How important are the dimensions of a room for you?

We want it to be big enough so you can fit in there comfortably. If it is too small, the sound will be too boxy. Even though it is close miked, you are still in a room, and the sound of that room will still come through the microphones.

What was it like to play with Bill Frisell again?

Bill Frisell is an old friend. We've made a couple of records together on the ECM label back in the '80s. He's one of the great guitar players of all time, and he works really well with people and always has something great to add.

We played together on "The House of the Rising Sun," one the first songs I ever learned on guitar. It also happens to be one of the first things that Frisell learned. We played it together at a gig in January, and I thought, "What would it sound like if we tried a jazz beat instead of the old 12/8 rock beat and extended the chorus to two measures apiece instead of one?" It ended up having this really cool form to improvise over, which I thought was more like Coltrane than the Animals. Then I played it for Bill, and I could really hear his low tremolo guitar playing that on his Fender amp.

Finally, what was it like mixing?

James came up with rough mixes as we were recording so we could leave the session with a CD of the takes that we had done. We mixed the entire record in two marathon 17-hour days. We were able to achieve this because the sounds don't really change on the instruments that much. James tweaked the sound on each tune a little bit here and there and mixed each tune in about two hours. It was key that we mixed in the same room that we recorded it—it came right back through the same board and went right to the master. If we had gone to another studio, it would have been harder.

Is that the natural room sound I am hearing on the record?

The room sounds great, but we are also using the big EMT plate that they have at Avatar. We might have used a little bit of Lexicon on some of that stuff. There is certainly some artificial reverb in there, though.

Did you learn anything making this record?

I learn every time. I'm not in the studio every day like some people, so every time I go in the studio it is a new thing. Pro Tools even now is a little bit of a new thing for me. We had a great assistant engineer who was the Pro Tools master, and when we were doing the overdub sessions with the horns, he was really great at going ,"I know exactly where the middle of the bass solo is where you want the horn," and we were right there. So I am always learning something.

19 Buzzcocks: A Different Kind of Session

Buzzcocks launched their career back in 1977 with a self-distributed, DIY EP entitled *Spiral Scratch*. Since then, after signing their first record contract on the day that Elvis died, they've blazed a relentless trail of eight highly melodic and energetic albums that have stood the test of time. Their trademark sound earned them the respect of bands both here and abroad, and it isn't a bit of a stretch to say they created the archetype for groups such as The Libertines, The Arctic Monkeys, and Green Day.

Two original members are now with the group: guitarist/vocalist Pete Shelley and guitarist Steve Diggle. Pete and Steve form the basis of Buzzcocks' trademark guitar sound, still instantly recognizable and original. I caught up with primary songsmith Pete Shelley to discuss their latest critically acclaimed effort, *Flat Pack Philosophy,* as their tour bus made its way to Albuquerque.

Buzzcocks' *Flat-Pack Philosophy,* released March 2006.

Are you enjoying the tour so far?

Yeah, I get a little bit bored looking out the window, though.

The response to your new album has been fantastic. Clearly your fans still appreciate what you are doing. How does that make you feel?

I think it's good. It's nice to look back on what we accomplished and show that we're still around and still capable of doing great stuff.

You guys have been going strong since 1976. What do you think the longevity of the band is attributable to?

I think it is the songs that keep us going. The songs have always been our greatest strength. At the moment we are touring and playing half our new album. The new songs are equally as good, but they've sadly been neglected as the tour progresses.

There are some amazing songs on the new album—including "Reconciliation," "Credit," and others. How is your approach in recording these new songs different from how you approached some of your classic early recordings?

I think we are now getting used to working with Pro Tools more, so that did help. On the last album we did—the untitled one—we recorded and mixed it in the same studio. This album we recorded in Southern Studios, and we mixed it in the same studio we mixed *Modern* in, three albums ago.

Was there anything special about recording at Southern Studios?

It's handy for everyone to get to and is actually very close to our homes. It's got the basic required equipment and a good engineer—that's all we need, really.

I would imagine that capturing a live feel is very important for you guys. In this day and age of DAWs, what is the danger in a band like yours going overboard with overdubs and frills?

It's interesting you should say that keeping the live feel is important, because none of it was done live [laughs]. Pro Tools is great for working through arrangements, obviously, because at the time you lay down the track, you may realize that you've got too many verses. If that's the case, you can easily reverse that, make all the verses disappear, and alter the sequence. This ultimately can result in a better idea.

Going back to albums such as *Love Bites* and *Another Music in a Different Kitchen*, were those albums done more live and immediate?

Yes, yes. We used to go in and do two or three backing tracks a day and then spend a few days doing the overdubs and vocals and mixing—that was it. This album took a lot

Photo by 2012.org.uk.

Buzzcocks' current lineup: Tony Barber, Pete Shelley, Danny Farrant, and Steve Diggle.

longer than the previous one we did. Part of the reason for that was by the time we finished the initial recording session, I hadn't come up with any lyrics for the vast majority of the songs. I had little bits here and there, but not enough to do a whole vocal track on. I thought "Well, we'll leave it a while," because it was still only a year since our last album had been released. So I got the vocals sorted out, and it ended up we didn't get back together until about a year later to continue working on the album.

Give me an idea of the duration it would take to record an album like _Love Bites_, one of your best efforts ever.

On the whole, it would take two or three weeks, including the mixing.

You guys have had some pretty heavy hitters produce your work in the past—people like Martin Hannett and Martin Rushent. What was it like to have one of your own, bass player Tony Barber, produce this one?

Tony produced the last three Buzzcocks albums. It's good because he understands the history of the band. Also, he's sensitive to the things that we are and are not. He didn't try to make us sound like the band that we aren't, which perhaps sometimes many producers are guilty of! [laughs]

Photo by Phil Guild.

The Buzzcocks performing live in 2007.

You and Steve have a very signature guitar sound. Can you tell us what your typical setup and signal chain are like?

I don't know; we just kind of choose whatever is at hand in the studio. On the road I usually play a Gibson, but I was given an Eastwood guitar by a man in Canada, and they are like an old classic guitar design but made by different materials, so I use one of those. On the album, Tony is always trying odd combinations—he's got a lot of old classic amps.

On your earlier albums you would have Steve or yourself in one channel, and the other in the other channel.

Yeah, that's the way the band is settled—so you get a sense of what it is like live. I often argue with drummers over whether the drums should appear in stereo as the drummer hears them or as the audience hears them.

Your voice is still amazing—do you have any difficulty laying down vocals these days?

We use any tricks that are available to us, especially double-tracking. I enjoy double-tracking myself. Also, to me, the harmonies come naturally. Musically, I have no idea what that is doing—it just feels right to me to sing it that way.

How does the writing process occur? Do the songs change fundamentally once you bring the songs to the band?

When the songs start, they are just sketches. In fact, a lot of the time the rest of the band doesn't know what the melody of the song is until I've finished singing the vocal!

Are you ever nervous about how your newer songs will stand up to your older ones—classics like "Ever Fallen In Love (with Someone You Shouldn't've)?" or "ESP?" You have a pretty strong back catalog to live up to.

There are times when it's only natural to be nervous about those things, but then a few days later the mood will change and I'll realize, "You can do whatever you want." Those songs that you mentioned as classics, at one point they were just ordinary songs—but they've since acquired their reputation.

You guys have been doing this for so long—and quite frankly, when you started out there were only a handful of bands doing very melodic, intelligent punk rock. Is this still an exciting genre for you to be in, and what do you think of the current scene?

In June we just played 30 dates on the Walt tour and there were loads and loads of bands doing covers of "Ever Fallen in Love," so on the last day, as we were doing "Ever Fallen in Love," all the rest of the bands got onstage with us to play it. I can't count how many people were up there.

How did you feel about John Peel?

He was just someone who was just passionate about music—he wasn't a celebrity DJ. The music was more important than him as a person. Also, he was a very engaging and amiable chap to be around. The public liked him because he knew his music and was passionate about it. That is very rare nowadays in a DJ. It was really fun doing the session with him because it was free studio time. So we used to try out new songs. Things like "Late for the Train" started out as a demo on a John Peel session.

You guys were one of the first bands to really defy the rules and go independent with your *Spiral Scratch* EP. Was that a difficult row for you to hoe back then, and do you think it's easier for bands now?

In Manchester, where we lived, there were no record companies. You had to travel down to London to even find a record company. We thought, "Why would they want to do our music?" because there was all this swearing, and the other music was a lot more commercial than what we were doing. But it ended up that people *did* like it, and so we started the ball rolling and managed to get something out there. And John Peel was good because he used to play the track so people could actually hear what it was like, then go try to find a copy.

It is a bit the same with the Internet. It's never been difficult to get the records into the store—the difficulty is actually getting people to know the record is in the store. With the Internet, it's easier to get your stuff to market, but you still have the same old problem: How do you get people to know about what you are doing? So I think there needs to be a lot more Internet marketing.

When Buzzcocks came out on the scene in 1976, most of the other punk bands were focused on lyrics that dealt with politics and other things. Your lyrics have always been about relationships and highly personal from the outset. What are your thoughts on this?

Part of the idea of punk was to make songs relevant to everyday life. So our songs weren't from some mythical stead or some mythical place. They were about everyday life, and it was about making everyday life into the art. I was just standing on the shoulders of giants, on people like Jonathan Richman. In the early days, I used to like Alice Cooper before he became famous, Sparks, and the Velvet Underground.

What about now? What influences do you have?

I don't know. It's harder to tell now. I am a bit more cynical and skeptical rather than so accepting and adoring, to be truthful.

Are you having fun on the road?

It's very tiring. It looks okay on paper. Fifty-one is old—yesterday we were playing in Denver, and I was having trouble keeping up with the breathing. It's a mile high, and you don't realize how it affects you until the middle of the set.

What was it like mixing *Flat Pack Philosophy*? Was it easy?

As for the mixing, I left this to Tony and came in only occasionally to make suggestions. We started mixing at Southern [U.K.], then ended up at Woodbine, which was better to get the sound that Tony was after. It was a lot more focused and more precise.

Do you have a stash of songs that haven't been released?

I've got stuff in various stages of development. Like a musical shed full of half-built songs— so if I ever need a song, it looks like I'm prolific because I can always find the bits and construct something. When I'm writing, I avoid recording a song entirely. I allow myself the luxury of forgetting. If I don't remember it, then it probably isn't worth remembering any- way. All of my songs have actually passed that one test with me. They are memorable, and therefore when other people hear them, they will remember them as well.

Sometimes you can get too precious and think that every note you write is fantastic. I get rid of lots of things, and it's just fun messing about with ideas sometimes. It's fun cap- turing everything and not being so pretentious.

Do you manage to get a lot of personal time for yourself anymore?

We will be full-on to the end of the year, then it will ease off again and we'll have a normal life.

20 Barenaked Ladies: Fresh Baked and Bare

Barenaked Ladies' release, *Barenaked Ladies Are Me,* is packed with the same brand of melody, wit, and clever instrumentation you have come to expect from the group, which has recorded and toured relentlessly for 18 years now. The new album has a few distinct twists in its approach, however—first, it was recorded entirely at Steven Page's [lead singer, principal songwriter] newly completed home studio, Fresh Baked Woods, in northern Ontario, and second, the group is releasing it independently through some fairly innovative distribution channels.

Steven Page coaxed Susan Rogers (Prince; Crosby, Stills and Nash) out of retirement from the recording business to lend a hand at producing, while bringing Bob Clearmountain on board to handle mixing duties. The result is a very organic and familiar-sounding record that significantly enhances an already prolific catalog of music.

Photo courtesy Chris Woods.

Barenaked Ladies (left to right): vocalist/guitarist Ed Robertson, bassist Jim Creegan, keyboardist Kevin Hearn, drummer Tyler Stewart, vocalist/guitarist Steven Page.

Steven, why should fans be excited about this record? What strikes you as particularly different?

The name of the new CD is *Barenaked Ladies Are Me*, and it's really for us about engaging with our fans on a deeper level. Kind of like the KISS Army. There are a few new things we are doing, and some of them are a little gimmicky. We're asking them to remix the songs—for about three bucks, they can go to our website and download 16-track masters in AIFF format and do with as they please, or they can access four stereo MP3 stems on our MySpace page for free. The songs can be mixed in ACID, GarageBand, Pro Tools, or whatever else. Then the hope is that we will take the best one of each song and make an EP that we will put out there for a charity CD.

How long has it been since your last record?

It has been three years since the last proper studio record. We did a holiday record in between—the last studio record, *Everything to Everyone*, came out in '03, which was our last record for Warner Brothers/Reprise. Then we decided to start our own label. Rather than resigning, we realized that at this point in the history of the music business, it is probably a good idea not to enter into a long-term relationship with a major label again.

It seems like the timing was perfect for you on that, especially since you are giving your fans a little more flexibility on mixing songs and material selection.

Oh, it's great. Especially in this time period—this holiday record, more than anything else, was a great way to test-drive how our system was going to work. I built my own studio—I have a farm just northeast of Toronto, and we built a studio there and we did the whole record there. It worked out so great for that that we ended up doing the entire new record at my place as well.

Do you have a name for the studio?

It is called Fresh Baked Woods—it is a reconstructed barn. It was originally supposed to be in the barn, but it had a mill roof and so on. We realized it would have been more costly to soundproof that than really do what was essentially a new building.

So it is properly isolated? Tell me about the design and construction.

Absolutely—I had it professionally designed.

How long before the band felt really comfortable in your new recording environment?

Almost right away. I was nervous about them coming to my place. We had worked in some fairly top-notch studios around the world over time, and I was afraid that my place might seem too rinky-dink. But it was funny—what we found was an answer to something that had been bothering us for years. We all have families—why do we all have to pick up, leave our families, and live in some crappy apartment with rental cars in Los Angeles or Nashville to make a decent record?

It's so much more about the performance, isn't it? How was the tracking process for this record? Were you going after a good live track first?

We did go for a good live track, first and foremost. I have one large isolated, well-designed recording room. I had the drums set up in there, and then our bass player, Jim, would stand out in the hallway—he's the only guy who got shortchanged because sometimes he was out there freezing his ass off. In the old days, it used to be a lot about "Let's go somewhere with great vibe," or "We've got to have lots of eye contact," or all these other things. We've played together 200 nights a year. We are at a point in our career where we know each other so well, and we can communicate well both musically and through talkback without sitting on each other all the time. I think a lot of that desire for eye contact comes from insecurity. We are finally at a place as a band where we've been together for 18 years, so we don't feel that way anymore.

Did you engineer this record?

I didn't. We had Susan Rogers. She did *Stunt* for us back in 1998, which was our biggest album. She is a former Prince engineer, and after she produced *Stunt*, she made enough money on that that she actually retired from the music business and went to school for animal psychology. She had moved up to Montreal to do her doctorate, and we said, "Do you feel like coming out of retirement to help us do our bed tracks?" She would commute from Montreal for, like, four days a week, and we would do all the bed tracks with her.

Assisting her with that part was a guy named Paul Forgues. We found him working at the Warehouse in Vancouver for a long time—he works with Garth Richardson, and he has been a godsend for us. We brought him out on the road, and he was recording all our shows. We've been selling all of our live shows as downloads—we bring a Pro Tools rig out, and we get to have a whole separate splitter and a whole separate mix. He knows us and the gear inside out. So he was assisting during the beds, then he did all the overdubs.

It must have been good for you, putting these technical jobs off on other people so you could focus on performing, right?

Exactly. I love the process of recording, and I love collecting gear. I like the process of engineering, but if I was behind the controls, I would be so stressed out and not focused enough on the music. I think we made the right choice. We can talk about what our decisions are going to be and what we want things to sound like, but Susan and Paul do a spectacular job.

Did you record to 2-inch tape or did you record right to Pro Tools?

We did both. We did all the basic tracks to 2-inch. I've got a Studer A820—that's one of the great things now. It's unfortunate for the studios, but as they go out of business, they offload this stuff. It has happened a few times in Toronto when I've been fortunate enough to be able to get some equipment out of it. We use the studio just for our own stuff—if we go on the road for a few weeks and come back, it is still set up. We don't have to worry about lockouts and all that stuff, and also I don't want a lot of people there—there is a lot of wear and tear, and as everybody knows, you can't really make a living running a studio.

What console do you have, and how did you choose it?

I had a Neve 8014 four-bus console loaded up with 1073s. I initially wanted to have that as my console, but I realized it was not going to work as far as how the bussing works. For an 8- or 16-track, it might have worked, but we record in 24. We ended up pulling all the 1073s and the compressors, the 2254s, and racked them up. Now we use a Control 24 as a monitoring surface. So we use that, but I have a few other things. I have some Telefunken stuff and some other outboard that we use.

Did you mix it at your place too? The mix sounds really open.

That's the one thing we didn't do. Bob Clearmountain mixed it. He came up to Toronto to do it—he rarely leaves his place. But we were pretty intent on recording this record as close to home as possible. So we mixed it at Metalworks Studio in Mississauga. My studio is just not equipped to mix outside of the box.

What did Bob do to the mix, and did his work make a big difference in the record?

It always makes a big difference. A great mixer just makes the record come to life, just like a good mastering engineer. We've had great luck the last few years with Bob Ludwig. These guys are like two sides of the same coin. They are quick, but they really, really listen to music, and they are very musical. Clearmountain makes it sound like a record almost right away. It's not like he sits there and works on the kick drum for a half hour. He just puts it all up and starts figuring out where the song is. He's also very experimental—he'll say, "Do you mind if I try this distorted drum kit on the beginning?" He will try what I would call more arrangement ideas.

Did you let Bob do his thing, or was there a nice interactive flow?

It was very interactive. He likes to have some time by himself to get the mix down the way he wants it to, rather than having us breathing down his neck. But we would come in a few times a day—we were actually in there still recording and finishing up overdubs in the next room. He is great and so not a prima donna. He knows that he is good at his craft, and he knows how all the stuff works. He knows it is our record—we are the artist and the producer, and he knows his role. He understands our point of view, and there were never any conflicts that way. I would work with him anytime, and we've been very fortunate to work with some great mixers.

Let's talk about some of the guitar work. You've got banjo and a lot of other nice sounds—can you share how you are recording acoustic instruments?

I have a couple of KM86s that I stumbled across. I did an acoustic session—I think it is called "Acoustic Café"—an NPR show. I was out there promoting my solo record, which was called *The Vanity Project*. They had the KM86 in the figure of eight so it would reject the vocal if I was singing and playing guitar. I thought the guitar sounded so great—so when a local studio went out of business, I grabbed couple of them on auction and have had great luck with those. They sure sound nice in the figure of eight on acoustic.

Tell me about the really great layered background vocals going on. Is this just you layering yourself or is it other members of the band?

We would all sing. A song like "Sound of Your Voice," which has the big Queen-style backing vocal, we would just all stand around the mic and sing and come up with what range we wanted to be in. Then we would go upstairs, sit around a piano, and write out our parts. It was fairly complex, but we needed to know that we weren't stepping on each other. Then we did something we'd heard Queen had done. We had four guys standing around one mic and singing the same part. Then we would layer that, then have two tracks of four guys singing the same part. Then there were just a couple tracks of individual guys, just to bring out the clarity. Then we would do it all again. On one track, we had something like 18 tracks of backup vocals.

We tried to sing backup harmonies the other way around, but realized that sometimes the tuning issues became hard to isolate. If you listen back, you go, "One of those is out of tune," and it's four guys singing four different parts around one microphone—so you have to redo the whole take. If there are four guys singing one part, you can decide more easily what isn't sounding right.

How long did the whole record take from beginning to end, including mixing?

Well, we started the writing process in the spring of '05. We started recording from October to December, then we hit the road because we had this Christmas album we were promoting. Then we came back in January and recorded until May. All in all we did 29 songs—there are 13 songs on the record. The great thing about Bob Clearmountain was that he mixed 29 songs in 15 days. It was insane—the nice thing is that despite this, the record sounds nice and varied. It isn't homogenous from track to track.

I heard you are going to be releasing these other songs that weren't included on the record. Is that right?

There are a few different ways. On iTunes and through our website, you'll be able to download a deluxe version that has all 29 songs. We're also planning a physical release of the "other half" early next year, and the songs will also be available on a USB stick. So it's been really fun trying a bunch of different stuff.

What is your typical pre-production process? These songs are really catchy, and I'd be interested in the process that you go through.

Ed Robertson and I are the principal writers, but Kevin Hearn, our keyboard player, has been in our writing quite a bit—he wrote or co-wrote a bunch of the songs on the record, and Jim, our bass player, wrote another song that is on the record. To record my demos, I will mostly use GarageBand—especially if I'm on the road. The mic on my Mac is fine, but if I need something more involved, I'll use an Mbox to do slightly more elaborate demos. If I'm out walking somewhere, I will call my voicemail.

When Ed and I were writing a lot of these songs, we'd do some fairly elaborate demos. We used to do very elaborate demos, but we've stopped doing that because it kind of stops some of the spontaneity when you're actually doing the recording. Also, because there are just two of us doing the demo, it stifles the other guys. The drummer already has an idea for a drum beat because I programmed one or played one—same thing with the bass. I want to give them the opportunity to really contribute to the song. So what we'll do now is just an acoustic guitar, a lead vocal, and some backing vocals, and for something like that, an Mbox will do just fine.

21 Josh Rouse: Nashville Vibes from the South of Spain

Josh Rouse released his new album, *Subtitulo,* on March 21, 2006. A young Nashville veteran with five albums under his belt, Rouse chose to record the acoustic/Brazilian-tinged album near Africa in the south of Spain, a country to which he had relocated just months before. Working with producer Brad Jones, Rouse shifted gears musically and geographically, creating an album that can be described as both romantic and intimate.

While the singer/songwriter didn't leave his Nashville roots far behind, Spain represents a new chapter in Rouse's musical career. The move also coincides with the launch of his new label, Bedroom Classics, the vehicle by which he hopes to reach a continually expanding fan base around the world.

Why did you move from Nashville to Spain?

Well, I have a girlfriend who lives here, so I moved here about a year and a half ago. That was about it. It's pretty laidback here. When I first got here, I got pretty inspired just by the climate—we lived right by the beach in this small town. I was going into town a lot, and I bought a nylon-string guitar and began writing a lot on that, just guitar and vocal. So that's where a lot of the songs came from. I think I was going for a soft kind of feel, while listening to a lot of Brazilian music like João Gilberto. I wanted to make a breezy, summer feel-good record—you know, lots of major seventh chords.

What was the transition like for you? You are moving from Nashville, which is a huge industry center, to a more modest geography.

It was good because I've recorded all my records in Nashville, where there are always plenty of people around to play. But on this record, I wanted it to be acoustic and wanted to play all the guitars. I wanted it to sound more intimate—not so "stacked," although we did have some strings on some songs. I wanted to keep it very simple.

Photo by Paz Suay.

It was very nice. We recorded this in the south of Spain in a little studio called Paco Loco Studios. It was just me, my drummer, and the producer, Brad Jones, who plays bass, the Rhodes, and piano. I wanted to keep it as a small group of people. In Nashville, if you ask people to come over and play…well, this was a little more homemade.

Can you tell me about the recording process? The recording sounds very intimate and close.

I recorded a demo with just an acoustic guitar and a vocal, which I sent to Brad. He had some ideas, then he flew over to Spain, and he, the drummer, and I sat around in a little semicircle and worked over the arrangements. When we had it all together, we'd record it—we recorded all the songs in exactly 10 days. We didn't practice them a lot or anything—as soon as we had an arrangement worked out, we would record a couple times and listen. Maybe we would change things rhythmically as far as the bass and drums, but many of the tracks are just me and my acoustic guitar, which was easy. It's really done kind of semi-live, like a lot of people do it.

I'm impressed by how quickly you put it together—I read that you wrote all the songs in a week and recorded them in another 10 days. That's fast.

Well, I had a lot of the ideas, but I hadn't completed all the songs yet.

Can you describe Paco Loco? What kind of environment was it like to record in?

Paco Loco is in El Puerto de Santa Maria and is way down south by Africa, actually. The facility is somewhat isolated; it's a little compound out there. There is a nice house where the musicians can stay, then there's the studio, which has a nice Calrec board. In fact, the whole sound of the record is pretty much a U 67 and the preamps in the Calrec. I used a 67 for all the vocals.

The studio itself was really basic. We recorded all in Pro Tools—nothing was analog, which was a change for me. The live room was pretty sizable; we had our drums set up in there, and there was plenty of room where Brad played bass. I'd sit next to him with a nylon- or steel-string acoustic, and we'd record the song all like that in the room together.

So you didn't record the drums to a click track and then do all the overdubs later?

No. And there wasn't really any isolation. As far as recreation time, there was a pool there, which was nice. We'd start every day at about 12, work for two or three hours, and then take a long lunch and go swimming in the pool for a couple hours. Then we'd come back and work 'til midnight, taking a dinner break at about 10 p.m.

Photo by Paz Suay.

It sounds like having a relaxed environment was good for you.

It's the best experience I've had recording. It's a great way to do it, especially for this kind of record, which is pretty laidback. It really was the perfect environment for it.

Also, you presumably didn't have A&R reps and deadlines breathing down your back, right?

No, I've started my own label anyway, and I was just trying to make a good record. I didn't care about what anyone else thought about it, really—there was no deadline or funny politics. I've already put out five records on another label. While my experience wasn't bad, I don't *own* any of those records. I worked hard promoting, touring, doing all the work, and my previous label continues to see most of the royalties from those records, which continue to sell. This time, though, since my contract was up, I was in a good enough position to try it myself. I had a big enough fan base and thought I could do it as well as my other label, and maybe see more money from the records.

There is just no reason artists shouldn't make money from their records, especially with the Internet and downloading—there is no middleman, and the money can go right to you. For me, as long as I can make my money back and enough to make another record, it's great. And then you make money down the road, years from now. You see that money. On my other records, I don't really see the money. Even though you like the records, you're like, "That happened, but...."

Have you been influenced one way or another by the local music in Spain?

I don't know. The lifestyle is a little different here—I didn't really get into too much Spanish music, and I still haven't. I know a couple of people who play in bands, but they sound like American indie rock bands [laughs]. I was listening to a lot of Brazilian music—that was the biggest stuff. Just rhythmically, the chords and the way the music feels. It just has a great sunshine vibe to it, and it makes you feel really good.

I still hear a tinge of Nashville, though, with things like the pedal steel.

Exactly. We wanted to mess with the geography a little bit, try something different. We would throw a pedal steel on something that was almost bossa nova.

What did Brad Jones bring to the record, and what was it like to work with him?

This is the third record I've done with Brad—he's a Nashville guy who has worked with lots of singer/songwriters. He has an eclectic taste and good pop sensibilities and he plays instruments really well. We work really fast together—he engineers and produces at the same time and does all the string arrangements on the spot. He doesn't write anything down—it's all done off the top of his head, so there's not a lot of sitting around in the studio waiting.

He's really helped my songwriting, arranging, and everything. He's just super musical and has a great feel. The Rhodes part on "His Majesty Rides" is a perfect example: It's funky as hell, and he did it in just one or two takes. I was like, "Wow"—it added another dimension to that tune.

Tell me a little about how the drums were recorded and what Mark [Pisapia]'s role was.

We miked up the kit in a pretty standard way with a SM57 on the snare and all, and then had two overheads about eight or nine feet above the drummer, kind of slanted, in addition to having a distance mic in the room. To achieve a good snare sound, Brad likes to go back and mix in another sound. For example, we might take a Stevie Wonder or an Al Green snare hit, real deep and dry, and combine it with the live hit. We did this on a couple tunes, all in Pro Tools, which can produce a great result.

One of the funniest things was that the only bass we had was this old Yamaha bass from the '80s—the strings were like an inch off the neck! So Brad played all those bass lines through this Fender Bassman, which had a blown speaker, ultimately giving it a sort of growl. We were like, "Okay, let's go with it." We were digging it!

I guess that proves that it's not the gear but the player!

Exactly.

The whole album has a minimalist feel. Were there a lot of overdubs?

It's pretty sparse. There are a few overdubs here and there—the biggest ones are the strings and the pedal steel. We kind of played as a three-piece band.

How is the reception so far?

Really good. My last two records were pretty popular, and this one is a little more subtle and laidback—this is what I was going for. It didn't have the same reception at radio, but I really wasn't making it for that purpose and really didn't have that in mind. The fans really love it, so I'm happy, and the response has been really good all over the world. A lot of hotel rooms and just running from city to city.

How involved are you on the business side, now that you have your own label?

My manager helps out a lot with the business side—he knows why I am on the road a lot. It takes enough energy to concentrate on the concerts and keep a healthy state of mind. It's all pretty smooth and takes care of itself. It's not too complicated.

What did you do different on this record technically?

We just worked really fast, and we don't slot two weeks for mixing or anything like that. In fact, we usually mix as soon as we finish a take. Like you say, it's such a minimalist record that we didn't have to work too hard to get the mixes where they needed to be. As a result, by the mastering process, the tracks were almost ready. Sonically,

I knew I didn't want any smoothing EQs, squashing dynamics, or anything like that. We tried to keep it as rough as possible.

How do you mic up the acoustic guitars? Is it any different recording nylon strings?

For acoustic guitar, we did a couple of different things. We tried moving the mic way back toward the butt of the guitar, just pointing it at the end. Other times, we miked it at the 14th fret, a couple inches off the neck. We'd also move it back, almost *behind* the guitar. All the time, we used an Oktava MC012—very inexpensive, but amazing-sounding. We didn't use any compression while recording the guitars. The guitar I play, which is a small-bodied Martin, has a pickup in it, so we'd mike up the guitar and also run it through the amp—it was probably a Fender Twin.

22 John Densmore: Breakin' on through to New Rhythms

John Densmore has always considered himself a jazz drummer, both before and following his successful career as drummer with The Doors. Now, he has finally surrounded himself with like-minded, seasoned jazz musicians who share his passion for exploring new musical directions—and who are helping him push his own boundaries as a performer.

The last time Densmore sat in the producer's chair was when The Doors co-produced their blues-oriented masterpiece *L.A. Woman* in 1971 with longtime engineer Bruce Botnick. On the new self-titled Tribaljazz album, Densmore had the opportunity to work alongside Botnick once again, along with some newer friends from the jazz world.

Photo courtesy Cory Lashever.

John Densmore today, playing with Tribaljazz.

John, how did you get involved with Tribaljazz? What was the spark?

I was doing a benefit for the arts and music program at my son's grammar school. Art Ellis, the alto soprano/sax/flute player was there, and that was the beginning of Tribaljazz. Art and I spoke, and we had the same vision—he had all these melodies, and drummers need melodies. So we played together, just the two of us. We then arranged all the songs and began getting musicians. I'm big on arranging—in The Doors, I had a big mouth about that.

Tell me a little about how the sessions went down and how you ultimately decided where you would record the project.

A lot of the sessions were done live, and most of it came pretty easily. Art knew of a studio called Stagg Street in the San Fernando Valley, which was big enough so that we could have sightlines for all these musicians—we've got a six- or seven-piece band. Franz Pusch, a jazz engineer, did several of the tracks, and they went really fast. On "Blues for Bali," the second cut, he used a binaural mic shaped like a head. It was placed just over the kit, where you would put overheads, with the head looking toward me. It emanated a really broad, ethereal kind of sound on my ride cymbal. Some other cuts were more manufactured, like "The First Time (I Heard Coltrane)." That whole track was built up—in fact, I even overdubbed the cymbals.

I understand you worked with an old friend on this one.

Yes. Bruce Botnick mixed several cuts—it was great to work with him again. We did all the mixing at Capitol Studio A, and we used their original reverb tank. Having Bruce and his ears, I didn't even have to be at the mix, but I want to be at everything.

How do you reconcile being both an artist and a producer? Is that difficult, and did you really want to play both roles on the *Tribaljazz* album?

In The Doors, we produced *L.A. Woman* with Bruce, our longtime engineer. By the third album, we knew how to make records. I certainly wanted to have a heavy hand on the production [of *Tribaljazz*]. A lot of laypeople think producer means money—they don't understand that it is exactly the same as a director of a film. It can mean some money, but it essentially means nurturing the performance out of the performers—either by creating an atmosphere or by sometimes telling them what to do.

As a drummer with a sensitive touch, how do you feel about all the devices that seem to have taken over music production, including drum machines and sequencers?

Drum machines have taken over the hip-hop world, and I fully understand that. Being a drummer, I listen to all these drum machines—actually, a lot of people now prefer metronomic drumming. If it's not metronomic, like a machine, they don't like it. That's a little disturbing to the human condition, because we aren't machines, are we? Thank God I played in the '60s. A long time ago, the original drum machines had a button you could push that literally sped up and slowed down the beats to make them sound less machine-like. Now, that machine feel is preferable to a lot of folks.

Tribaljazz live.

Tell me about The Doors' 5.1 remixes that have just seen the light of day. You have to be nervous remixing these songs, which are indelibly stamped in everyone's mind. How did that process go and how involved were you?

Bruce handled all the mixing on these himself, and I would go to his studio and offer my comments. He's a genius—he's smart enough to know that you don't just stick the audience on the back speakers and the whole band on the front. That would be a first impulse for a novice. He recorded all these records, so he knew every rattle, shaker, and rhythm guitar and was very artful in spreading them around. The mixes really put you in the middle of the band, and you can distinguish the sounds better when they're spread out like that.

Strange Days lends itself quite well to 5.1. It was our second album, and we were relaxed in the studio, having fun with backward piano tracks and fooling around with phasing when it was first invented. It was a bit more electronic, so he had fun spreading that one around in the mix.

What was it like to work with Paul Rothchild and The Doors, and how were production decisions handled in the band?

The stress that came in the studio came from Jim [Morrison]—the last few years he was bent on self-destruction. Rothchild taught us how to make records and he was a great guy—except by the middle, he was such a perfectionist that he would get dictatorial. By the third album, for example, he made us do 100 takes of "The Unknown Soldier." There were two sections, so let's say 50, but it was ridiculous. It got to the point where I *knew* that there were earlier takes that were better, because they had more life in them. We weren't exhausted by trying to fulfill his perfection.

It was a pleasure to produce the last Doors album by ourselves because we knew how to do it by that point. Botnick produced it with us and said, "Listen, you guys know what you're doing." We only did a couple takes of everything on *L.A. Woman,* and there are mistakes—but we didn't care about the mistakes. Miles Davis had a big mistake on *At Carnegie Hall*, and he said, "I don't care, the feel is so good." We had immensely good times in the studio—it was techno heaven.

Was there any Doors session you'd characterize as particularly special?

When we recorded "The End" on the first album, Paul ritualized it and lit some candles and incense. The mood is definitely captured on tape. The fourth album [*The Soft Parade*] was fun because we had strings and horns—even though we got a lot of flack for that. We wanted to try our *Sgt. Pepper's Lonely Hearts Club Band*, and we always talked about having some jazz solos, so Curtis Amy was at the end of "Touch Me." It was fun, and that's why we got back to the garage in *L.A. Woman*, back to basics, where we started. *Morrison Hotel* and *L.A. Woman* are just back to the Blues quartet. We had to go through *The Soft Parade*—we wanted to change our sound and just experiment. The last one, *L.A. Woman,* and the second one, *Strange Days*, are my favorites. On those albums, the studio was like the fifth Door. We were very relaxed while fooling around with all the technology.

How did songwriting go down in The Doors, and was it a generally pleasant process?

Jim didn't know how to play a chord on any instrument, but he had melodies as well as lyrics. He said, "How do you write songs?" So we all sat down together and we'd say, "It's an E flat," or "It's a waltz." We just really hacked it all out together. Then he said, "Let's just split everything." So even the songwriting credits were "Music by The Doors" for every album but one. It was a complete democracy, and that afforded everyone the

Interior shot of Sunset Sound during The Doors' recording session.

inspiration to put in 200 percent each. Everyone was equal, everyone was eager, and there were no egos because we were splitting everything we were doing—any idea was accepted.

Bruce Botnick, engineer for The Doors, mixing a session.

Jim Morrison himself is actually a performer on your new *Tribaljazz* album. Tell me how you came to take the whisper track from "Riders on the Storm" and breathe life into a new song.

The original whisper track for "Riders on the Storm" was Bruce's and my idea. Jim did a couple of vocal takes for the song, and we had it. So we then said, "Hey Jim, go back into the vocal booth, do it once more, and *whisper* the whole thing." We placed it so subliminally in the original tape—if you listen to it now, you'll probably hear it. For the people who don't know it's there, you point it out to them and they say, "Wow, there it is!" So I got this idea to put it under the flute on the *Tribaljazz* LP, and I called the record company and the estate, and they said, "Take it. Go!"

As a member of The Doors, is it difficult to maintain your own identity while being cast in such an iconic context?

This band is called Tribaljazz, not Tribal Doors, if you know what I mean. I'm playing with monster musicians who are forcing me to keep pushing and improving. It keeps me young, and I'm playing better than ever, getting off on taking new risks. These young bucks are making me really want to play.

23 Tony Bennett: Master of the Mood

Tony Bennett's contribution to recorded music during the last century is immeasurable. His rare ability to impart a distinctive and instantly recognizable mood to every song he sings has earned the greatest respect of his contemporaries. Not surprisingly, the success Mr. Bennett achieves in the studio has less to do with the equipment being used than with his enduring and seemingly effortless vocal performances.

On his latest album, *Duets: An American Classic*, which broke the *Billboard* Top 10 album chart just weeks after his 80th birthday, Bennett shares the mic with many of the world's most successful pop artists—indeed, every person on the record has made a permanent contribution to the genre. While each of the artists on the record has likely spent hundreds of hours at the world's top studios, each may have learned a thing or two from Mr. Bennett about technique. For starters, the vast majority of the record was recorded live.

How have things changed over the years in recording, and how has your formula stayed the same?

There have been major changes. When I first started about 50 years ago on Columbia, there was no splicing. You couldn't take the first performance, put it on take 15, and splice it together so it sounded like one record, for example. You had to memorize the song so you could sing it from the beginning to the end. To be honest with you, the public would get a real good shot of the artist because they received a full performance of the song. The take that you would hear is the one that went down on tape—just like a regular solo performance.

There is a wonderful authenticity about that, and you can really hear that it is about the performance as opposed to creating this multilayered production.

As a result, through the years, I stuck with that approach because it was just better. To make an analogy, I visited the Library of Congress in Washington, D.C. recently and found that the older items on the shelves were made of better materials. For example, the earliest books were written on cloth, and they were hand-printed—they were made to last forever, you see?

Photo by Reuben Cox.

Tony Bennett with Phil Ramone, Dae Bennett in the background.

Do you think the live approach that you have employed over the years presented a challenge to some of the other folks you sang with on the album?

They thought so when they first came in. The artists I was working with on this record weren't expecting to record live. When I said after only three takes or so, "That's great, that's just right," their eyes lit up and they said, "You're kidding!" I would say, "Why are you looking at me like that?" And they would reply, "Well, we usually take, like, 25 *weeks* to record," and they'd be adding a trumpet, a piano, or whatever else to make it just perfect. I said, "No, no. Singing jazz through the years with greats like Stan Getz, Bill Evans, or Count Basie, I've found that throughout my whole catalog, the more spontaneous it is, the better the record becomes."

I told them that a live performance on a record is more vibrant, more permanent, and that it never gets dated—it doesn't get filtered in any way. After all, when it starts sounding like it's *too* perfect, there is something wrong with it. There needs to be a little dirt in there somehow.

The duet that you did with Barbra Streisand, "Smile," sounds so natural, as if it fit like a glove. What was that take like?

It was wonderful. We did that song at her home out in Malibu on a beautiful day. We recorded it in one or two takes in her living room, which happens to have a spectacular view of the ocean. Barbra didn't really understand why I chose that particular song, so I explained that even though the song was written many, many years ago by Charlie

Pictured from left to right: Danny Bennett, Phil Ramone, Dae Bennett, and Tony Bennett.

Chaplin for the movie *City Lights,* one of the great movies that he made, it still has particular relevance today because of 9/11. Take the lyrics "When there are clouds in the sky, you'll get by if you smile through your fear and sorrow"—it's all about pulling through. I said, "Barbra, this is the kind of thing you believe in!" I got through to her, and she sung it beautifully—she smacked it right out of the ballpark.

You sang with so many wonderful artists on this album. Maybe you can share with us what it was like to sing with Paul McCartney over at Abbey Road.

It was beautiful. Paul and I get along great—he's such a natural. I've known him since the early '60s, when I gave the Beatles their first music award, before they were playing in stadiums and became such a phenomenon. In fact, my son, Danny, who manages me, has in his office a huge mural of me giving the Beatles their first award! Paul's got it— he's just a natural, and I love him. He's got a great sense of humor and a great heart. He really wanted to do "The Very Thought of You" by Ray Noble. Ray Noble is the Cole Porter of Britain—he wrote the best songs, and at the same level as Cole Porter did during the Great American Songbook era.

One of the nice things about this record is that you are dealing with so many different voice characteristics—how were you able to mix and match all this talent, and what struck you as interesting or desirable when you were choosing the talent?

It was this whole process. I was a little apprehensive when my son Danny came up with the whole idea—I said, "What are you doing?" But once we started getting these phenomenal, institutional artists—you know, people who are going to be around for the next 30, 40 years—I just got a big kick out of it. As soon as NBC heard we were doing it, they wanted to do a special TV show as well. It was the first time in the history of television that they did a musical that was made on film. It took a month in Los Angeles to do each section with each artist—people like John Legend, Diana Krall, Stevie Wonder, and Barbra Streisand.

What about your song choices? They are all from the Great American Songbook. What was behind the songs you chose?

I have been fortunate enough to have introduced about 35 songs into the American Songbook that are now standards. We gave each artist four songs of mine, so they could choose one that they really liked personally. The Dixie Chicks chose "Lullaby of Broadway." They had never done a swing song in their life. After they finished making the record, they said, "We love doing this! We should make an album!" I said, "Do it; it will be fun!"

What is it like working with Dae [Bennett, owner of Bennett Studios, and Tony's son] at his studio, Bennett Studios? Is there any "father and son" synergy going on there?

I never liked Allan Freed's theory: "This is your music, and your parents like the other kind." It broke up the family life in America, and I never liked it. I found out years ago from the managers of the Paramount Theater, which is now the Hard Rock Cafe, but in those days, that's where Sinatra, Dean Martin, Jerry Lewis all played. The management there said, "Look, you're doing seven shows a day, which is quite inhuman—just sing great songs and don't sing demographic songs and play to one audience. Just sing to everybody. By singing great songs, I got the young people in the audience in the morning, the senior citizens in the afternoon, and the married and engaged couples at night. So we sang to the whole family just by singing great songs. By doing great songs, the whole family likes it—it's actually a better business.

What makes Bennett Studios a special place?

I've met a lot of great jazz musicians there, and they love it there. They are comfortable there, and so am I. Ever since Dae was a little boy, when stereo was just beginning, he would just sit between the speakers and listen. Soon enough, he got great ears, and he knows just when it is right and when it is not right. He did all the sound engineering on the NBC special—that's high-definition sound.

This album we did in the studio, but every other record I've done with Dae, I've recorded in the theater. It's amazing there because we use the natural reverberation, and it is kind of old school, so it's perfect. Dae works with me 100 percent. I'm proud of both my sons—they both work great with me. Danny is brilliant as a businessman, and Daegal gets the best sound for me. Dae knows when something is right or when it's not right. He gets the best sound for me, and if something's not right, he speaks up. I'm also in on the mixing with him.

Photograph by Jeff Touzeau.

Dae Bennett pictured at Bennett Studios.

Do you have a favorite mic you like singing into?

I like the Neumann. I've always liked the Neumann. The whole idea is to get full fidelity, true to the natural sound. Everyone has different reasons why they use different mics, but for me it needs to sound as close to a live performance as possible. That microphone does it for me.

What was it like working with Phil Ramone, and how did you select him?

He did the first Sinatra duets album, and then we did an album, *Playin' with My Friends: Bennett Sings the Blues*, with Ray Charles, and after that we did a duet album of blues, a jazz album. This one is so different because of the great stars that are in it. All of them are going to be the institutional artists for the next 30 years—there's not one who's going to drop out or lose his or her popularity.

What was the dynamic between you and Phil Ramone, and what do you look to in a producer of that caliber?

Phil made everybody comfortable. At one time or another, he's done something with each one of them. When they knew Phil Ramone was doing it, it made everybody comfortable, so it was very natural.

When you are singing a duet, what kind of chemistry has to occur in the performance?

The main thing that we were looking for was contrast in voices. A good duet album has voices that are different from one another—the same principle applies to live performance. We arranged the songs to the appropriate keys and matched the harmonies so they sounded just right with each artist.

Tell me how Elton John did when he came in.

Elton John was so prepared that he did it in one take! He came in, sat down at the piano, played "Rags to Riches" once, and then said, "Let's do one." After we did it, I turned to him and said, "You can't get better than that!" James Taylor surprised me because he had an ear for improvising. He just did everything intuitively, and it was just right. Frankly, I was surprised at the performance of all of them, because unfortunately, when you get to be my age, a sort of attitude sets in among musicians—"It's not as good as it used to be," and that sort of thing. But actually, what I found out was that all of these people were professional. They were ready on time, they knew what they were doing, and loved doing it— Bono, Sting, each one of them was just terrific to work with.

You are known as someone who has a very professional attitude in the studio. Can you share a little bit about your personal ethic in the recording studio?

They didn't expect this, but I grew up in an era where there was no splicing about 50 years ago. You had to make a record right from beginning to end—that was then the record that you made. Singing with great jazz artists throughout the years, like Bill Evans, Stan Getz, and Count Basie, I learned that the more spontaneous it is and the closer to a live performance it is, is what makes the record good. It sounds alive.

If you do it in 15 takes, looking for perfection, you're not really going to get it because the musicians get tired after five or six takes. They don't want to have to play it again, again, and again, making it tedious. When you do it in four takes it's spontaneous. It may not be perfect and it might get a little grungy every once in a while, but it doesn't matter. I look at this album as the first vocal jam session—it was done spontaneously, and everyone involved did it in three or four takes. It makes it real and like a live performance.

Was this recorded live?

Yes. The band was with me, and everything was done at the same time. Some of the artists couldn't believe that we worked that way. They said, "Sometimes we take 17 weeks or 25 weeks 'til it comes out." Sting and Bono, they all said, "We should record this way." They considered it old. I told them, "This is the way you do it; this is the way it is supposed to be."

Are you pleased with the response to the record?

I can only go by the sales, and so far the reaction is unbelievable. The first day it was out, it sold 200,000 copies, and it is still way up on the charts. It is number one for this week.

24 Crowded House: Coming Out on Top from Down Under

After an 11-year hiatus and the untimely death of original drummer Paul Hester two years ago, Crowded House has returned with an album of 14 new tracks and a worldwide tour. The new album, *Time on Earth,* picks up seamlessly where the band left off from its last studio album, 1993's *Together Alone.* Neil Finn's songwriting continues to mature with gems like "Silent House" and the first single off the album, "Don't Stop Now," which also features a guitar performance from Johnny Marr of The Smiths fame.

The album, which originally began as a Neil Finn solo effort, took about eight months and was recorded at Finn's own studio in New Zealand, as well as at RAK and Real World Studios in the United Kingdom. Though *Time on Earth* was recorded at three studios with two producers and four drummers (including Ethan Johns himself), Crowded House's sound is instantly identifiable. *Pro Sound News* talked with founding member and bassist Nick Seymour about the album and the tour.

Your new album, *Time on Earth,* has come out after quite a long hiatus. When you were together originally, you had such a great run of recordings. Was it difficult to find your groove together this time around?

It evolved over a period of about eight months before we even realized that we were making a band album, and at that point we called [multi-instrumentalist] Mark Hart, then auditioned drummers and found Matt [Sherrod] to complete the record. So what began as Neil ringing me and saying, "Do you want to get together and record these new songs I have?" ended up as a Crowded House album.

I assumed that it was going to be another Neil Finn solo album originally—which I would have been quite delighted to do. I was happy to just be a musician and get paid to turn up at a studio. I hadn't had a bass gig since Crowded House, really. I've been producing records and soundtrack-type work at a studio I had in Dublin, Ireland.

Crowded House's *Time on Earth,* released 2007.

We worked together for about eight months in three different sessions: one with Joey Waronker playing drums and two with Ethan Johns producing and playing drums—and guitars and whatever else he could put his very talented hands on!

So Ethan actually recorded some of the songs on the new album in addition to playing drums?

Yeah. After a while, we realized we had made an album that sounded a lot like a band—Ethan wasn't about to throw away his A-list producer moniker and join the band as the drummer, so we thought, "If we're making a band album and it sounds a lot like Crowded House, perhaps we should just throw ourselves into the abyss and see what happens by ringing Mark Hart"—and auditioning a drummer so we could go into the studio and record a few more songs. We wanted to be able to take it to that next level and have a band identity.

How many tracks does Ethan play drums on?

Probably on about eight tracks on the album, Ethan Johns is registered as drummer. Then there is a track by Joey Waronker; a track by Ricky Dutch, a drummer we found in New Zealand; and about four tracks on the album were played by Matt Sherrod. We didn't re-record anything once we found Matt. We knew we had a couple of songs or maybe three songs that we had attempted prior to Matt joining the band—we re-attempted those songs and found they had a new energy, a new lease on life. This also made us realize we had another record in us, and we had to get back into the studio and do some more recording.

When you were in the studio, did it feel like a similar vibe to the last studio album you did years ago?

The last studio album we did in New Zealand, called *Together Alone,* captured a particular energy in the band when we recorded it. There was a lot of drama, a lot of neurosis; it was probably one of the easiest records for a producer to make because the band was absolutely on fire when we recorded that. We had such a momentum. Just recently, I was listening to all the demo tapes for that album and I realized that Youth just fell into it at that record. As a producer, I would give my right bollock to record with a band that were in that shape at that time. He went on to produce The Verve, who got really big in the States—it was a very controversial period for him.

The new album has a much different energy since we just had *carte blanche.* There were no expectations, and everyone was in pretty good shape with respect to how they felt about themselves and also their talents.

Did it feel good to interact with these guys after so many years?

Absolutely. It was like putting on an old coat and finding a tenner in the pocket.

How did you choose where to record this album?

Neil has set up a fairly traditionally architect design studio in a building that he found in Auckland, New Zealand. A lot of it was recorded there, but once we found Matt Sherrod and we realized that we were on fire as a combo, we had to find a studio available for us with Steve Lillywhite—we really wanted to work with Steve. That studio is in London and it is called RAK—it really hasn't changed since the early 1970s. It was just a delight to be in a place that had that much thrown together, "laid-backness" in its design. It's been used so much since those days that it's never really been renovated.

Which is kind of nice, because you are going back into a familiar environment.

Absolutely. It had all the old analog gear, including an API desk. However, we did actually do those last four songs straight to Pro Tools, whereas the first part of the album was recorded onto a 16-track 2-inch machine to get the big squelchy bass and drums sound, and then transferred to Pro Tools to do overdubs. A lot of the vocals were kept, though. A lot of the original tracking vocals that Neil did, he couldn't beat the performance when he went to do vocal overdubs. It's about a spell—you enchant with a certain character when you've been jamming all day. Often when you're doing vocal overdubs, it's hard to find that character again in a kind of clinical environment.

Photo by Kerry Brown.

Crowded House, left to right: Nick Seymour, Neil Finn, Mark Hart, Matt Sherrod.

Was there any trepidation or nervousness among you guys doing overdubs in Pro Tools, since you had become so used to analog tape over the years?

Not really. Pretty much all four of us now have a Pro Tools machine somewhere in the world, and it's a pretty bulletproof system. The only thing you question is sample rates and all that kind of thing, and I'm not about to get into that. We were listening to the way this sounds when monitoring, and they sounded just as squelchy and as good as what we're hearing in headphones, so you've just gotta trust us! [laughs]

These tracks really gel together, and you didn't overdo it with layering. Did it feel as natural as it sounds when you were laying down tracks?

Pretty much. We were doing it in the old-fashioned way of getting the best take we could—if someone made a mistake on the take, you would actually stop and do it again. We tracked it all live and ultimately chose the best take—a very traditional manner. We would end up getting about two songs to tape a day. Often it would just be one take, then we'd go listen to it after dinner, and by that time a lot of red wine would have been consumed and we would have been very happy.

What was special or striking about Ethan's recording approach?

He had what I thought was a very unusual technique of drum recording. I've never come across a four-mic setup on drums before, but apparently it's quite a traditional technique that is used by a lot of guys he knows out in L.A. recording a room sound. Ethan is a real drummer—he would tune his drums, place them in the best position in the room to get a great sound, then place the microphones accordingly. As long as the drummer was enjoying playing and enjoying the space itself, that would be relevant to the tone of the track that was coming out the other end.

Do you remember anything special about his mic setup?

The only mounted microphone was the kick drum mic. The other mics were floating, and they'd be moved accordingly. He always had a fairly robust old Neumann, maybe an U 87, sitting to the right of the floor tom about three feet in the air. Then he'd have a forward mic that was probably about six feet away from the drums that was getting even more of the ambience. A lot of the sound would be from the actual room itself.

We were recording these tracks in Neil's studio, upstairs in his temporary workroom that was an old ballroom in what was once a Masonic lodge. This building that Neil has found, he's built the studio on the second floor, but the third floor was a ballroom with a sprung dance floor. It had probably 15-foot-high ceilings, wooden floors, and fabric baffles to slightly deaden the room.

Was the mixing desk in there, too?

No. We would all track in that ballroom area and we had a desk in another room that we'd built, which had a big double-glazed glass frame so we could see each other.

When you did that, you probably didn't realize these tracks would end up on a Crowded House album.

Exactly. Having said that, the last studio album that we'd made as Crowded House, *Together Alone*, was recorded in a big, open-plan beach house—so we were used to the idea of making a room space work. It's a movable feast—if you go into a space and set up your instruments and you jam for a while, you start playing to the room sound. You might move your amps around, you might realize you don't need to be so loud, and often that is a great basis for recording if you have that luxury. We are blessed that we have these resources. No one seemed to talk about a budget—they just said, "Get going."

That's very interesting. So the room itself can influence how you play as individuals and actually change the dynamics of the band's performance.

Absolutely—it's the difference of a bass player playing with a pick or with his fingers.

What is your take now that the album is out and you're looking at it from the 10,000-foot view? How do you look at it now that you aren't in the middle of recording it? Are you pleased?

I am. I do realize that we have a natural order of recognizing when to stop—recognizing that we've achieved a spatial quality to the sound and haven't had to clog it up with a lot of musical parts. It still has a simplicity that works dynamically. Every song has a structure that will lift or drop according to a combination of the musical parts and the lyrics, including the character of the vocal. All of those things seem to be as good as they can be—I think by this stage in our lives we have pretty good standards in recognizing when something has defined its character.

When Neil brings in a song, how flexible are the arrangements? Do you guys work on the songs and change stuff around?

We do. It is a result of the way we connect as musicians. We seem to have a very intuitive chemistry with each other that is somewhat unpredictable, but at the same time, we know when we are hitting on something that has a mutual resonance.

Are you going to take this out on the road now? What are your plans over the next several months?

For the next six months, we're going to be touring various parts of the world—Australia, the U.S., and Europe. We're in the States in August and September for six weeks.

Do you have a preference on touring or recording with Crowded House? Did you miss it?

I missed touring with Crowded House terribly when we first called it a day. The first five years of not being in a band, I missed the whole touring regimen and the lifestyle of it. I love being able to get up onstage and play every night; it is a big adventure. The fact is, I'm really delighted to be touring again, but at the same time I'm so glad that we have a new album. There wouldn't have been much point for us to get back together to do some retrospective catalog tour just for people to reminisce. I'm really happy that there is actually an album that is taking us to the next level.

25 The Unique Electronic Textures of Ulrich Schnauss

Ulrich Schnauss is a synth-based composer from Germany who has become well regarded due to his combining of audio and visual performances. He is a synth composer in the classical sense inasmuch as he takes great pains to make sure his songs translate to a simple piano before he adds his low- and high-frequency oscillators, pads, and other treatments.

Schnauss' compositions are reminiscent of his distant European cousins Tangerine Dream, Klaus Schulze, and Jean Michel Jarre in that they are often in excess of 10 minutes and contain swirling rhythms, textures, and sonic variations. While Schnauss' audio requirements are very stringent, he recognizes that the song, arrangement, and performance must come first for the audio to matter at all. I spoke to Ulrich following a New York City gig at a place called Joe's Pub.

Where are you coming from artistically and musically? I hear a lot of Klaus Schulze or Tangerine Dream influence.

The first thing I got turned on to as a kid on the verge of turning into a teenager—and I think that is a very important phase for people to develop their musical taste—I was really into a lot of stuff that was happening at that time in England, both electronica and indie-rock wise. From then on, I discovered a lot of the things you mentioned through that in a way as well. There was also a band called LFO I liked on Warp Records—the album was called *Frequencies*. They were listing their all-time influences on the record sleeve. They had Yellow Magic Orchestra and Tangerine Dream—that's how I discovered those things, and they became a very strong influence as well. I think people discover older music through current things.

Has keyboard always been your main instrument?

I took piano lessons for about eight years, and throughout the entire '90s I was playing electronic music entirely. It's only up until quite recently that I've had the opportunity to play in a band as well.

What is the process you go through when you are creating a tune? Your songs are very melodic, but I am wondering whether you start with the rhythms or even other abstract sounds.

The basic process is always the same. I always sit down at the piano and improvise. Then occasionally you come up with an idea that could be the core idea of an interesting song.

So you can generally hear the connection between a piano and what a song might turn into electronically? Do you visualize where it's going to go?

Totally. This approach is quite important for me because as much as I enjoy soundscaping and sound design, the core of my music should be something that could survive on piano just as well. I want to have that element, and I don't want to be totally focused on the soundscaping idea. I want to have all the elements.

Obviously you have a good technical command of your gear, which is a necessary part of your craft. Tell me when you got a handle on this aspect and whether there was a significant learning curve for you.

I was probably about 14 or 15 in a small town where I grew up in the north of Germany, Kiel. I got to know a guy who was like a techno DJ, and he had a small studio with a sampler. It was in this studio where I had the first opportunity to work with synthesizers, so I saved my pocket money and got my own.

Were you into soft synths originally, or did you go right for the hardware?

At that time pretty much both. To be honest, when I started going into that studio, I didn't really know what the difference was anyway. I just heard these wonderful, weird sounds and thought I would like to do something like that as well.

What was the first piece of gear you bought, and was there anything in particular that propelled you forward?

One of the first things I got was an Ensoniq ASR-10, which is a great instrument and sounds wonderful. The filters are amazing, and it's a very complicated instrument. It took me a long time to figure it out—I wish there was a soft synth of this.

On your new album, how did the composition process go? How do you actually go about creating the sound components once you have your song together on the piano?

Once I have the rough structure figured out on the piano, I've got a couple of favorite sounds I use for sketches. I play the chords and I use them as a basis, then I erase them and start with a baseline for melodies, backgrounds, and atmosphere. It's very cliché, but you could say I approach it the same way as a painter—I build it up from a rough sketch.

Photo by Jason Evans.

Ulrich Schnauss.

What is your platform of choice?

I am a Logic user.

What do you like about Logic? You could probably work in any program you like.

There are probably two things about it. First, which is a more meaningless point, I am a Mac person—therefore, Logic is obviously the choice. Besides that, I do think that Logic has some really big advantages when you are trying to integrate a lot of hardware in your setup. I find it very comfortable. For example, I bought some Apogee audio interfaces recently, so I've got 16 in and 16 out and can put all my hardware effects into the setup in the Logic environment where you set up the audio files. You can come up with very interesting and complicated setups. The environment is my favorite window.

What about all soft synths and native sound generators that come with Logic—the soft synths, the ESX 24, Ultrabeat, and all the others. Do you find yourself using these as a regular practice?

To be honest, not that much. My music is very much based on sounds where the source materials are coming from hardware synths. What I do use a lot are plug-in effects, which I use quite excessively.

What are some of the key pieces of hardware in your setup?

Well, my favorite synthesizer of all time is definitely the Voyetra 8, an American synth from the early '80s. I just think it is a wonderful instrument, and whenever I play it, I am just amazed at how organic it sounds. The OB-8 is about the best synth that I've owned for the longest time. It is a very good friend of mine. I use that very much as a starting point—it has a very nice basic sound. You switch it on and you play it, and it sounds very inspiring.

What about for your rhythm tracks?

They are mostly made out of samples. I like taking individual sounds from the '70s fusion jazz stuff. The sequencing is done in Logic, and I'm still working with a hardware synth as well. I tried switching to a soft sampler recently, but just soundwise, I wasn't 100-percent convinced.

What about recording? For your latest album, are you actually recording into Logic as well?

I record to DAT still. Once I've got it in the DAT, I bring it into Pro Tools to do some final editing.

So you don't use Pro Tools as a creative tool for altering your compositions or changing arrangements? It's only for refinement and basic editing?

Yes.

Let's talk a little bit about plug-ins. What kind of tools are you working with to shape the sonics?

There are two things that I am using the most. One of them is Cycling '74's Pluggo package. Cycling '74 is a small American company in California doing some really interesting stuff. Most of their stuff is granular synthesis–based, which I find very interesting. In fact, that is the main reason I wanted to have a computer. I wouldn't really use a computer that much for classic things like modulation, effects, and reverb—I think that is better with hardware. But I am really fascinated by all the granular stuff. I also use Native Instruments' Reaktor, which offers a lot of things along those lines as well.

What about EQ? Do you prefer any particular plug-ins for your sounds?

Yes, there are probably two things I use the most. I've got the classic Waves EQ, which I find is very neutral-sounding, and I also use a Universal Audio card that includes the Sonnox Oxford EQ, which I also use.

The sonics on your pieces really exploit the entire frequency range—you hear sub-bass and very, very high frequencies.

For this latest album, I definitely wanted to layer sounds to the extreme and almost create a static wall of sound. I wanted an ethereal sound that was almost hypnotizing.

How do you manage things like panning—placing your sounds in the stereo field and creating depth—with the tremendous variety of sounds you are dealing with?

With this album, I was much more radical than on my previous productions with respect to sound placement. I would have a dry signal on the right side and have massive reverb on the left side, which is a good method of layering. I am much more hardware-based for reverbs still. There are some great reverb algorithms from the early '90s that you can still get for very cheap. The Roland SRV-330 and the SRV-3030 are completely overlooked and are all really good. My thesis is that in a couple of years people will really regret that they are throwing these pieces away for such little money.

Do you get into the esoteric gear at all? Do you have a lot of stuff lying around your apartment?

Yeah, I've acquired a lot of stuff by now. I'm always surprised my girlfriend isn't complaining about it!

What do you monitor through?

Throughout making this album, I monitored through headphones. When everything was in its final structure, I ran it through a pair of Tannoy monitors that I really like. They pick up the tiniest details, and if you did anything in the wrong way, it will sound awful. They are very mean speakers and really tell you the truth!

26 John Fogerty: From Creedence and Beyond

Since emerging in the late '60s as front man for the inimitable Creedence Clearwater Revival, John Fogerty has written more than a handful of songs that have become time-tested American standards: "Proud Mary," "Lookin' Out My Back Door," "Who'll Stop the Rain," and "Bad Moon Rising," just to name a few. With the release of *Revival*, a collection of 12 brand-new songs, Fogerty has recaptured the spirit and passion of what he shared with us so many years ago.

Despite having nearly every piece of modern recording technology at his disposal, Fogerty decided to stick to a tried-and-true recording methodology that served him faithfully during his years with Creedence—capturing the essence of the tracks live with a four-piece rock 'n roll band. Fogerty handled lead guitar duties with Hunter Perrin accompanying on rhythm guitar, David Santos on bass, and Kenny Aronoff on drums.

When I spoke to John, he was more than happy to cover both old and new. He is very proud of his days in Creedence Clearwater Revival and shared candescent memories of both his early guitar setup and some of his recording experiences with the band at Coast Recorders, where the first album, containing "Susie Q," was recorded.

How do you go through the recording process now? So much has changed—has your own methodology changed as well?

Well, this time I very much made it a point to rehearse ahead of time. In fact, I picked the four guys from my band. Even though my band has six people in it, I just wanted to have two guitars, bass, and drums—a lineup that I've always considered to be the essential rock 'n roll lineup, going back to Elvis, Buddy Holly and the Crickets, the Beatles, or Creedence Clearwater.

Photo by Nela König.

John Fogerty.

I've found that to be the most useful, versatile lineup without any extra stuff. I wanted that group of four guys to rehearse the songs that I had written and pretty much arranged—although if you have time to rehearse, you also have time to move things around, explore, and all that. I very much wanted to make sure that those four pieces were presenting the song, and they had to find it within themselves to make the arrangement valid, if you follow what I am saying. Because in times past, I've gone in with just a drummer or a drummer and a bass player, and you are sort of being vague. You have an arrangement that you think is rhythm section, but then you say, "I'll put in a guitar line here, and I'll do a solo there. Maybe I'll do a background vocal there." It's not really set in your mind exactly what it is going to be.

How does this impact spontaneity? You are a great lead guitarist, so does this bring you more flexibility?

Well, I think it is better to know. This last way was much better, and it is the original way that I used to make records with Creedence. You want specific, but then it has to hold up. You've got to make everything count, knowing that you're not going to add a bunch of other stuff later. Because when you say you're going to add stuff later, even though you don't know what it is yet [laughs]—a lot of records get made that way. I daresay even most. But I wanted it to sound like a band, and that is a whole different statement.

Back in the days of Creedence, you were almost forced to be more decisive when you were laying down tracks because you only had limited tracks—8, 16, or whatever it was in the day. Now with DAWs, there are unlimited tracks—but it sounds as if you are keeping that self-discipline and you want to nail the track going down instead of relying on what you lay down later.

That is absolutely correct. I was totally rejecting the technology and basically just using it as a tape recorder. The idea was that these four guys are going to present this song, and we are going to play live. So the discipline or mandate was around the music rather than around the technology and all the unlimited availability that comes with that. The song has to be valid with these four pieces, and we're just going to play live and record it live—that's pretty much how it was done. I must admit I overdubbed the lead vocals because the drums were crashing, and I obviously couldn't get the isolation. A lot of the soloing—for instance, on "Creedence Song"—was live from the get go, front to back.

So this is one of the first times since Creedence when you likely held to the discipline, right? It was more or less a template that worked for Creedence for so many years.

Well, that's true. And it wasn't so much that I was trying to imitate or copy Creedence, but I just felt that having that band "feel" was important. You play a certain way, you're going for it, and you're reacting to each other, so you can tell immediately what is a good take. If you are judging everything that is there right when you are playing it for the four guys, rather than saying, "That will be okay after I add piano, an organ, and the Tabernacle Choir"—if you are judging based on what's there right now, that's very much like the old days, and again, it's a band having to stand up, live with, and go with what they just recorded.

How important is the environment in which you record? You have doubtless been in the best studios—I think you recorded a lot of your Creedence records at Fantasy.

Fantasy was built because of Creedence [laughs]. That building did not exist when I was making those records. "Susie Q" was recorded at a place called Coast Recorders—I think it has since changed its name, and I don't even know if it is a recording studio anymore. Parts of that first album were also recorded at Sierra Sound in Berkeley. The second album was recorded most notably at RCA in Hollywood, when I had gone back after our initial success to start the second album. I had very high hopes for our second album. I had the arrangements, I had the band rehearsed, the writing included—songs like "Proud Mary" and "Born on the Bayou." At that point, I just felt I had outgrown Coast, so we recorded at RCA, and it was a great experience. Then Wally Heider opened his San Francisco studio in time for *Green River* and the rest of the Creedence albums.

How important is the environment today? What kinds of things do you look for, and where did you record this album?

For this album, the live tracks and backing tracks were recorded at NRG in North Hollywood. It's a cool rock 'n roll place—a lot of bands like Linkin Park, Offspring, and Slayer recorded there. It's a pretty rockin' kind of place. I did the vocals at another location that was a lot smaller and more intimate. But I liked NRG a lot—the drums sound really great in Studio B. I'm old-fashioned in that sense; I'll walk into a room and clap my hands and say, "There's a certain live air to it." Obviously with new technology, I suppose you can add a lot of things like echo and delay, but I just wanted that nice feel for when we were doing it, because it feels good.

The essence of a room is so important, and a lot of folks overlook that, right?

I think so. Lots of pop records are made that other way with machine drums, keyboard bass, a lot of sampling and stuff—that's okay for that kind of music. The one thing I have really noticed is that they have not invented a machine that plays rock 'n roll drums. Many, many companies have been working on this, but those kinds of sounds don't sound good coming out of a machine—they sound very robotic. The hip hop stuff, the Beyoncé stuff, that all sounds great with machine drums—that music has grown up that way. But for rock 'n roll, there is something about the human feel, the certain way of being on the beat, a little ahead. The drummer is anticipating what's going to happen two seconds from now, but you can hear that anticipation—that is part of the excitement. You get a little nervous and sweaty, because here comes the chorus!

Let's talk a little about your guitar sound. How much time did you spend getting the right sound, and is there a typical setup?

I have a lot of guitars—I am one of "those people." I am a guitar collector, and I love old and new guitars—I'm not a snob about it. I have great old vintage and valuable guitars; I've got a huge collection.

Back in the Creedence times, everything was very simple. Creedence started out very much as an acoustic/electric rock 'n roll band. Both my brother Tom and I were playing Rickenbacker electrics; I was doing lead on the Rickenbacker. Sometimes that sounded good, like on *Green River*; other times it sounded a little thin. I also used a black Les Paul custom that I mostly tuned down to D. I tuned every string down a whole step so it gave it a great big resonating sound with those humbuckers—especially with chords. That's what you hear at the beginning of "Bad Moon Rising." That big chord strumming—also at the beginning of "Midnight Special," that great big sound. I basically learned that trick from the old folk artists like Leadbelly. They were getting that big sound on their 12-strings because they tuned down to D. If they tried to tune that guitar up to E, it would blow up! [laughs]

I loved that sound, so I just started doing it on electric, and it turned out to be this serendipitous happy accident that everybody thought was a great big sound. In the beginning I used a Kustom amp—a solid-state amp from 1968, the old tuck and roll things. I never had colors and sparkles; mine were black. My brother Tom played through that as well. They didn't break up. They had a lot of headroom so they sounded so clean and clear on strummed rhythms—they sounded great. Then to play a lead I would stomp on the internal fuzztone that Kustom had, it was called the Harmonic Clipper, and it was an absolutely great sound. It didn't do the tube overdrive thing—it was yin or yang, you know? "Susie Q" is really those two sounds.

A little bit later I began to get into small Fenders: Deluxe Reverbs, and I think I had a Concert Fender, so I was breaking it up a little bit. Nowadays, it's anything and everything. All over the new record I used a PRS single-trim guitar and a Cornford amp—in fact, I used that on a lot of songs on this album. That's what you're hearing on "Summer of Love" and the lead on "Somebody Help Me." For "Gunslinger" and "Broken Down Cowboy," that's a beautiful three single-coil pickup Strat-like guitar made for me by Ernie Ball—it's absolutely beautiful. I think it's the best-sounding guitar I've ever heard, so I use it a lot.

With all these sounds you hear in your head, you doubtless rely on an engineer or engineers to make the sounds a reality. Can you tell me who engineered this record and what the engineer's role is for you?

My engineer is Jim Scott. He's worked on a lot of great projects like Dixie Chicks, Tom Petty, and others. He was on the same page as I was. For most of the stuff, I will say that you've got to have the sound coming out of the guitar the right way. I said this way, way back in the Creedence days: It's not what's coming out in the control room; it's what's going on on the other side of the glass out there in the room, you know?

Creedence's sound was very simple, but it was the right choice of simple things. The snare drum in those days was a direct and definite choice, as was the kick drum. That formula, or that mandate, still prevails now. On different songs I use different snares, of course, but my drummer, Kenny Aronoff, is a wonderful drummer and knows how to hit a drum in a million different ways to get a certain sound. But again, it's got to sound right out in the room. Given that, Jim Scott was very good at capturing what these instruments sounded like and using the right mic to do it. We recorded direct to Pro Tools—things are so good nowadays that the issue is not so pressing anymore.

Yeah, it's been an ongoing argument. But you can't let it hold you back from moving ahead, right?

Yeah. When I made *Blue Moon Swamp*, I was fighting digital like it was some sort of infernal plague. But in '96, '97, they didn't really have it down. Our editing was by cutting up pieces of tape.

I told Kenny, "We didn't have to do any drum editing on you." Which is a remarkable statement in this day and age. Everybody goes in and tries to make their drummer sound like a drum machine. I love the way Kenny plays—when we had a take, we just had a take. It sounded human and good—that's what I wanted. I didn't want Beat Detective or whatever in there to turn him into some sort of drum machine, sterile or whatever. I like when things move.

There were a couple times where I moved a guitar part or a whole section into another position. But this wasn't Frankenstein, and we didn't do it on drums. We didn't start out a song with three verses, two choruses, and a solo and then suddenly change all that around—we didn't change the form of the songs. It is a great tool, though—I really learned that you can get lost in that endless, infinite array of choices. I've sat there like everyone else going, "Do I like this snare sample, 'ping ping ping,' or do I like this drum sample, 'bunk bunk bunk'?" Then hours go by; you are glazed over, and whatever inspiration you had is gone.

Even though I allotted plenty of time, there was still always that subtle nudge of pressure saying, "You've got to get this and move on." That really helps the urgency of the whole thing—I don't mean recklessness; I just mean urgency. We're going to do a take here—we've got all day, and I've got a bunch of world-class musicians here.

Most of the time we would rehearse a group of five or six songs, then we would go in and record. Basically, we would play several of the songs that day—we didn't just concentrate on one and beat it to death all day. We would do three or four takes on the first song, and if it wasn't right or wasn't coming, we would move on and do a little bit of the second song—maybe four takes or so. Then we'd move onto the third song.

The next day we would come back and try that first song, and then it would pop and you'd say, "Okay, that's great." It turns out that one of the songs on the album, "Longshot," which was the second song we tried on the first day of recording, just had that magic—here's a band playing rock 'n roll; what more do you want? It was all there. That was pretty much the method. Then on the third day, we would insert or inject another song into the mix, now that we already had a take. By the end of five days, you'd have five takes.

In the case of "Broken Down Cowboy," because that song is so meaningful to my wife and me, I had what I thought was a very good, wonderful, studio-perfect take. We had even gone to the point of overdubbing, adding acoustic guitar, and I may have sung a vocal. I played it for my wife, and she said, "Gee, I like the demo better." I'm sitting there rolling my eyes, saying, "Oh God! Beat the demo!" She doesn't know about that syndrome, "Beat the demo." [laughs] She was there in the studio, and we all listened to what was basically one day of rehearsals that had been recorded. But of course, she had been going around listening to that demo in her car, on her computer, and in her player for a month and a half. But she's my wife! [laughs]

Even though we recorded the demo on separate tracks, there was a lot of leakage since we were only rehearsing. So we thought, "Maybe we can strip out a couple of the guitars." But it turned out that what she was hearing was the vulnerability and hesitancy—that's what she was hearing and what she liked better. Even though we had a wonderful, world-class studio take, even slick, it was missing something.

So I reminded everybody of that song, "Walk Away Renée." It was written by a garage band, but they rose so far above themselves with the material. I said, "That's what we want to do with this song—make it sound like we're not quite so sure of ourselves." So we allotted one empty day in the calendar, and it had to happen. We came in and we nailed on take two. I looked at her with that question mark on my face, and my wife said, "We're done." [laughs] And from me, you've never heard such a sigh of relief. You're going for something that's so elusive—you're trying to bottle that emotion, but you usually go past that.

Do you have any sonic preferences when it comes to microphones? Let's take vocal mics.

I have a wonderful vocal mic that was made for me. It's a Brauner microphone, but it's the Klaus Heine model. He rebuilds microphones, and I think he had quite a career doing that with all the old legendary microphones like the U 47s. I discovered those late in my career, around the *Blue Moon Swamp* time.

I always thought, "Ah, microphone schmicrophone." But I heard one of those one day, and I went, "Oh my God." They're not so crystal clear, and no two are ever the same, but they have this airy fog in them or something. There's tons of character, and it sounds like a finished track when you sing into it. I was sworn on those, and then I called Klaus Heine, who knew my voice. He said, "Look John. I know your voice. What I want to do is make the microphone exactly for you." So he did—and he used a certain diaphragm and put it together in the old-fashioned way. It just sounds finished, and it's an integral piece of gear.

John, can you tell me about any sessions with Creedence that just left your hair on end? Tell me about one special moment that blew you away that you can't erase from your memory.

When we went down to RCA in late 1968, the session I most fondly remember is "Proud Mary." The engineer, Hank McGill, lived on a boat [laughs], and I thought that was fascinating. I probably met him in Marina Del Rey, but I can't really remember. I thought it was amazing that he lived on a boat. He was a very hands-on, adaptable engineer who was going for sound. We rolled into RCA. It was a big, big room—I think it was studio A. Basically, he just built a little gobo room around the four of us, so that the drums were in one place and we were just sitting there next to our amps—the way we always rehearsed. I'm playing a Gibson 175, kind of a jazz box. Tom was playing a Rickenbacker at that point, and Stu had a Rickenbacker bass. Doug had his Kemco drums.

We just put it down the way we sounded at rehearsal. We heard the playback—which was on an eight-track, by the way—and it sounded just like we did out in the room. We were hot, and it sounded good.

That song didn't just influence the music world, it also influenced American culture. Were you surprised when you saw the effect it had on people once the record came out?

I knew when I finished writing "Proud Mary"—the morning I was working on it, when it was done, I was practically shaking. I knew I had written a standard—meaning like Cole Porter or Irving Berlin: "Smoke Gets in Your Eyes" or "White Christmas." I knew it was far above anything I'd ever done before. Did I know it would still be around and revered 40 years later? Of course not. The funny thing about "Proud Mary" was that when we were doing "Rollin', rollin' on the river" at the end, the tape ran out. It actually pulled off the reel about three seconds after that fade-out that you hear. It was just amazing how all that worked. It was probably like take two. But we all knew in the studio that it was really good.

What about "Susie Q?" That's a special track—there are great drum sounds and a really great vibe.

For that one, we were trying to go from being a top-40 cover band that plays in bars to somebody who could be on the radio overnight, in one fell swoop. Up until that time, we were gollywogs; Tom and I would write songs, and the original songs were okay, but there was just something that was not quite there yet. I chose to go with an old song so I didn't have to worry about whether the song was good or not. I "psychedelicked" it up. I arranged it purposely to be played on the San Francisco underground station, KMPX, which was basically the first place where the freeform underground thing was happening, with Tom Donahue and a host of others.

It was a long jam, but I organized the jam. I had specific parts taking place at specific places in the song, and then I kind of mapped it all out. I don't read or write music, but I mapped it out like a timeline. It was very visual: 1492, Columbus discovers America. 1527, John goes to the bridge! [laughs] It was a long timeline over a sideways couple of sheets—I had to tape two sheets of binder paper to get it all in. I kind of knew what was going to happen with the arrangement, but of course the playing had to be good in the first place. We practiced that thing for probably a month and a half or two months. We would play it in our own little rehearsal place that we called "The Shire"; we also played it out a couple times in the clubs. Finally, when it was time to record, we went to Coast Recorders in San Francisco.

Part of the trick of the sound on that was I had two speaker boxes plugged into that Kustom amp. So we miked both of them—so there is a little bit of funny phasing you hear. The amps were also tilted in so that I could go and stick my head in. If you've ever seen a woman's vanity, there are three mirrors, and the middle one is the one she's in front of. But there are two wings that fold in toward her, maybe so that she can see the left side of her face and the right side of her face. That's how the two cabinets were positioned, so I could stick my head in with a guitar, and that would make it start to feed back. There is a lot of acoustic feedback going on. By the way, "Susie Q" was take one, I'm pretty sure. We went in and said, "That's it, we're done."

27 Raul Malo Takes on the Classics

Malo's *You're Only Lonely* takes the listener on a romantic stroll through 12 classic love songs from an eclectic collection of writers, including Willie Nelson, Ron Sexsmith, Don Everly, and many others. Working closely with accomplished producer Peter Asher and expert engineer George Massenburg, Malo's smooth tenor is the centerpiece and focal point of the album. Malo delivers a distinctly original feel to some well-known songs, while preserving and respecting the emotional intent of the originals. When I spoke to Malo, he had just completed the album before embarking on a short East Coast tour with his band.

On the album Malo took several risks, covering standards and classics not often attempted by others. For example, he did a male vocal rendition of Etta James' "At Last" that was respectful of the original version, while adding unique touches to the arrangement and delivery, making it all his own. With master engineer/producer George Massenberg at his side, Malo delivered from both a performance and a sonic perspective.

Photo by Kristin Barlowe.

Raul Malo.

Raul, I understand you are already touring with this record and you played New York City a couple of nights ago. How did that go?

We just played the Bowery Ballroom the night before last. It's been going great. We are doing an East Coast run, and the record has just been released. We are kicking things off with the new record, but we've been touring since the beginning of the year. It's just been one kickoff after another.

This is a very big-sounding recording, and you should be very proud of it. How much time did you allocate for this album?

We did spend a lot of time. The first thing we did was pick the songs—we probably had about 50 or 60 songs to choose from, and then we started doing pre-production, then the recording. There were different phases in the recording, too. We did the recording in blocks for the most part, partly to accommodate everyone's schedule, but also because it was a nice way to work, giving you a little time to sit back and listen to the first batch and evaluate. Doing it this way enabled us to clearly see what was needed and how the record was shaping up.

Let's talk about the song selection. You came up with a really nice variety of tunes—I'm sure a lot of these tunes must have been near and dear to you. How did you arrive at these songs?

Well, the initial process was, "Let's just make a list of our favorite songs"—songs I've wanted to record and songs I thought I could record. Once we had this list, the big test was at our hotel room in Dublin, Ireland, and I had my acoustic guitar. Basically, we went song by song, and if I could play it on the guitar and sing it, and if it sounded believable, that was basically how the songs were going to make the record. I sat there and played Peter the songs one by one, and he had a checklist—it was kind of like the schoolmaster and the student, and we were doing a test [laughs]! That's how we picked them. If I could sit there and play them on the guitar, they would make them on the record.

There is a very strong emotional overtone in all these songs, and I would imagine that some of them were very risky to undertake, such as Etta James' "At Last." Were you ever nervous about living up to the original versions?

Well, sure. All of them are iconic songs, and we were a bit nervous about tackling some of them. I was especially a little nervous about "At Last," just because it's such a famous song and an iconic performance. But we had one thing going for us, and that was that there were no male versions of the song around at the time. Essentially, we treated all the songs as if they were demos; if you heard them for the first time, how would you do them? It's really hard because you want to treat the song well and pay the respect it deserves, but you also want to put your own spin on it. There's a fine line.

You really preserved the emotion—take a song like "So Sad." It leaves me with the same feeling that the Everly Brothers' version left me with, but it's executed in a completely different way.

Thank you. That's exactly what we were trying to do. With songs like these it's a fine line, like I said. But you also have to have your own spin on it. It's a real challenge, I think.

Can you share with me your approach on the arrangements? Take a song like "Angel Flying Too Close to the Ground," which really builds with a fantastic choir. Was this approached collaboratively with Peter?

Peter was just fantastic to work with and was extremely open to ideas. On that one, I remember we were toying with it and playing with it with the band, and we thought it would be nice to build it up into almost a gospel-type thing because we didn't have anything else like that on the record. I thought the song would lend itself to that sort of treatment, making it a little different from Willie [Nelson]'s version. Peter was fantastic in that regard, because he wasn't like, "This is how we do things in L.A." or whatever. [laughs] The record was truly collaboration, and working with him was indeed a pleasure.

Let's talk about the tracking in Nashville at Ocean Way. How did the initial tracking sessions go down?

Well, Ocean Way is a fantastic studio. I love that big room and I love the board they have, that old Neve. We tracked a lot of that stuff live—even the vocals. We would work out the arrangement with the band. A lot of the time we already had an arrangement.

So were you right there in the live room, or were you in an iso booth?

I was in an iso booth, but a lot of them were tracked vocals. We would start going through the songs and the arrangements, and Peter would direct the band. He wouldn't let them play here, or would let them play here. He worked in a really interesting way because, coming from an environment where everybody gets their licks in no matter what, he didn't let anything get in the way of the vocals. In turn, what happened was whenever there was a little lick or a drum fill or some other sort of musical moment, it became part of the hook line or part of the song.

Or possibly it builds the vocals in some way—were these little treatments ultimately acting as a bedrock for the vocals in some way?

Yes, exactly. And that's how he works. For me it was great, of course. Nothing got in the way of my vocals. But it also meant you can't hide behind anything! [laughs] Peter is also very respectful and accommodating to musicians, and would listen to everyone's ideas. If an idea fit, it would be implemented. It was never his way or the highway—never that sort of environment. It was fantastic.

What kind of interplay was there between you and Peter in tracking the vocals? How involved was Peter in terms of microphone choice, and how much direction did he give you as a singer?

Peter is not a technical kind of producer—his forte lies in the performance side of things. He was very instrumental in directing the performance, and most of the time he basically just stayed out of the way. Honestly, I would sing the song, and if we got it, he'd simply say, "Let's move on; that's fantastic." On "At Last," there was a little bit of back and forth because we were trying to achieve a crooner type of performance. We tried a couple of mics, and I think we ended up with a U 67 for the most part. I know I did some vocals out in L.A., and I think we had a Soundelux—the 251. He leaves the technical stuff to the engineers, and luckily, he works with great engineers, of course. With people like George Massenburg, he knows who to hire.

Malo and Massenburg relied on a Neumann U 67 for many of the recording duties.

What was it like working with George?

Geez, George is a genius. It was fantastic because whenever I would throw a suggestion out or tell him what I wanted to hear, he would not only do it, but he'd make it better, surpassing anything I even had in my head. He knows his tools and his craft—watching him work, I was just in awe. He is a gentleman and a genius engineer. He mixed the record at his house out in the country before he had his room at Blackbird.

What was it like working with him out there?

It was great—it's beautiful out there in the country. I got to run my motorcycle out there. It was so funny when I first got there because I had never worked with him. I was expecting this super high-tech laboratory environment, and it wasn't like that at all. His mixing room out there was basically his garage, but he makes it work. It was interesting because he mixes at a really, really low volume. More so than any other engineer I've ever heard. I thought, "Man, I can barely hear that!" I've always been involved in the mixing and production of every record I've done, but working with these guys was great because I got to lay back and let them do it!

It's so clear that he got the vocal right where it needed to be—it is front and center and sounds perfect on every track.

Well, that was the whole point of this record to do that. That was the kind of record that Peter set out to make with me, and that was never lost throughout the whole process, including mixing.

From a performance perspective, how much work did it take for you to nail the vocal takes? Did you have to do a lot of work on the front end before you even went in with the intent to record?

I don't want to sound too pretentious, but it doesn't take me long to get the songs down in the studio—especially if we've played them a few times in pre-production. We did quite a lot of pre-production, and I was pretty familiar with them—we had played them a couple of times. I wanted to go in and capture a live performance as we were tracking wherever possible, since that's usually going to be the best take if you can catch it. But some of the songs, like "Feels Like Home," were so new to me that we went back in and did it again, even though I had laid down a track vocal. Which was okay, but I wanted to go back and get it just right. So that one took a bit of work and a couple of times.

I'm not one to do 30 vocal tracks and comp, though. I'll do two or three performances at the most, and that's about it. You can tell when a vocal is being comped, and for the life of me, I've never understood why. When you hear some of the great performances from people like Ray Charles, his performances aren't perfect, but in its imperfections and nuances, there's an emotion there that most engineers today would suck the life out of. I don't have the patience to comp vocals. If you can't sing a song from top to bottom without stirring it up, what are you doing there in the first place?

Why did you decide to do a duet with Martina McBride? How did that unfold?

Well, that was a fortuitous event that just happened. She happened to be working at Blackbird one of the times that we were working there, and George Massenburg just happened to be working on a record at the time with her husband. So there were many factors involved, plus the fact that we wanted someone who could belt out a song like "Feels Like Home" with me. All those things played into it, and it just happened to work out. She was in town, it made sense, and she agreed to do it. Sometimes those things are difficult to make happen, but this one wasn't that hard.

Looking back on the record as a completed piece of work, what is it like? Does hindsight or being away from it for a while give you any new perspective?

I'm proud of it—I'm very pleased with the end result, to say the least. Having worked with someone like Peter, I feel like I've learned a lot and gained a friend. The overall experience was just fantastic, and I'd do it all over. The making of the record was great.

28 Band of Horses: Creating a Sense of Freedom in the Studio

Band of Horses' spectacular second record, *Cease to Begin*, sees front man Ben Bridwell honing his craft both as a songwriter and a performer while once again working alongside veteran Seattle-based producer Phil Ek [The Shins, Built to Spill]. The result is an intense, sonically focused effort that has since coincided with a nearly sold-out North American tour and a new European tour starting in February.

Having recently relocated the band to South Carolina from Seattle, Bridwell wanted to find a studio closer to home to record *Cease to Begin*. He happened upon Echo Mountain Records & Recording, a converted church in Asheville, North Carolina, that provided the perfect atmosphere and laidback environment he was looking for. *Pro Sound News* spoke to Ben as *Cease to Begin* continued its climb up the charts and as Band of Horses continued its stampede through venues across the country.

Photo by David Belisle, courtesy Sub Pop.

Band of Horses, left to right: Ben Bridwell, Creighton Barrett, and Rob Hampton.

In what ways do you think you have developed as a songwriter over the last few years?

With the first record, I had help from Matt Brooke [former band member] to give me guidance on the songs. I wanted to make sure that I had the confidence of someone else reassuring me, "That change is good!" or "That lyric is fine." On this record, everything was much more on my shoulders—I knew I had to carry a lot of the weight myself.

Sometimes I can write a song in one sitting, and it can be done. Other times, I'll have a melody dancing around for a couple of months before I actually sit down and put some music to it and figure it out. On the whole, though, I don't know when my songs are going to come or how. For the most part with both records, it was me forcing myself to mess around with new ideas, while looking for some sort of melody. Once I had a good idea, I would introduce it to the guys; if they didn't cringe, I knew we had a little song on our hands.

Tell me what it is like to work with Phil Ek—this is your second record with him.

It's great. On the first album, Phil and I didn't really know each other that well, but I knew what to expect the second time around, and we get along really well. He can be a bit direct when trying to get the results that he thinks he can get from you. As far as that is concerned, I guess I wasn't as sensitive this time as I was the first time around—I took less offense at him being a perfectionist and pushing me. It was easier in that sense because we knew going in that he was going to be tough, so we just kept our nose to the stone. Phil is fantastic—I feel like a lot of our sound is owed to him and that he's another band member. He influenced [*Cease to Begin*] so much.

Was the approach in recording *Cease to Begin* simpler or more complex than the approach for *Everything All The Time*?

I think perhaps the songs are more simplistic this time around. It's all relative, but maybe the more direct and simplistic the song is, the more room there is to build on it. Take "Is There a Ghost," the first song, for example. There are a million guitars on it, and Rob Hanson played every guitar track and the bass tracks on that—so it can be a combination of using different players on the tracks, or it can be the simplicity of the songs. Phil has a vision, and I just take direction—we just do whatever he wants us to do until he feels that it's good enough.

What is different to you on this album versus on *Everything All the Time*?

One difference on this album versus the last one is that we weren't sure what the instrumentation would be on some of the songs or what tempos we were going to use; therefore, we weren't sure what the overall outcome would be when we started. We also knew we wanted to keep this record more laidback and avoid using things like click

Lead singer and writer Ben Bridwell of Band of Horses, performing at New York's Terminal 5 in 2007.

tracks. It was important for us to try to play more and try to get as much live feel to it as we could—even though we knew Phil [Ek] probably wouldn't let us keep most of the live stuff. All in all, we tried to maintain a more easygoing approach—the first record was a bit stressful, even though I'm the only one from the last record that is on this second record.

Creighton [Barrett], our drummer, doesn't work well with click tracks, so by not doing them, it helped reduce some of the stress. We just said, "Let's play it like we normally do, and we'll be fine." I believe in the end this approach served us really well. It helped erase predispositions and also created a different kind of vibe in the sense that, "Well, the songs are all there. Let's just record them and not really worry about it too much— let's just try to have fun with it." That's exactly what we ended up doing—we had a lot more fun this time around.

Can you tell me where your head was when you finished *Everything All the Time* and how much time you took between that one and *Cease to Begin*?

Right around the end of the last album it was the holidays—around two years ago. The album was done, and the promos had been finished. I guess it was March. There were a number of months in between going to work for the record and it being completed, so there was a lot of downtime.

Band of Horses' *Cease to Begin*, released 2007.

Did you feel good about *Everything All the Time*?

Yeah, I felt really good about it. I didn't know what was going to happen, of course. I just wanted to get back to work as soon as possible on a follow up before any of the press started to pay attention to us or any of that stuff. I wanted to keep the flow going and keep writing songs.

I found this little red caboose on the Washington coast where I had planned on going to write songs. I had already written "No One's Gonna Love You" at that point. It was a little red caboose that somebody had turned into a little hotel shack. It's on the beach, and you can live in it or rent it by the night. There is no TV—there is electricity, a little wood stove, but there is no phone reception or streetlights. There is nobody around—at least during the off season, anyway—so I went there to write some songs. That's where I came up with "Ode to LRC," which is "Ode to the Little Red Caboose." That and "Detlef Schrempf" were written there, just in one sitting.

"LRC" wasn't the rockin' version that appears on the record—it was really mellow. Between those three songs, I thought I had a really mellow record on my hands.

I love how "LRC" came out, though. It comes in very strong and hits you right over the head—the perfect opening track for an album.

Yeah, I like it, too. But at the same time, I actually miss the way it used to be.

What kind of guitar did you write with? I assume an acoustic guitar.

When I started doing this whole thing, I didn't know how to play guitar. I was lucky at the time—we had a bit of a gearhead in our band, and he would bring all this stuff: vintage Les Pauls, pedal steels, and things like that. I didn't know how to play guitar, so I just tuned the guitar to where I wanted my hands to be, basically. So still, anywhere I go, I have to have like 10 guitars and all in different keys. It's my curse and my blessing because it has made those songs what they are and a little bit different. What I'm doing even today, I have my guitar lesson because I am trying to learn how to play guitar like a normal person. I have no idea how to play my tunes in a standard tuning or even how to go about it.

How did you write the first album?

I wrote it on those same guitars—two Les Pauls and the pedal steel.

Tell me about the demos you put together that are now known affectionately as "Dumb Dick Blues."

We recorded them at the Jam Room. There were seven songs by that point, including "No One," "LRC" and "Detlef." By this point we had "Window Blues" and "House of the Setting Sun," which later became "Cigarettes, Wedding Bands," and "Islands on the Coast." Then there was a song called "15 Krona," which didn't make the record. I basically had the basis for the record. We didn't have "Is There a Ghost" yet, nor "The General Specific," or the instrumental "Lamb on the Lam (in the City)," which was just an album filler.

I wish that the "Lamb on the Lam (in the City)" had continued on beyond 40 seconds or whatever it is. It is one of the more melancholy and interesting chord progressions on the album.

I know, I know. I had written it as a pop song, and I was trying really hard to put together some sort of words for the record, but it just never happened. It could be one of those things you come back to later and rewrite. Anyway, we had seven songs. We thought since we were this far along, we might as well go in and start doing a demo—time to book studio time. The album was finally shaping itself, so we went down to Columbia, South Carolina, and started messing around with them. The engineer was Jason Caffey. We didn't really use click tracks very much—we just wanted to identify the problem areas before we got into the real deal.

This was a completely different band from the first time around, right?

Exactly. The only people we had in the band at the time were me and Creighton Barrett on drums. Rob Hampton was playing bass and guitars.

How did you come across Creighton?

I actually met Creighton in Charleston when I was like 18, at a party. There was a Dinosaur Jr. song on at this party, and we became best bros and moved in together after that. I left for Seattle, then I moved him out there later.

When you were in The Jam Room, did it gel together and feel like it was going to work out? What was the vibe like?

I remember thinking at the time that that was one of the better things the walls of that studio had ever heard. I was very confident and thinking that this album was going to be great—I wasn't stressed at all. I thought all the performances sounded great. To think that even a year ago, I was singing hard, forceful, and really raspy. I was also smoking the whole time.

The new album just sounds very polished, and I love your voice on this album. It seems like you tightened up so many things, and you can hear it on the new album.

Phil Ek, who produced both of our records, is really good at getting me to do it correctly and sounding good. It takes a lot of work to get there, but I quit smoking because of that record, and it's amazing to hear the difference from the demos. I've also realized that I shouldn't be singing really loudly or forcefully.

What was the setup like in the Jam Room?

There was no stress. I remember there was an upright video game that had a menu of these old Atari games, but it had this song that was playing all the time—we couldn't turn it off. It was the creepiest, awesomest little tune—we wanted to cover it. I remember it wasn't until like the sixth day, we decided that we could unplug it and not hear it anymore. It was strange, because you'd do playbacks of the demos in the control room—you'd hear it while the song was going on, and it was very weird.

The best thing, though, was that we got an old friend of mine that I grew up with to come around to the studio and see if he would lay down some keyboards for us. I called up this dude, and he came in and just murdered it. Now he is in the band and has been in the band since then. He's really come into his own in this band—he has always been a fantastic songwriter and performer, but instead of doing the Columbia club circuit, he is touring the world now.

Then later, we went to Echo Mountain to record it and we met Bill, who is also meant to be in this band as well. He is now our bass player. Then through Bill, we met Tyler, who is playing guitar for us. For this album, we chose all the right little avenues to go down, and we met the best people.

Take me from recording the demo until you recorded the album. Did you take a lot of time off and think about the tunes before you went in again?

I sent Phil the demos immediately, just to see what lyrics were stupid and the different ways I could try to muster up some energy to make them better. Around this time, we were still touring a lot—we would go on tour for three or four weeks, then go straight to the studio and record for two weeks, then go back on tour. It was just constantly so much work around that time.

That was good. We were realizing that some of the songs were different because we had already been playing them out before we started recording. Once we started recording, we'd say, "This song needs to be so much bigger now." So we would stay away from playing it, so we could figure it out. Phil does that to people—he makes the songs sound better than they are supposed to, and then forces you to play them live better.

But there were a good few months before you went back into the studio?

Yes, exactly. We definitely had some time before we went back in.

Band of Horses performing at NYC's Terminal 5.

Tell me about your choice of studio to record the new album—I'm assuming that you could pretty much record wherever you wanted to at this point?

Yeah, kind of. You don't want to blow a bunch of money on making your record; they give you a healthy budget if you need it, but you have to pay it back, so there is no reason to go bonkers. What happened was that we were on tour and met the bassist from Archers of Loaf, one of our all-time favorite bands. His girlfriend ran this studio, and they asked us if we wanted to come by the studio and hang out for a beer. We said, "Absolutely," because we really wanted to hang out with that guy.

They gave us a tour of the studio, and we just fell in love. It is Echo Mountain, in Asheville, North Carolina. I grabbed a pamphlet and got it to Phil. He went online and checked out all their stuff and liked their gear and the setting, so he and the label were pretty supportive of it. It was obvious where we should be, and it was a great experience compared to the first record—it was so much more laidback than the first record.

They were just getting started at Echo Mountain, and I wasn't sure how many people had recorded there yet. Steve [Wilmans] is a veteran of recording; he bought that church and converted into a pro studio. I always had it in my head that I wanted to record there, and location was important, too—we wouldn't have to travel out to Seattle for seven weeks or something like that. We could do all the basics in Asheville, then do our overdubs in Seattle, where Phil has the comfort of being home in the studio that he likes to use.

What was the biggest thing Phil brought to the project?

He makes you play your songs better than you've ever played them. He forces you to—and he convinces you that every song is as important as the next. You have to give it all you've got. We wouldn't be in the position we are in if it wasn't for Phil crafting our sound at the same time.

On this album, it's noticeable that there are really no weak songs. The lowest common denominator is very high.

I don't think Phil would agree. I think he felt that some of the songs are underdeveloped or less than inspired. But Phil overanalyzes everything.

What were your first days like at Echo Mountain?

The first two days in there, Phil couldn't figure out how to get a good drum sound out of the room because there was so much dampening, so we had to brighten it. The main live room had been dampened to the point where Phil couldn't pull out any natural reverb from this nice, big, wood room—it was very strange. At the first sign of this happening, however, Steve, the owner, jetted over, got his tools, and just started taking panels down off the walls. Within an hour and a half, we had our drum sound—in the end, we just had to give the church some of its natural reverb back.

Phil doesn't like to add artificial reverb—he likes to use as much of a natural sound as he can. If he has to fix something with other things he will, but he knew he needed that natural room sound to make the record—otherwise, we were going to have to scrap the whole two-week session there.

Everything ended up being good, but the beginning was a little scary. We didn't know if we were gong to have to scrap the first two weeks we had to start with. Phil is a little bit picky, and he had that look in his eyes of being stressed, a look which I know well. But he was right. It's funny; he knows what he's doing, so you trust him even when you think everything is okay. He usually ends up being right.

For many people, the sound of the room is very important—even more so than the gear. It seems like Phil was very sensitive to the sound of the room.

He crafts those records just as much as I do.

Let's go through the new album track by track. What track did you do first?

God, I can't remember. We just tried to get the drums down first, and then we put the bass down. "Is There a Ghost" started as a demo when I was trying to learn how to use GarageBand on my computer. I had never learned how to do that, so I thought while I was living alone at this house I was living in, I should do that. So I wrote that song, those words and a little melody with an acoustic guitar.

It's ironic, because once we had put down most of the songs, Phil thought that we still needed a more poppy one. "15 Kroner," which is on the demo, didn't make the record because the lyrics are stupid and it's just kind of a crappy song. So we took that away, and he said we needed something poppier. So I had all my demos on my iPod, and I said, "Go through these, and if there are any you like, feel free."

While Phil, the rest of the guys, and I went to lunch, Creighton and Rob decided to stick around and work on the demos. We came back, and they had found the groove for that song.

The nice thing about that is that it is so minimalist and there are like 15 words.

Yeah [laughs]. It is funny. The one that you throw together at the last minute ends up being the single for the record. To me, that song represents the band coming into its own. With this band, I feel like we take just about any song and make it great. That song is a glimpse of the future for us, I think.

Rob said, "I'll take care of this one." I didn't even try to learn the chords. He was like, "I'll do it!" and Phil just kept on saying, "Let's add another one." I just added a light synthesizer in the background that just goes along with the chords. You can barely hear it. That song was easy.

What about "Ode to LRC?" How did this evolve from a nice, quiet-ish demo to sounding more like The Clash where it comes in with the commanding drums and guitars?

Phil wanted to make that one massive. I'm sure I doubled my guitars, and Rob probably doubled or tripled his. Ryan had done his keyboards, and the bass had been done already as well. A lot of the guitars were done with Rob and I overdubbing in Seattle after all the other tracks were down. You just keep building a house with it. One of Phil's friends played violin at that song just to add another dynamic to it.

I think I double-tracked my vocals the whole way through on that. With Phil, it's hard because he's on you for everything. If you are off the meter of it, a little flat, a little sharp, or if he thinks that you're just not into it, he'll make you do it again. It does take time, and the hardest part is getting the double-tracks exactly right.

"No One's Gonna Love You" is a departure from the last album—it's a little quieter than most of the songs on the last album. Tell me about writing and recording that.

I am playing a Univox on that. Ryan played a Mellotron on that, which is that nice whistly sound in the background. Rob came up with a nice complementary guitar, but unfortunately, my guitar had to carry that one. I really had to work for that. It is based on a delay setting, a delay pedal that has to be spot-on, otherwise the meter is wrong.

What kind of amps did you use in the studio?

Whatever we could borrow—we would use mostly Marshalls and Fenders and a few odds and ends here and there. "No One's Gonna Love You" is the oldest one of the bunch—it's probably two and a half years old. It wasn't directed to anyone as much as it was just the words sounded right for the melody. It seemed like that was what the song was asking for.

What about "Detlef Schrempf?"

That was written at the LRC just as the end of Seattle was approaching. I had decided I really wanted to move and get out of the "scene" a little bit and get to simpler times. It was not simple times in Seattle at that point, and that song was a melancholy jammer, just discussing relationships falling apart, and it was named after Detlef Schrempf, who was a hero in Seattle—I couldn't think of a better name for it. It's really my least favorite song on the album. I love Detlef so much that I hate to tarnish his name with the song—I don't think it's that great.

Take me through "The General Specific."

I had the melody for that as a rock/pop song. After a show I went to with Rob on his birthday, we came back to our rehearsal space and jammed to that. It was so bad that I vowed to never do it again. But near the completion of the writing of the record, I needed more songs so I went to my bank of everything I had messed with. I worked with Ryan, our keyboardist, to give it more of a piano groove. He helped make that song simpler, and it allowed the melody to come out more. I had to rewrite lyrics, and Phil told us to keep working on it. We did the stomping and the hand claps all at the same time.

The stomping and clapping reminds me of "Twentieth Century Fox" by the Doors on their first album. How did Phil capture these sounds?

He wanted to mic up the whole rooms. He had distant and close mics strategically placed throughout the room. We all had our headphones on—I'm pretty sure it was the four of us: Rob, Creighton, Ryan, and myself. It was actually really hard to do it in time, and I don't even know if Phil used a full pass. He might have made a loop. I felt that track was the closest we ever got to "Exile on Main St." This was our honky-tonk jammer. Our hands were actually sore from clapping so much, because Phil was such a slave driver.

Tell me about the guitar sequence on "Lamb on the Lam." It is a short song, but very moving.

That is actually from GarageBand—I still don't know what I'm doing in GarageBand. I think Phil put my iPod into the board and just messed with it. That is just the demo—he had to do some work on it, and it was added just like "Ghost" was. I had mentioned to Phil that I wanted to have little interludes between the songs if possible, but this never really panned out. I was probably using my Super Reverb on this one.

What about "Islands on the Coast?"

That one was written back in Seattle—we had performed that for a couple of tours, I think. This was another one where I messed around with the delay settings and a weird detuned guitar. I made a bouncy little pop tune, and it reminds me of The Shins or something. I didn't know what I was saying until it was time to record it—I just had a lot of garbage lyrics. I never actually say "islands on the coast"; I say "when eyelids want to close." It was kind of more about leaving Seattle. I thought it would be fun to confuse people a little bit by changing the title.

I remember thinking that this was going to be the single—which I'm always wrong about. I've been wrong about that now for two albums in a row. When we did basics,

I thought the label would want to go with it. But it ended up being nowhere near the single.

Phil thought they were going to choose "No One," and I thought he was probably right—it was my least favorite, as was the first single off the last album, "Funeral."

"Funeral" was your least favorite?

Yeah, I thought it was cheesy. I didn't like that song at all, and I didn't even want to record it. Ultimately, they decided on "Is There a Ghost" because they thought it would be better for radio play or whatever.

What about "Marry Song?" This is another really slow one, and you have what sounds like a Fender Rhodes going on, carrying the chords underneath.

I wrote that one on an autoharp in Boise, Idaho. We were staying three nights in Boise, and I was being cheesy and sat under a tree and wrote a melody on my new autoharp that I still can't play well. I wrote the first line, then never finished writing any lyrics and never picked it up again. So this was another one that was rediscovered at the end of the writing process—we did a demo of it, and everyone liked it, so it was a keeper.

That actually might be a Wurlitzer at the beginning. That was the only song on the whole record where one of the original live sets was kept, besides drums. We didn't even know if that sound would work for the song—Ryan was just playing along so he could get the drums tracked. We were all playing in the same room. When we listened back, Phil said, "That's perfect, I love the sound, we're not changing a thing." So Ryan was done.

That song could be seen as not very ambitious, but that was one of the things I liked about this record. I didn't care if anyone liked it—I wasn't going to shy away from it, and we just played it. I also remember that one as being pretty painless, and it was from the gut a little bit more. I had worked out the harmonies in advance.

Let's move on to "Cigarettes, Wedding Bands."

Okay. That one was written at home—I had the melody for a little while, and this was originally slow. I showed it to Creighton and Rob, and we tried to turn it into a Crazy Horse sort of number—we wanted to play it as loud as possible; it was also influenced by this band we were just on tour with, The Drones. They have a loud guitar sound, and I wanted to try to incorporate some of their gnarliness.

What about "Window Blues?"

That was written at home on a banjo, just sitting out here on our back porch overlooking this very picturesque little lagoon that we live on. It was a homecoming, lazy jam of being back in the South, I guess.

The banjo was really hard to get—it is hard to find people who can play banjo slow and in time. Even on "Marry Song," we were trying to get banjo on it. We tried two different guys playing it, but it just didn't work out, so it got scrapped. This one we got, and it faded in at the end of the song. We wanted to keep this one and "Marry Song" as simple as possible—a less-is-more approach.

Tell me about the mixing. Did this take a lot of time?

Right when we were done doing the vocal tracks, it was time to start mixing. Phil mixes as he goes, and the whole time he is getting an idea of what he wants. We kind of let him do his thing unless something is sounding totally ridiculous. You just trust him.

During the mixing, I am doing crosswords and reading. He'll sit there and stare at me, and I'll be like, "It sounds fine." I'm already so over the record and sick of hearing it by that point. I should try to have a better attitude than I do.

I have to say that "Is There a Ghost" is one of the best sequencing decisions I've ever heard. By putting it as the first track, it just breaks through everything and opens up the entire record as soon as you put it on. How were the sequencing decisions made?

Well, we knew even at Echo Mountain, before the overdubs, that that song should be first. We also knew that "Window Blues" should be last, since it doesn't have any chorus and it's kind of aimless. Phil and the label discuss the sequence, though, and suggest the order. Whatever they think works best, I will listen to it. Because at this point, I don't want anything to do with the album. I don't even want to hear it.

What are you focused on now?

I am taking guitar lessons and trying to play guitar like a normal person. I'm also trying to write, but so far it's like a square rabbit in a hole. I can't quite pull it out.

29 Jesse Harris: Capturing the Feel of a Performance

Jesse Harris' latest album, *Feel*, was a departure of sorts for the songwriter, who is best known for his contribution to Norah Jones' *Come Away with Me* and *Feels Like Home*. He is no stranger to great songwriting, having won a Grammy for his 2003 single, "I Don't Know Why," as well as recently writing and recording the score for Ethan Hawke's film *The Hottest State*, which featured performances of his songs from such diverse artists as Willie Nelson, Emmylou Harris, Norah Jones, Cat Power, Bright Eyes, and many others.

On *Feel,* Harris' seventh album, his songs are enhanced by the tasteful grooves of percussionist Mauro Refosco, who lends a relaxed Brazilian musical aspect to the album. In fact, at one point Harris considered doing the entire record in Rio de Janeiro, using local Brazilian musicians, and decided against it because it would have been too demanding on his schedule. He ultimately decided in favor of recording at New York's Loho Studios during a very brief touring break, using some tried-and-true musicians he worked with in the past: Tim Luntzel on bass, Andrew Borger on drums, and John Dryden on organ, among others.

Jesse, tell me about the new album—I understand it went down fairly quickly.

Recording and mixing went down in exactly seven days.

How did you find all the musicians you used?

Well, I played all the guitars, the banjo, and the harmonica. But the rhythm section is Tim Luntzel and Andy Borger. The other main musician on the album was Mauro Refosco, who played all the percussion. The album was tracked at Loho Studios, which is on the Lower East Side, and mixed at the Magic Shop.

Had you ever worked at Loho?

No, I never had. Tom Schick, who recorded and mixed the album, recommended it. I first met Tom on Norah Jones' album *Not Too Late*. He also recorded the majority of the music for the soundtrack that I just did for Ethan Hawke's film, *The Hottest State*.

Photo by Lyle Owerko.

Jesse Harris.

We did a bunch of stuff together on that album, including Willie Nelson's and Norah Jones' tracks—I loved what he did with Norah Jones, so I asked him to do my album. I really like Tom's vibe in the studio—he is relaxed, fast, and creative. He likes to move quickly, and I like to move quickly. Also, he's never uptight, and we seem to have similar taste. I really trust him.

Keeping things moving along during a session is always a challenge, especially since so much of the technology can really be an impediment to the process. How did you keep the process so fluid?

If you have good musicians, they are going to have good sounds already. And if the engineer mikes things properly, it's not going to take very long. I love Pro Tools because it's faster and because if you do need to change some little thing, you can do it very easily. And I don't change a lot of things, but if you're doing live takes, there might be one thing that is off—or one thing in the vocal you want to switch out. When you do that with Pro Tools, it's so easy, and you can keep moving quickly.

When you guys tracked this, did most of it go down live?

Most of *Feel* went down live. We would put down the track, and when we had a track that we liked, unless the live vocal was so indispensable, I would usually sing it about two more times, then make a comp from a few takes of the song. I'd never focus on a single line, though—I'd sing the entire song. Then we'd build upon it with percussion and violin, organ, and piano later.

Can you walk me through Loho and describe how you were situated there?

Loho is not an extraordinarily big room, but it was big enough that we had the drums and the percussion in the same room, with a bit of baffling in between. In the corner of the room was our bass player, Tim, who usually played electric—but if he played upright, he was still in the room. The bass amp was isolated in a booth, and I was isolated in my own booth, where I was playing guitar and singing at the same time.

And do you remember anything about how the miking was handled? Were they looking for a little bit of bleed recording drums?

He used two Coles mics for drum overheads and a 57 on the snare. The usual kind of drum miking, but not over the top—he didn't have, like, 15 mics on the drums. Then he miked the percussion separately.

The percussion is one of the more interesting parts of this album. Was this percussion aspect new to you, and had you ever explored this percussion in previous albums?

No, no. This was the first time that I ever really had a percussionist throughout the entire album, and especially someone on the level of Mauro. Sometimes Andy would record percussion with him, and Mauro also played vibraphone. I'd just say to Mauro, "What do you want to do?" and he'd know exactly what to do. Honestly, I don't even know everything that he did—he's got so many instruments. A lot of them are Brazilian instruments—he played pandero, tambourine, cowbells, maracas, then he's got these Brazilian drums that are played around his neck and other ones that are played on the floor. I think the percussion helped bring everyone to a different level. The songs all have a really strong groove, and the percussion was really important in achieving this.

Did having all these percussion tracks complicate the mixing process? How did you go about mixing them and placing them in the stereo field?

With mixing, I let Tom do his thing, and if I had some kind of thought about it, I would say something—usually if something was too loud, too soft, could use a little more reverb, or whatever. Mostly, the mixing was all Tom—technically and aesthetically, he would make most of the decisions.

The Magic Shop has this beautiful old Neve board that looks like the cockpit of an airplane because it comes around in a semicircle. The sound and the vibe there are great. It's a really good room to mix in because you can hear so well—it's very accurate.

It's not as if you mix it there, then take it home and it sounds completely different. Tom and I just did another record there, which was a compilation of young contemporary female singers performing a Billie Holiday repertoire—it's a great place, and I've done three albums there, at least in part.

What was Tom's mixing style?

Tom is really fast—he seems to deal with the entire mix at the same time. He's not one of those mixers who works on the drums for an hour, then introduces other things. He does the whole thing at once and begins to shape it.

Was this the first album where you recorded the entire thing in Pro Tools?

It was, actually. I've done certain tracks before in Pro Tools—for example, certain tracks off the soundtrack album were all Pro Tools. I produced an album for a singer named Sasha Dobson with Terry Manning, and that was all Pro Tools. I think records done in Pro Tools can sound just as good as those done on analog tape. It is also so much easier—oh my God! It's very trying even just physically to have to take that tape around. It's also cheaper and more convenient—if you need to go to a new studio, you just take your little hard drive, and you're ready.

Terry Manning is an amazing guy.

I've done three albums with Terry. He did my last two records, *While the Music Lasts* and *Mineral*. I did Sasha Dobson's *Modern Romance* with him as well.

What was your overall vision for this album—you've done seven now. What did you want to do differently on this one?

I wanted to release myself a little from being too "over precious" with it. Not that I have been so precious in the past, but I would find myself working on my own stuff to get too hyper-focused or uptight—do you know what I mean? Psychologically, I just wanted to relax and let it happen. Working fast for me usually came out of not having enough time and money, but now I'm more or less used to doing it that way.

I've had bad experiences in the past where you get this pressure from the label: "You've got to keep working on it," or "You need a hit song." Sometimes we were in and out of the studio for a year. Luckily, I have not had that kind of pressure from the labels now. I was on Verve Records for a couple of albums, and for the most part, artistically, they left me alone. For this latest record, I made the album first and showed it to Velour—they liked it and asked to pick it up.

Why did you choose to go with a label this time, rather than going it alone, such as on your last one?

I decided to go with a label this time around because last time my manager was doing all this footwork, I was paying all the bills, and it was just a little too much for both of us. It is hard to sell records. So we decided to leverage someone else's infrastructure; they have a staff, and they've all done it before. If they want to pay for the promotion, it takes a huge burden off of me.

I knew the guys at Velour, and I think they really know what they are doing. They operate on a level that I really liked, selling between 10,000 and 100,000 records, depending on the artist. They seemed like a solid and relaxed organization.

Now that the album is done, what is it like to look back?

I am really pleased with the record. As usual, though, the album has been done a few months now, and I'm already writing new tunes and thinking about the next thing. *Feel* is already starting to feel old to me [laughs].

30 Joe Jackson: Raining with Talent

While Joe Jackson's songwriting has always been predictably brilliant, his strategy in recording the *Rain* album was slightly less conventional. Jackson teamed up with his old friends, Graham Mabey and Dave Houghton, the original rhythm section of the Joe Jackson Band, and they holed themselves up in an East Berlin studio with what he considered to be the bare essentials: piano, bass, and drums. Their objective was to record a collection of songs that rose above the mediocrity of many today's releases.

Sonically, Jackson had a simple vision: big. By sticking to sparse arrangements, simple instrumentation, and selective overdubs, he surmised that he could deliver on this vision and put out a record that the entire band could be proud of. While *Rain* is a refreshing departure from his previous works, Jackson's brilliance as a composer and performer is instantly recognizable as the album ushers listeners through a wide range of moods and tempos.

Joe Jackson's *Rain,* released 2008.

Tell me about the recording environment where you recorded *Rain*.

Well, it's a bizarre place. It used to be a major East German radio station that employed 20,000 people. Since we recorded the album, I learned that it was not only a radio station, but it was also a center for the Stasi—you know, the secret police—where a lot of their wiretapping went to. So all kinds of people were being bugged from this place as well—some serious Cold War stuff! We used that studio because I moved to Berlin, and I wanted to record there because that's where I was living. When I went into the studio, I already had a very clear idea of what I wanted the record to sound like. So if we had done it somewhere else, I think it would have sounded pretty much the same.

Joe, the record sounds very minimalist in a good way. You only have three instruments, and there aren't too many overdubs.

What is interesting about it is that I think it sounds really big. It sounds bigger than the last album I did, where there were four of us. It just creates a lot of space, and you really hear what everyone is doing. The sparseness, if you want to call it that, is very powerful. If you put a guitar in there, for instance, it wouldn't add anything that was really needed and would just clutter it up. When you take the guitar away, the piano sounds huge.

You've been working with these musicians—Graham Mabey and Dave Hartmann—for decades. Is the chemistry like clockwork, and did the takes go down relatively easily?

We didn't have to work that hard to get these tracks down. I probably had to work harder than them. These guys are so good that I struggle to keep up with them sometimes. But then again, I'm not only the piano player, but also the singer. I have twice as much to do, really, and the vocals are the hard part for me.

Can you share any special miking techniques?

Well, we recorded to 24-track analog, and for the drums we didn't do anything special. We had one mic up in the air in the middle of the room—it was a quite a big, fairly live room. We also had a mic in a little chamber in the back of the room, which was sort of a drum storage room. We found that when we put a mic in there, we got an interesting drum sound that we mixed in. We didn't really do anything special—it was a very straight-ahead, old-fashioned recording.

With such a relatively simple mic setup and such sparse arrangements, was it easier to mix the album?

It took a little while to get the right context for the mix because I wanted it to sound big. It was just a question of me, Sean [Slade], and Paul [Kolderie] mixing it and getting on the same wavelength. So the first few days were rather experimental, and we realized

Photo by Frank Veronsky.

Joe Jackson.

that we all wanted it to sound like you are listening to a trio, but it is in a big space and you are sitting in the front row. That's the kind of effect we wanted, and once we knew this, it went pretty smoothly.

There are a lot of different flavors on the album that range in style from Debussy to some serious rockers. Did you deliberately want to change it up for this effort, or is this just how the tracks came out this time around?

Nothing is deliberate—it just comes out as it comes out. I just happen to be a diverse and eclectic kind of musician, and that's the way it is. I just let it go where it seems to want to go, and then after the fact the press can come along and pick it apart if it makes them happy.

You are one of the few artists to avoid becoming pigeonholed. Your first album fit squarely into the punk and new wave era with all its energy, and subsequent efforts have been very diverse. What do you think, looking back on how your career has evolved in all these different areas?

I don't really feel that there are a lot of different areas to the extent that other people seem to. To me, it all feels like part of the same thing. I am aware that it is a bit more diverse than what some people do…but what the hell, you know?

Is there a typical process flow you go through when you write?

No, there really isn't. My writing process is quite mysterious, even to me. It's always changing, and the songs all seem to start from different places. It might start with a bass riff, it might start with a little melody, or it might start with a line of words, which could come from anywhere. It could come from something I read in the newspaper, it could come from something I overhead in a bar, the song could start with a title—that's happened before. There are really no rules, and quite a lot of my songs are sort of pieced together over a long period of time. I could have an idea that could just sit around for a year or two, and then have another idea and think, "Ah, idea B fits with idea A." So some songs, you could take four years to write. Others might come out all in one go. But it is very rare that I sit down and finish a whole song right there and then. That almost never happens.

These records sound so magical to us. Does any one memory in the studio stand out to you as particularly poignant? What moments in the studio have been most special to you, if any?

You put me on the spot here. People are always looking for magic and mystery, and there is plenty of it, but people tend to look in the wrong places, I think. When I go into the studio, it's to do a job that I know how to do. I go in having all the songs written, having all the arrangements worked out, and knowing what I want the record to sound like. It's just a question of getting it done, because I don't want to spend my whole life messing around in a recording studio. I don't find it a particularly great environment—it can be fun when it's all going well; it's great. But my method has always to get in and get out as quickly as possible. What I really enjoy is playing live to an audience. That's where the magic happens, to me.

Many of the songs on your new record you have been playing live since around 2004. How are they translating live, and how have they changed?

They work great live—that is more or less how they are conceived. The album is basically live.

How important is the producer's role to you? You are very capable yourself, but do you rely on other people around the studio to help you take your recording to the next level?

I don't work with a producer—I've been producing myself for a very long time. My bandmates are old friends, and I know the way they play well enough that I am almost able to communicate with them in shorthand. I can say, "Do something like this," and they know what I mean—they're pretty sure to come up with something I like. I can also anticipate what they're going to do. There is a great balance and a certain amount of freedom, but I am always in control because it's my project and I am a dictator. But I am a benign dictator [laughs]. You can ask Graham and Dave—I think they would say that.

Your piano has a striking, shimmering sound. How do you prefer to mic it up?

It is a combination of fairly close mics and distant mics as well. We always put a mic up at the top end—the area right at the top of the keyboard, where there are no dampers on the strings. There is always a mic right on that area because that's where you get a lot of air and a lot of harmonics shimmering around. In terms of the actual mics that we use, I tend to leave the technical stuff to the engineer. I know if I like the way it sounds.

What about Graham's bass? What is behind the sound he gets?

Graham usually has a blend of direct and amped. But do you know his distinctive sound comes from the way he plays? There is a certain way he plays that is very clearly articulated, very deliberate, very driving and just smart. He is a brilliant bass player. A lot of people don't even listen to the bass, but I try to make them listen to the bass when he's playing.

Joe, tell me more about recording vocals.

I wouldn't say recording vocals is easy, but I always have a very good idea of what I want. It's not always easy to get it because I really challenge myself technically. When I'm writing I tend to be in composer mode, and then I have to switch to performer mode and hope that I can keep up with my composer self. Sometimes it's quite difficult. I write things that I think, "Well, that's great, but I don't know if I can actually sing it." And sometimes it's pretty tough, but I seem to find a way.

When did you know the songs were fully baked and that it was finally time to record?

When I felt that I had a whole album of songs that were the best I could possibly do. I really wanted to make an album where every track was great and something I could be proud of. There are just too many people making albums with one good track and seventeen crappy tracks. I'm just trying to do my bit to the best of my ability, rather than putting an album out that is half-baked. I waited until I felt that I really had a whole album's worth of really solid, indestructible songs, and I feel that this is the one.

31 Kaki King: Dreaming of Perfection

Having just released her fourth album, *Dreaming of Revenge,* Kaki King has become known as a young, innovative guitarist who is pushing the envelope of solo guitar with her rhythmic, fret-tapping style. *Dreaming of Revenge* sees King collaborating with producer Malcolm Burn, who is also featured as an instrumentalist. In fact, the two played nearly all the instruments on the album, including drums.

The interplay between artist and producer resulted in a very melodic and technically appealing collection of songs. For King, it was also a challenge as she continues to push herself both as an artist and as an engineer. *Pro Sound News* spoke to King following the release of the new album and just before she debuted her new material during a show at New York's Bowery Ballroom.

Can you tell me a little about the new album?

I recorded it with Malcolm Burn at his studio. He's really gotten it down to a science—he knows what he needs to use to make an album. For the drums, he never used more than about three or four microphones, and most of them were sitting about two or three feet away from the drum set. Other times, he would run a keyboard and a guitar through the same amplifier and just throw up a mic and press record.

He didn't really care if there was a buzz coming from the amplifier; he was just really good at creating this aura in the studio. At first it was shocking, because any other engineer I've ever seen would just freak out about this stuff, but he and I really understood that capturing the feel was most important.

What was different about your studio experiences on this recording versus the last several albums you've worked on?

It was set up so wonderfully—it is this Victorian mansion up in Kingston, New York, and you live on the third floor. Then the second floor is sitting rooms and the kitchen, and on the first floor is the studio. It was just very beautiful—I could get out and ride my bike around, and there were no distractions.

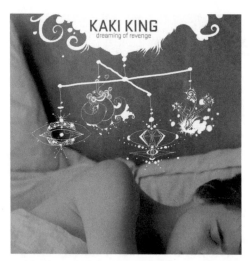

Kaki King's *Dreaming of Revenge,* released 2008.

Was it less pressure working in this way?

Yeah. The interesting thing was that we didn't anticipate finishing the record by the time we did. We thought we were going to get most of the album done and come back and finish it after my tour—I had a really long tour to go on. We realized during the process that we were actually going to finish the record.

Then of course there was a mad scramble to get the strings together, because that was the last thing we had to get done. Because there was less pressure, we were actually more productive and got more done.

There is lots of instrumentation on this record. Tell me about some of the effort you put forth, since this is clearly not just a solo guitar record.

Most of the album you hear is either Malcolm or me, and most of it is me. I played most of the drum tracks—I think Malcolm played drums on two tracks. We didn't worry about who was doing what, though. Malcolm would play bongos here, and I played shakers there. If it was my idea to play shakers, I'd do it. We weren't too precious about who was doing what. Once we came up with a melody we liked and would record together, I would play guitar, he would play keyboards—we would play the same melody and the sounds would overlap. That was our process.

It's funny because I was shocked at certain things he was doing, and he was shocked at my method. When I need a really, really good drummer, I hire one, but I don't really want to hire someone who might not work out. I think on my second record, on the few drum tracks there are, there are three different drummers on the record and three others that didn't even make the record. I thought, "This is absurd. I can do this." Why don't I do this because I am here, and if we don't like it, guess what? I'll do it again.

I think Malcolm played more of the bass parts; I played all the guitars and most of the drums. For anything we couldn't play, like synthesizers and violin, we brought people in. For the things we just physically weren't capable of playing, we didn't play. But for everything else, it was just me and Malcolm.

Photo by Louis Tehran.

Kaki King.

Being such a technically capable guitarist, one might think it's possible to lose sight of slow, tasty melodies. But this album is really rich with well-constructed—and not always technically complex—melodies.

It's interesting because I was trying to return to some of the more challenging guitar work that I had been doing earlier. It felt like over the course of the year or so, my creativity with guitar had just fallen off a bit. I reinvigorated myself, and I wrote new songs and learned a new way of picking. There is a lot of underlying music on this record that is quite challenging—but I've never been one to show off, because that doesn't make good music. It was Malcolm who said, "You've got these incredible harmonics—why don't we create these melodies?" So the whole record is really colored with these beautiful melodies all over it.

Have you gravitated to any certain mics over the years?

Every studio is different; every engineer has his own way. But one thing I've always done and have always insisted on having done for quite a few records now is putting a mic at my ear or above my head. This is because when I play my guitar, it sounds absolutely amazing to me because of the way I'm holding it—the vibration is traveling a certain way. So when I record my acoustic guitars, particularly the Ovations, I put a microphone either at my ear or right above my head—as if it was another ear listening to the guitar, pointed where my ear is pointing.

Is that usually a small condenser?

No, it's usually like a Neumann 87.

Then are you picking it up in front of the guitar as well?

Yeah, we'll always throw up a couple of mics in front of the guitar. I've had four microphones in front of me at times, in addition to the mic by my ear. If the sound wasn't right, it wasn't right. He'd come up and make it right.

There is a lot of dimension on the album—the aspect of near and far. For example, you'll have a slide guitar with a wet reverb mixed down really low, but then you'll have a dry acoustic up front. Were you trying to create more space when mixing the tracks this way?

Certainly. It was kind of like unfolding a map, and Malcolm is an expert at that; he is super good at balance. I personally hear the melody a lot more than how I hear the acoustic guitar.

Now that you've done so well for yourself touring and selling records, what new goodies have you been able to get? Has your choice of guitars changed?

Onstage I have two Trios—the identical black Ovations that are to my specs. I set them up a certain way and put certain strings on them depending on what I am doing. I don't want to have to be changing stuff too much during a show.

I am really learning how to play an amp—I've played through Twins and Mesa Boogies. You have to make sure the personality of the guitar is coming through the amp. Fender amps are all different, and they all have their own personality. They all sound really, really good because now I'm learning how to get a good sound out of them. Before I thought you could almost plug a guitar into anything that was decent. The last thing on my learning curve was learning how to "play" an amplifier as an instrument. Now that I've learned how to do that, I'm really happy.

Photo by J.B. Mondino.

Kaki King.

I would imagine you have different guitars for different applications. For example, you probably use different guitars for studio and live use. Do you have a particular favorite guitar you like to use at home, just kicking around? For example, Bob Marley wrote a lot of his songs on an old Hohner.

I just bought this guitar that I love, and it has become my favorite. It is a Guild Freshman. It's basically a hollow-body electric, but super, super slim. It weighs almost nothing, and it has one pickup. It actually sounds really decent not plugged in. So I've been using it for a lot of radio appearances. It has this cool, really compressed little sound to it, but it is really fun to play. I'm totally in love with it, and it sounds sweet plugged in, too. I've been playing a lot and writing on that.

How much DI do you rely on when you are recording acoustic?

It depends. If I'm doing a one-off thing for radio, we'll take a direct signal. I have a preamp in my Ovation that sounds really good; it really puts out a lot of bass. I don't use any microphones onstage. I'm only going through this preamp, and it can sound quite amazing. Recording can be different—engineers will want to put up amazing microphones, but I do typically like to take a direct signal just to add this big, odd, plasticky fullness that seems to come out of the preamp.

Where do you get the most pleasing results—live or recording?

They are two totally different things. On a purely sound level, in the studio because you take the time to make the right mic choices and get the exact sound you want. At the same time, when you are playing live and you are pushing air though big speakers into a crowd, that is a whole different experience. You can't really compare them.

Where would you like to grow as an artist?

I think pretty much everyone has their Mbox, their Pro Tools, and their Logic setup. I have many people who want to help me out, and companies who have given me the software and plug-ins. I can sit and work with Pro Tools all day long, but I am not a studio expert at this point. One of the songs on the record was done on an Mbox in my parents' garage. But all in all, I would like to learn to be more competent as an engineer. Not on some grand level—I don't want to start making records from my house—but I would like to be a more rounded, better studio musician. I've been approached by a few people to do film scores, and I have a couple of these lined up; it's something that I will be working on.

I'm not saying I want to be the girl with the golden ears, but I'd like to at least trouble-shoot my signal chain, be faster, and be more competent. I want to be able to plug in my MIDI keyboard and know exactly where all the right sounds are for my plug-ins. If I can take the time it takes me now, reduce it to half, and improve the quality by 100 or 200 percent, that is my goal.

You're right—it really is up to the performer, but I do think there is a relationship between engineer and artist or producer and artist that it is really complex and essential to have when you are going to make something that is really, really lasting.

Is there a typical lifecycle of a song from when you are sitting down writing until it is finished? Does it happen quickly for you?

It always depends. Sometimes it just comes out immediately, sometimes it's six months, or sometimes you have an idea you forgot about that you return to because it was a good idea. It is never the same.

Are you a first take kind of person?

I'm definitely a perfectionist. Malcolm will go through a lot of takes to make sure we have it, then he will say, "Now that we have it, let's do it again." And a lot of the times that last performance, or the first one, will be the one that we use.

The type of music that you play would not lend itself to punching in, right? So I would imagine it is much more critical for you to capture an entire performance to avoid an editing nightmare or spoiling the continuity.

For the most part, yes. I try to come to the studio very, very prepared.

What kind of trust and interplay was going on between you and Malcolm? Were there instances when you didn't think you got a particular track and he did?

Absolutely. I would say, "I don't think so," and he would say, "Don't worry, it's fine. We're done."

32 Spyro Gyra: Still Going Strong

Twenty-six albums and three decades later, Spyro Gyra is still mixing up the best jazz rhythms in the business. Founder and saxophone player Jay Beckenstein's journey has been interesting—both as a musician and as a studio owner. Until 2006, he owned Bear Tracks Recording, an idyllic, world-class studio nestled amongst the trees in upstate New York. That studio hosted acclaimed artists and producers such as the Goo Goo Dolls, Phil Ramone, and Dream Theater over a period of many years.

During that time, Bear Tracks also served as home base for Spyro Gyra, who would rehearse and record there in between their exhaustive worldwide touring schedule. For their new Grammy-nominated album, *Good to Go-Go,* the band was forced to break the mold because, alas, Bear Tracks is no more. This introduced challenging—but rewarding—processes for each member of the band. *Pro Sound News* caught up with bandleader Jay Beckenstein.

Tell me where you guys did the new recording. I know you were used to recording at Bear Tracks for all these years, which has now closed.

Good to Go-Go was recorded in several new environments. When we were all together recording it, we used a studio called HarariVille Studios near Hoboken, New Jersey. That was a very nice studio that allowed us to cut as a quintet. Another half of the record was done in our homes, which was a pretty new experience, considering this material was going to be part of the final product. We'd always demoed at home, but never had the mindset that what we were doing was going to be final.

Tom, out in Vegas, has built a small home studio for himself with a drum room, and Bonnie, our drummer, cut a bunch of drum tracks out there. In terms of the whole overdubbing process, I cut a lot of my sax stuff in my bedroom. Everyone is using Pro Tools, a couple guys are using Digital Performer, but everyone is able to send files back and forth. We found the whole process interesting and glitch-free.

Spyro Gyra, from left to right: Scott Ambush, Tom Schuman, Jay Beckenstein, Bonny B, Julio Fernandez.

Tell me about how much preparation you had to go through before you actually went into the studio.

We went to a little rehearsal studio in Nyack, New York, where I live, and we spent four or five days learning things. But again, a lot was sort of tossing the ball back and forth and learning as we went on the tunes. All in all, it has been a year and a half since I've been out of Bear Tracks. It is a weight off my shoulders. Running a big studio like that required an awful lot of noncreative work, so I'm happy to be rid of it.

I was shocked that the process outside of the big studio went as smoothly as it did. And I found elements of it that were better. Speaking personally on recording saxophone, in a big studio the playback is either through the headphones or on the other side of the glass. It is very hard to hear the nuances of what I'm doing—intonation, or what the horn is sounding like, how what I am playing is fitting into the sonics of the tune, all that stuff. I really found that sitting there with the computer on one side of me, the microphone in front of me, and playing and listening, playing and listening, I discovered a lot of things about playing that I hadn't discovered over 25 years. Like where it's good to stand in relation to a certain mic and play softly and where in relationship to a certain mic you can play hard.

I'm sure this applies to where you are playing in relation to the bedroom or wherever else you are recording.

Or the attitude I was playing with—I got a lot more instant feedback doing it up there. I found that in terms of quality, what I might have lost was minimal enough that I liked what I was getting more doing it that way.

Photo by Jeff Touzeau.

Jay Beckenstein pictured near his famous studio, Bear Tracks.

So recording this way really forced you to adopt an entirely new process in terms of file transfers and working in the context of a new production methodology.

This new production method goes for my entire business. The change has been so rapid and so unkind in many ways that everybody is learning new processes. The downside is that maybe people aren't as comfortable, there isn't as much time, maybe you are losing some things, but there is an aspect of people being tossed into new environments and having to find out new ways of doing it, particularly in the music production end because technology has allowed different processes. It kind of stirs up the pot a little bit, and for us it made the process a little less blasé.

Even though you are working with these new processes and often working apart, I would assume that because you all know each other so well and have been playing together for so long, the styles still translate.

They do, but there is a certain amount of back and forth. I might get some stuff from Tom, our keyboard player, and I'll play on top of it. It will go back to him, and he will think, "Oh, had I done that, that would have sounded good," and he'll change something there. If you are talking about it being a construction project…you know, there's still that wonderful thing of setting up live and having wonderful accidents happen. I still swear that gets you the most exciting stuff. But you can definitely make beautiful constructions with this file-sharing thing. You can go back and forth. It sort of reminds me of oil painting—there is really no end to the process. You can paint over and paint over, and change and change. In fact, one of the things you have to learn in all of this is when to stop.

And how to maintain that original vision—I'm sure you had an overall vision for this record that had to remain true.

I think the individual composers on their individual tunes guide the tunes through the process, and if something is straying in a way they don't like, they simply say something. We are all very good at cooperating with each other.

We are getting ready to do a Christmas album and thinking of doing old-fashioned, straight-ahead jazz. We are going to go into a studio and cut it—both kinds of processes can be rewarding.

Jay, tell me about writing now. I know you have often preferred to write on the piano in the past.

I often write using the computer. I write from drum tracks up; I write from saxophone down. I'll play piano for pleasure, and sometimes ideas come off of that, but they always end up going upstairs to where my computer is eventually. I try to approach writing from all different angles. I don't try to do the same thing all the time because maybe that makes it easier to come up with something different.

The interesting thing again about this new process is that when I am trying to put tracks down to realize my new ideas, I am a lot fussier because I am realizing that just maybe some of those tracks might get on the record.

So you've got to spend a little more time choosing the right sounds.

I've got to work it little bit more carefully and have it recorded properly. I'll think, "I can build this into something we can actually use." Whereas before, it was always, "I'll build this into something that will show the guys what I want." That makes the writing process more difficult because you are being fussier, but it is also nice to have it in one piece. Your writing is going right to the realization.

Does the fact that this album has been nominated for a Grammy kind of validate all the effort you put into this?

I really enjoyed making this last record with the guys. It had a great vibe and it was like family. The music came out really buoyant and interesting, so the record is a success for me—whether it sells a lot or wins Grammys, that's wonderful. But it was a success the day we finished it.

Jay, tell me your mic preferences and placement for recording the saxophone.

I always used to use a Neumann TLM 170, and on this one I used a Soundelux U99 large-diaphragm. There are so many variables for a saxophonist before he even gets to a mic—mouthpieces and all that. There has always been this mindset that a microphone makes a saxophonist sound good. No! The saxophonist makes the microphone sound good. I swear, I can take any microphone and change my variables.

So you almost have to play a certain way for a certain mic?

It can be done in a certain spot in a certain room, with a certain mic, you can play a certain way. Some mics sound good when you are playing softly; other mics sound good when you are playing loudly. But if you move in the room, all of that changes. The variables are endless. I found with this one mic—it's not a cheap microphone—I could get everything I wanted, but it was me that had to change.

Do you typically use any kind of compression going in, or do you prefer a clean signal chain before you hit tape?

I am using one of these Rupert Neve Portico 5012 dual mic preamps. I did a lot of guitar recording and a lot of saxophone recording here in my room using those preamps, and they all sounded great.

Tell me the choice of roles within Spyro Gyra. Are you the producer or are you all sort of producing?

The whole "who is the producer" thing has always been fuzzy with us. There is an overriding producer role that I play, which involves picking material, making sure everyone is getting along, and all that, but when it comes to the tunes, that is very ambiguous. I have some say, the composer has some say, and the band members are all opinionated, too.

The engineering role is becoming more ambiguous, too. Sometimes Tom Schuman and I would do the recording. There was no engineer here when we were doing the recording.

How are these tracks translating live? Are you playing all of the tracks live yet?

We are a live band. Inevitably, when you go out on the road with material like this, you beat the crap out of the record. You are so beyond what the record was trying to say about these tunes. It's so much more fun, and everything gets stretched out and morphed into better things. We say it after every damn record process. After we've put out a record and toured to support the record, at the end of that process we say, "Damn, I wish we were recording this stuff now. It sounds great."

Maybe you should tour the next record first, then record it.

Yeah, but there are two downsides to doing the tour first. One is that if you do that, then you put the record out, you start new material, and you're playing the same stuff forever. Also, when you play music that is going to be on the next record, it just doesn't work.

We've played with the idea of taking a live recording setup out on the road, integrating new tunes and recording what we're doing live, and getting it that way. Then maybe editing or whatever later.

What is the direction in the band now, and how is it evolving?

To find new places to go musically is something we all consider. We're always open to change and any kind of new thing that comes along and sounds exciting in our world. We all look forward to evolving as we've always evolved. On the other hand, as a band that's been together for 35 years without any exceptions, we have all really enthused people who feel like they are doing some of the best stuff they have ever done. Just to go out with a unit that is feeling that way is a really great thing, and it makes for really good, lively music. I think the band is in one of its best places psychically that it has ever been. If we can just maintain that for a long time, it will be great.

What other artists are out there now that you have a respect for? Is there anything that appeals to you in contemporary music?

I'm pretty tired of the same old, same old. The industry just tends to turn out widgets. Somebody might be creative, then you get a million copies of it until it becomes banal and you don't want to hear it anymore. I have two young adults and a teenager, and there is plenty of good music going on around here. But most of it falls in a few categories, and it's not that interesting. I really like the stuff that Herbie Hancock has been dabbling in—*River: The Joni Letters* and the one before that, where he had all these really interesting artists playing for him, *Possibilities*.

I really like the way he was looking for unusual combinations—something different. I thought that was a breath of fresh air in this corporatized, desperate process. For so many years now, the big record companies have dictated what people are listening to in some ways, as much as the listener was dictating to them. These big corporations had a very uncreative way of doing this. If something works, do it again, if something works, do it again. Now you see them still doing it even as their revenue stream is shrinking to nothing, and they still don't get it. There needs to be some kind of inventiveness or creativity coming from them about what they are presenting. It just can't be more of the same, and more of the same, and more of the same.

33 John Starling and Carolina Star: Risin' Again

John Starling has been playing acoustic music with Mike Auldridge (resophonic guitar) and Tom Gray (bass) for more than 30 years. Bluegrass fans around the world will likely recognize the trio as the core members of the original Seldom Scene—part of an innovative Maryland-based acoustic group who ushered in a progressive new style of bluegrass during the 1970s. If being one of bluegrass music's trailblazers and influencing the likes of Emmylou Harris, Ricky Skaggs, and Linda Ronstadt isn't enough, Starling has also maintained a prolific career as a medical doctor, retiring only 18 months ago. Since his retirement, he has put most of his energy into a brand-new project: John Starling and Carolina Star.

Both new and existing fans will appreciate the band's honest, no-nonsense approach on the new album, *Slidin' Home*. The song selections, performances, and especially the recording sound as natural as ever—with the help of none other than producer/engineer George Massenburg at the helm. I caught up with John Starling as *Slidin' Home* continued to make sparks in the country bluegrass scene.

How did this whole album come about?

It all started with George. George Massenburg and I go back a long way—to the early Seldom Scene days. He was the engineer on our third and fourth albums back in the early '70s, and I've watched his career unfold over the years with some degree of amazement, as all of us have. When he did our third record, he was in his early 20s—we brought him back to do our fourth album because we were all very happy with how the third one sounded. When George was 16, he recorded a Country Gentleman album, then he went from that to the Seldom Scene. On our fourth record, he was living in Paris at the time; he said he loved Paris, but he hated French music.

During the recording of our fourth album, it just so happened that Linda Ronstadt had gotten sick on the road, and we knew her—she knew I was a doctor, so she called me up and said, "I have a fever of 105, and I'm canceling my last tour dates in Washington and New York—I'm going to come stay at your house." It just so happened that her fever had broken up at the time for a short while, so to make a long story short, we were in the studio doing album four. She would come to the studio with Lowell George, and he kept saying, "This engineer is unbelievable."

John Starling and Carolina Star, from left to right: Rickie Simpkins, Tom Gray, John Starling, Jimmy Gaudreau, and Mike Auldridge.

George and I also worked together on the two Trio records, with Dolly [Parton], Linda [Ronstadt], and Emmylou [Harris]. Over the years we kept in touch, and it was sort of his idea that we put together [*Slidin' Home*]. He wanted to do some work to try to determine whether if you go above 96 kHz in the 24-bit/96-kHz format, you hit a point of diminishing returns, audio-metrically speaking. He wanted me to get some acoustic musicians and bring them into this room he had put together with Pete Wasner, a keyboard player who was playing with Lowell George when he died. Pete has a house near Franklin, Tennessee, nearby where George lived, and the two of them took George's outboard over there and spent a lot of money putting it together to make the room sound unbelievable. George was always a big believer that the room dictates probably 90 percent of how something is going to sound.

What makes this room so special?

You'd have to talk to George about that, but it's a fairly large room with a very high ceiling, and it has wood panels throughout—they even put the vertical stringers farther apart than they usually would for an outbuilding so the wood would vibrate a little better. It's just one of those rooms where you walk in, snap your fingers, and go, "Whoa!" All the reverb is built into the room; you don't have to add it. It's perfect for acoustic instruments—that's what it's built for. On the first four or five takes, we put some baffling around the instruments, and the second time we took the baffles away. In the long run, it didn't make a whole lot of difference either way.

The bass has a wonderful low end. How did you get so much dimension in it?

We did four tracks to begin with and six later. The first group of tracks was done with baffles; the second group was done with no baffles. George was listening also in terms of implementing a surround mix, which eventually may be done when he gets time to do it! He loves doing that kind stuff, but there's not a market for it.

Did anyone have a preference as to whether the first group of tracks was better than the last group?

I don't think in the long run it really made quite a difference. The whole idea was to put together an acoustic group, so I talked to Tom Gray and Mike Auldridge, who played with me in the original Seldom Scene. We even wanted to get the other surviving member of Seldom Scene, Ben Evers, to record with us, but we couldn't work out the logistics. The way we all learned music together was by just picking in the parking lot or just sitting around playing in a little circle in a living room.

For *Slidin' Home,* we wanted to practice ahead of time, before we got into the studio, and then try to do everything as live as possible, head on. Whenever possible, we also like to play some live shows with the tracks we're going to do before we go in, rather than working them up in the studio. The essence of music is live performance—and that's what we were trying to get.

The way we learned music was by picking in a parking lot—just sitting around playing. Anyone who has ever played acoustic music and just sits around in a circle in a living room knows how good that sounds when it's live.

And you can hear how natural that is.

My whole thing is to practice ahead of time, before you get in there, and if possible, play some live shows with the tracks you are going to do before you go it—then sit down and try to do as much as possible live, head on.

My favorite singers are singers who are playing while they are singing. I've been involved in doing vocal overdubs until you and everyone else are sick of listening to it. In the same way, I think the essence of music is live performance, and that's what we were trying to get.

You focused it around the three of you as a core, then added other instrumentation. How did you decide on the instrumentation for the additional tracks?

Well, as with all collaborations, it's a matter of making chicken salad out of you know what. A lot of it came down to who was available. For the second session, we brought some Washington-area musicians together to finish the project, then put a little group together to go out and play some shows. I've made too many records that sound great without having played the shows on the road.

Emmylou Harris appears on this record. Obviously you are no stranger to her. Can you tell me what it felt like to work with her again in the studio?

I think in the long run, Emmy and I go back so far, and we communicate on a fairly regular basis. It's not a matter of approaching her; it's more like, "Hey, Emmy, we're going to be out here doing this, and we want you to come in!" [Laughs]. I thought that "In My Hour of Darkness" was a good choice for her, especially considering that I didn't realize until after we did it that she co-wrote the song with Gram Parsons.

We worked that song up a number of years ago when we did a benefit concert in New England for a gentleman who was the dean of a college up there. He was Gram Parsons' dorm counselor the only year he was at Harvard, and they became very close friends. We worked this song up in the hotel room before we did the benefit show, and since then I could never get it off my mind—so that was one of the things we did. At the time, we were just making music and not necessarily thinking about what we were going to do down the road.

Tell me about mixing *Slidin' Home*.

The way it was mixed was very interesting. George and I have mixed together in the past a number of times. It's always been my feeling that when it comes to the way things sound, that's George Massenburg's function. He mixed it at Blackbird in this room he's using for mixing and recording. It is very startling. Once again, George's whole thing is the acoustic view of what you record is 90 percent of what it is going to sound like.

I am doctor who likes to play music, and a closet audiophile. In a journal for surgeons, I read about a German term called "Functionslust." There is a tendency to overuse something just because you can do it. It is something that applies to surgeons, but it can also apply to musicians, recording engineers, and many other professionals. The idea, once again, is try to make it live, get it in a really good-sounding room, and then record it with as good of microphones as you can. If you do that, you're probably not going to need a whole lot of outboard gear. Some of my favorite recordings these days are live performances.

What are your feelings about digital recording?

Digital, particularly Pro Tools HD, has been the miracle of my generation. It makes recording live performances that much better. One way in which digital recording has finally gotten to the point where it is an advantage over analog recording is that trying to record live back in the analog days was such a hassle. With digital, it's not. When it comes to live recordings, we have gotten to the point where digital has made it possible to capture the live feel. That, to me, is a big advantage. When it comes to mixing, we were able to email mixes. He'd direct me to a site where I could listen to the mix.

I've gotten to a point with my computer where I can almost hear better there than I can anywhere else. What I am interested in as a musician are the dynamics. I was able to listen to a mix, email him back, and tell him what I didn't like about it. Then he'd send me another one. When we finally arrived at a place where we thought we should be, George would FedEx me a CD of the entire file, which I could take to a Pro Tools HD–equipped studio here in Fredericksburg, Virginia, and break out the tracks, sit there, and fine-tune the dynamics.

When it's finally done, I take it to a mastering engineer, Billy Wolf here in Washington, who I've worked with before—he's an absolute genius. The two of us will sit together and do a little more fine-tuning of the dynamics, then we're done. Then I'd send it to George Massenburg with a note: "Please tell me we didn't screw it up!" [laughs]

The other thing was that Billy was nice enough to make me a DVD of the final master, which I can play in my car and at home. I don't know if it's the placebo effect, but to me, once you've listened to DVD audio, it's okay to listen to the CD audio again, but just in terms of audiometrics—because you can get so much more information in there—it sounds much better to me than a CD. But I may be imagining things. At the Audio Engineering Society convention in San Francisco last fall, I brought this up and asked a panel whether I was just imagining things, or did the DVD really sound better? They answered, "Probably a little of both."

How long did the whole project take from beginning to end? Were there a lot of breaks?

We started the project in April of 2003, when we did the first tracks. Then we went back after about 18 months and did the second group. We weren't in any hurry—I was still practicing medicine. I just retired a little over 18 months ago, and that's when I started to put some time together, and George and I decided to go in and finish it up.

How have the production dynamics between you and George changed over the years? Your working relationship spans more than three decades.

I don't think our approach has changed since the early '70s. The first Seldom Scene recording was done with a two-track head on, five guys just sitting around. Once the last note was played, it was mixed. You had to have somebody who knew how to mix as you went along. We used to have a rule that we would try a particular track three times—if we weren't happy at that point, we would stop, take a break, go to something else, and come back to it later. Two-track head on in terms of analog—you didn't have to go down a generation. So everything sounded very immediate.

I bet that rule you had would still hold true today—if something doesn't work the first two or three times, then come back to it later.

I think that's the idea. Like everybody else, once we got into multi-track recording, then we started to want to layer everything and try to make it sound perfect, to the point where it just lost all its dynamics. That's what, to me, digital recording is now bringing back the possibility of doing—just going in there and doing a two-track head on. If you get a really good-feeling track, even if the bass is a little out of time, you just move it.

So one of the core requirements for the album was to have the three of you play at the same time, then do other overdubs.

Some of the tracks on the album were done totally live, head on—such as "In My Hour of Darkness," except for a small piano overdub where we had to fill it out a little bit. On some of the early tracks we did, I talked to the guys and asked if there was any other instrumentation we could add that would help. For example, on "Cold Hard Business," I asked the fiddle player if he could hear anything, and he said, "Yeah," and he went back and added a little pizzicato fiddle toward the second half of the track.

Tell me about the track selection. How did you pick out what songs you would do?

I would occasionally play some shows during the time I was a practicing surgeon, learning different tunes and playing with other people. There were many songs and artists that inspired me along the way—we tried to include some of those songs on this record. Most of the songs were just songs that I just felt comfortable sitting around and playing.

In the last five or six years, Eva Cassidy was one of my biggest influences, in terms of a singer. She was probably one of the best interpretive singers who ever lived—she died in her early 30s of malignant melanoma. If you ever find the record *Live at Blues Alley,* which was recorded live in Georgetown, or *Songbird,* which was an album that became the world's best-selling record four years ago, pick them up and have a listen. She knew how to do it.

34 Supergrass: Diamonds in the Rough

S upergrass is the championship fighter in the ring who refuses to go down. Despite the band's advancing age, each new recording effort seems fresher than the last and indeed more energetic. Their latest album, *Diamond Hoo Ha,* sees the Midlands, U.K.—based outfit at their most explosive in years. Bassist Mick Quinn says that this time they let it all out in the studio—and you can really hear it. The performances are raw and unrestrained, but the songs are solid. It isn't a stretch to say that Supergrass is one of the most exciting acts in the world today, and this album—at least in this writer's opinion—rises above anything by the band's contemporary peers: Arctic Monkeys, Arcade Fire, The White Stripes, Manic Street Preachers…*fill in the name here.*

Interestingly, Supergrass insisted on recording the album in a completely different geography, and they have done so many times in the past. The album was recorded in Berlin at Hansa Studios, which has hosted everyone from David Bowie, to Iggy Pop, to The Cure in the past. Mick Quinn talked about how tension in the studio is not always such a bad thing.

Photo by Andy Willsher.

Supergrass left to right: Rob Coombes, Mick Quinn, Gaz Coombes, and Danny Goffey.

I know you had an accident last year—are you okay now?

Yeah, that was after the recording, actually. We did the recording, and we were mixing in L.A. for the record. Then I went on holiday in France and fell out a window in the middle of the night. I did myself in pretty badly. I'm glad I'm still alive.

Where did you record *Diamond Hoo Ha,* and how did it all come down?

We had a bit of a longer lead of time to write all the stuff this time around. So we spent about six months on the back end of being in China and finishing the tour to talk about the writing from our houses. There was quite a long period of writing songs, and because they were so well prepared, it took a much shorter period of time to record it. We got this studio in Berlin; it's called Hansa Studios.

So you decided not to go back to the barn in France this time, where you recorded *Road to Rouen.*

No. If you do the same thing every time, you just get into routines and it's not very creative. We've done France for the last couple of goes, so we thought we would try another flavor. It was really just a barn, just a very temporary studio—we bought some gear, borrowed stuff from various people, and basically set up the studio for that record. It wasn't hard-wired— we moved the gear in, recorded the record, and moved the gear back out again.

What was it like to record in Berlin this go-round?

It was really good, actually. I went out a week early, before anyone else came in. I had a holiday in Berlin and did the whole tourist bit. It's such an amazing place—the east and west are still distinctly different, and it's really fascinating. You have all the history of Bowie and Iggy Pop and the '70s recordings. They recorded *Heroes* there, and Iggy Pop's *The Idiot* was done there…Siouxsie and the Banshees and a whole bunch of other things.

What is your recollection of the room?

Well, we were on the top floor in Studio Four, which is a lot smaller, but we set up as efficiently as possible. It hadn't been redecorated since the '70s, I think. We had a few technical problems, but it all worked out.

I've seen you guys live several times, and there seems to be a great chemistry. I am assuming you are all friends and that this translates to the studio, too. Can you tell me a little about what the vibe is like among each of you during sessions?

Things can get tense, and there is often creative friction here and there, but generally, I think we give each other enough room to maneuver—we know each other really well. There is never planned fighting in the studio—even before we get going, there is intense thought about what we are doing. But at the end of the day, we all go down to the pub and laugh about it, really. But we are all quite serious in the studio.

I was so impressed with _Road to Rouen._ When I heard you guys were coming out with a new album, I thought, "No way can it be as good as the last." But you've done it—tell me where your head was and what's different about this one.

Yeah, it was really quite a shocker. I am really a bit stuck into _Road to Rouen,_ and I really enjoyed making that record. And it was kind of a wrench to make this one because I got so stuck on the last one. But it's good not to repeat yourself. If we tried to make some more of _Road to Rouen,_ it would just be a pile of limitation. We put a lot of singles out, and we didn't want to do an LP of singles through the whole record— otherwise, it's going to compare with your "Best Of," and then your career becomes a parody of yourself. For this, we wanted to move back to where we were and take what we learned from _Road to Rouen_ and do something different again.

There is an amazing energy to this record, starting with the opening track, "Diamond Hoo Ha Man," then flowing right into "Bad Blood."

Yeah. I basically let it all out a little bit on this one—usually I'm holding back a bit in the studio, but this time we just opened it up and really went for it. We went through lots of takes and just went completely nuts, and we took the best out of that. Danny [Goffrey] is quite an interesting drummer because when he's relaxed, he can play in a really controlled way. But when he is nervous, you can wind him up like a motor until he goes completely berserk. He went on the Keith Moon end of the scale on this record.

What did Nick Launay bring to the table in terms of the production? Was he somebody you are used to working with?

No, he came in just for this record. It was difficult to know how we wanted to approach things coming off of _Road to Rouen,_ and we brought Nick in to keep us very focused on what we wanted to do and to keep it lean. He wasn't overbearing, and he brought the best out of what we were all telling him. He was really good at bringing us all together and helping us keep focused on what we were doing.

Does Gaz [Coombes] have really strong ideas when it comes to writing? Does he come up with most of the tracks, or are you building them up in pre-production?

It depends which track. Some tracks Gaz brought in, and they were completely finished, like "When I Needed You." He'd already recorded a demo at home, and the song was done, note for note. Rob [Coombes] came up with the important chord changes for "Butterfly," and we didn't have to do much tinkering with that. Rob had half the melody line, and we built an extra chorus for it, but that was essentially Rob's song. And that's a great song. "Whiskey & Green Tea" was just a scratchy guitar riff that Danny had kicking around for years. We put that together in the studio and added some special effects–type things to it. Everyone comes with accomplished ideas.

The backing vocals add so much more texture to it—can you tell me about these?

Danny put a lot more backing vocals on this record, but the key ones for me were the Motown-style vocals we did in "Rebel in You." Gaz and I just sat at around a mic, and he was enjoying doing the backing vocals more than the lead vocals. Gaz has listened to a lot of soul music over the years, and during the last couple of years I've been getting really heavily into Al Green and the old soul music. You can really dig those records and get a lot out of them.

What do you think about the music landscape these days? Having done this for 15 years, there are many bands who imitate you or who at least are influenced by you.

Nothing in the charts immediately grabs me, but I like Arcade Fire—I keep coming back to that band. I know it's old news now, but I keep listening to *Funeral* and getting more and more out of it. It's just a stunning record. Beyond that, I'm still appreciating Arctic Monkeys—they're interesting. There's a lot of interesting stuff out there, but I am less and less keeping my finger on the pulse. I think if bands are good, I'll eventually get around to buying their record. It's a really terrible thing to say, but I don't feel the need to rush out and get the latest thing. It's not like that for me. That said, I don't think anyone should wait to buy our record [laughs]!

How long did you have to rehearse before you were at a good level and were ready to start tracking? Did you tour with any of the material?

This is something I am quite interested in doing on the next record, but we didn't actually road-test any of this music at all. We kind of just relied on our own instincts, and we just pared down the music and made it as lean as possible. In fact, that is probably the only similarity to *I Should Coco*—the leanness of the music.

How much of the instrumentation with you guys is a tried-and-true approach? For example, on the first song, "Diamond Hoo Ha Man," you have got this spectacular fuzz bass going.

I played that with a plectrum and played the other songs with my fingers. I go through my Hiwatt stack, which I also used on "Bad Blood." I got the best bass sound I ever had on that track. We were recording that and we got the final take, and then my bass head just blew up. It worked because it was just about to blow up—I had the best bass sound in the world and I'll never get it again. The take was on the record, and it's the best take. I'm not too precious about what bass head I use; I just know when it sounds about right.

What about Gaz with his guitars—anything unusual with his setup?

I'm not sure what he's using mic-wise; he certainly had a much more straight-ahead approach than we have on previous records in terms of miking up stairwells outside the live room and stuff. It was more straight ahead and direct. I was also using a small Vox Tweed amp, and I actually managed to drag out my brother's Stratocaster, which hasn't seen the light of day for a few years. Strats are extremely unfashionable, but I think occasionally they're nice to pull out of the bag.

You guys are obviously selling a lot of records these days and selling out tours. Does having greater financial freedom translate to more relaxed recording sessions? Was there a lot of tension?

We always try and switch the goalposts on everything we ever make. The worst thing you can do, if something was easy last time, is to go right back in and do the same thing. You just get comfortable and you think it's going to be easy, but it never is. It's always difficult making a record. If you do something novel and you do something that you haven't done before, it kind of pushes you through better than you would if you were in a relaxed surrounding. Also, we knew we only had two and a half weeks to cut the record from beginning to end. We had to get it all done in that time.

Why did you choose to mix in Los Angeles?

It was more for Nick Launay, I think. He was more comfortable mixing there. In Berlin, he was a little out of his element in terms of being able to get hold of his gear and what he needed to use. I think we ended up using an SSL desk in Los Angeles. We flew in on a 2-inch tape machine and were coming in and out on that. When we were tracking the first couple of songs, we couldn't get hold of any 2-inch tape [laughs], but the rest of the record we did on 2-inch, then flew it into Pro Tools from there.

The sequence flows very naturally on this album. How did this happen?

Gaz kind of sequenced this record, and I think he did a really good job. It was kind of frightening because there was this big epic at the end ["Butterfly"], and I wasn't sure this was how we should end the record. Eventually he talked me into it, and it's a good thing he did.

You guys have been together a long, long time. Where is your head and are things going well for you as a band? Are you as excited as you were when you started?

Yeah. We're excited about different things. We just finished doing a big tour in the U.K., and big tours used to be so daunting, trying to work out what lights you wanted and approaching it all. On the last tour, we're finally getting it right after 15 years! It has been effortless and enjoyable for the first time in ages.

You have a big tour schedule coming through the U.S. this summer. Are you excited about that?

Yeah, it's kind of odd—we're going to a lot of places we haven't been and we're playing with the Foo Fighters. We're going through a lot of interesting places like Colorado and the Midwest, so I am up for that. I'm also looking forward to playing with the Foo Fighters!

Can you think back on any particular moment that was special for you in the studio?

Certainly. Very early on in the studio when we recorded "Wait for the Sun"—this was a big realization for our band. We had recorded *I Should Coco,* and we were up to the point where we needed B sides. They booked us some time in a tiny little studio and gave us a date to record, but they didn't book any sort of producer. So we produced it ourselves, and after that day, we thought we didn't need a producer and could do whatever we wanted. We didn't need anyone to tell us what to record or how to do it. If you want to record anything, you can. All you need to do is make the time for it.

Index